ALSO BY BARRY LOPEZ

EMBRACE FEARLESSLY THE BURNING WORLD

EMBRACE FEARLESSLY THE BURNING WORLD

—

Essays

BARRY LOPEZ

RANDOM HOUSE | NEW YORK

Published in the United States by Random House, an imprint and
division of Penguin Random House LLC, New York.

Random House and the House colophon are registered trademarks of
Penguin Random House LLC.

Many of the essays in this work have been previously published.
A publication history can be found on page 323.

LIBRARY OF CONGRESS CATALOGING-IN-PUBLICATION DATA
Names: Lopez, Barry Holstun, 1945–2020, author. | Solnit, Rebecca,
writer of introduction.
Title: Embrace fearlessly the burning world: essays / Barry Lopez;
introduction by Rebecca Solnit.
Description: First edition. | New York: Random House, 2022.
Identifiers: LCCN 2021046217 (print) | LCCN 2021046218 (ebook) |
ISBN 9780593242827 (hardcover) | ISBN 9780593242834 (ebook)
Subjects: LCSH: Lopez, Barry Holstun, 1945–2020—Travel. |
American essays. | LCGFT: Essays.
Classification: LCC PS3562.O67 E43 2022 (print) |
LCC PS3562.O67 (ebook) | DDC 814/.54 [B]—dc23/eng/20220208
LC record available at https://lccn.loc.gov/2021046217
LC ebook record available at https://lccn.loc.gov/2021046218

Printed in the United States of America

randomhousebooks.com

4 6 8 9 7 5 3

Book design by Susan Turner

BARRY HOLSTUN LOPEZ

January 6, 1945–December 25, 2020

That, friends, is the sum of my wanting.
Next to nothing, close to everything.

—PABLO NERUDA, "I Ask for Silence"

CONTENTS

INTRODUCTION

The Quest for the Holy Grail

> Attention is the rarest and purest form of generosity.
> Absolutely unmixed attention is prayer.
> —Simone Weil

THE WORD "ESSAY" COMES FROM THE FRENCH *ESSAYER, TO TRY,* and though Barry Lopez wrote book-length nonfiction and short stories, he was in some sense always an essayist, moving toward an apprehension of the natural world and our relation to it. To try is to explore the outer boundaries of one's own capacity as well as the world beyond oneself, and the meeting of these two things drives much of his work. Every essay is a document of the writer's endeavor and an invitation to the reader to pursue their own explorations.

This collection of his essays has, as well, scattered through it fragments of an autobiography, and in that autobiography are traces of a quest, another form of essaying. Though Barry chose in his writing to look outward more than inward, the two directions are never truly separate in his work. We learn from both what resembles and what differs from ourselves; we learn about being human from the nonhuman, though we may choose to learn about the nonhuman for its own sake and for the joy of enlarging our understanding and deepening our relationship to the world. Other essays are both windows that take you out of yourself and mirrors that show you back to yourself, and so a flight is also a return.

The autobiographical passages in this volume are themselves a guide to the work and its aspirations. From them you can glean a practical sense of who Barry Lopez was and why he was so passionate about place, travel, and the nonhuman world. *Embrace Fearlessly the Burning World* contains two accounts of his long childhood ordeal of sexual abuse by a family friend, "A Scary Abundance of Water" and "Sliver of Sky." In the first, he makes it clear that the natural world itself—what he could ride to on his bike, the flight of his tumbler pigeons and their daily return, the light and space and water of the San Fernando Valley, north of Los Angeles, where he then lived—was his sanctuary and his support when he otherwise so desperately lacked both.

The first essay, which came out in 2002, had a huge impact on me. The sheer generosity of recognizing how unexceptional his ordeal was, of weaving it into a broader recognition of the suffering of others and of what is redemptive and beautiful in the world around us, suggested to me more than any book-length memoir what memoir could be, and how the intensely personal and the larger world could be spoken of together in the same breath.

The act of widening one's focus is itself an act of generosity in situations like this, not as a way of ignoring one's own life but as a means for connecting it with others' lives. If disconnection is the devastation that allows an abuser to abuse, a family to deny, a child to suffer in silence, connection is itself curative. We might need to go deep, the piece seems to say, but we might also need to go broad, and it does that as well. Even in the titles of the two essays about this abuse—referencing water and sky—Barry reaches beyond, not to avoid, but to reach out the way a drowning person might reach for flotsam in the waves.

In the earlier essay, rushing into the untrammeled space of the San Fernando Valley, when much of it was still undeveloped or agricultural, was running from something. It was also moving toward something, and journeying to that something would be what Barry would do for the rest of his life—to what he loved most steadily throughout two dozen books and more than half a century of writing.

The love of place can sustain a life, and we usually talk as though it's an unreciprocated love, a one-way street. These essays show why that is wrong. The places love us back in how they steady and sustain us, teach us, shelter us, guide us, feed us, and that old image of the Earth itself as a mother is a reminder that we depend upon the unearned bounty of the biosphere. So, in a sense, in learning to love the Earth and particular places in it, we are learning to love back what loved us all along. Learning to love these places, by studying and understanding them, was one of Barry's lifelong tasks.

Those of us who write about the natural world cherish some sense of being fed and cared for and protected by places and the living things in them, of a communion with the nonhuman world that matters on corporeal, ethical, emotional, imaginative, and spiritual terms. Which is why we have often tried to talk about both how these realms are being objectively threatened—by climate catastrophe, extinction, exploitation—and disappearing from our consciousness, as human beings become more indoor, urban creatures, and what kind of loss the latter is.

We have tried to provide readers with a sense of what it means to be connected this way, both to give them a chance to access this connection through our own recounted experiences and to encourage them to seek out their own experiences or to examine them in new ways. And in hopes that by encouraging attention to and finding value in the natural world, we might move people to recognize the many ways in which it is immeasurably important not only to our survival but also to our spirits and imaginations, to justice and hope. What gets called nature writing is sometimes about animals or encounters, but often as well about the land itself, about place itself, ultimately about the Earth itself.

There's a passage in E. M. Forster's 1910 novel named after the country house at the heart of it, *Howards End*. That old house in the country gives the main characters refuge and a space in which to be themselves and to be connected to rural life and community. Forster wrote:

London was but a foretaste of this nomadic civilisation which is altering human nature so profoundly, and throws upon personal relations a stress greater than they have ever borne before. Under cosmopolitanism, if it comes, we shall receive no help from the earth. Trees and meadows and mountains will only be a spectacle, and the binding force that they once exercised on character must be entrusted to Love alone. May Love be equal to the task!

By "Love," Forster means the feelings between human beings, and he argues that we need more than that, and portrays with tenderness and power what "more" can mean. "Help from the earth" is how places love us back, but first we have to connect to them. In the essay here titled "Love in a Time of Terror," Barry writes, "Whenever I'm asked what I love, I think of the aggregate of relationships in that place that summer." Which is to say the subject of what is often called nature writing is, inevitably, nature, but also love, and the latter means that what the writing academics tried to herd into a corral of that name is often something else. It might be geography or sociology or history or anthropology, but it is often also the values, desires, emotions, and orientations that make us human, and in that sense, quite often, it is theology.

I often felt something intentionally priestly about Barry's presence, when he spoke to audiences—a kind of formal way of presenting himself, but also an intention to bring us the way a priest might bring a congregation to something transcendent or immanent. He was unafraid of taking moral positions and stating principles, and he wasted no time on that chimera of neutrality that has bedeviled so many white

American writers. This committed stance is present in his work. When his mother remarried, to a man who moved the family to New York City and away from his abuser, he was sent to a Jesuit prep school. There's a lot about Barry that remained Jesuitical or perhaps priestly—and as a young man he considered a monastic or priestly vocation. As he narrates it in "Madre de Dios," he did not end up pursuing that path, and the former altar boy moved on from regular attendance at Catholic church. But also, he writes:

> In those many years of travel, long after I had lost touch with my Catholic practice, I continued to rely, anyway, on the centrality of a life of prayer, which I broadly took to be a continuous, respectful attendance to the presence of the Divine. Prayer was one's daily effort to be incorporated within that essence.

His writing celebrates that the "presence of the Divine" is to be found in many places and phenomena, here and now, not in some disembodied heaven. The work is in some sense a celebration of abundance, from the desert to the Arctic, and a warning about its erosion.

He finds this presence in and as places, mostly wild and remote ones where the natural order seems intact, and as specific moments of witness, particular encounters. Places not as passive stages that life moves across but as the lives as well, as all the presences, living and otherwise, in a place, its animals, plants, weather, geology, and hydrology, the lay of the land, the human presence, and how they all interact. Sometimes he also describes the disciplines and rites of being present and regularly the other humans there, who are often guides of one kind or another.

You could describe his as a lifelong quest for the Holy Grail in which the quest itself is the Grail. The Grail is the journey, the search for something, and the something is outside oneself—musk oxen in a blizzard or algae flourishing under Antarctic ice, or an image of a stone horse laid out in the desert long before white people came along, or the annual autumnal return of the salmon in front of his house on the McKenzie River. But in his writing, this cosmology, the Grail is not just the travel to these places but the stillness and patience after arrival.

It is also the act of paying attention to these things, of entering a state of concentration, of focus, a state of being open to epiphany and rapture and communion. It is a seeking, so to speak, of the capacity to seek, with a kind of devotion that steadies the concentration. You arrive at a place, then you arrive at an awareness, then perhaps arrive at an understanding, which opens up the world to you and opens you up to the world. Finally, perhaps, you arrive at a relationship.

One word appears over and over in these pages: "attention." The word has the same roots as "attendance," which means showing up, serving, and caring for, with roots in the French *attendre*, to wait. Waiting, attending to, and paying attention are in some sense the same thing, waiting to understand, waiting to know, staying until connection is formed, the taking-care-of that begins by taking notice of. Perhaps it's all encompassed in the "continuous, respectful attendance to the presence of the Divine." Attention is something

Barry admires in others, exhorts his readers to practice, and describes in his own interactions.

One of the hallmarks of his writing is a sense of being unhurried, of the sheer luxury of time and the way that the old ways were the slow ways, and that this slowness is what it takes to know something, whether you wait for hours for the animal to appear or you return to a place over and over to know it under many conditions.* In that sense, it's an act of resistance to our hurried, harried, distracted era. In the essay on his friend Richard Nelson, the Alaskan writer and anthropologist, he notes, "To be patient, to pay attention to the world that is not yourself, is the first step in the neophyte's discovery of the larger world outside the self, the landscape in which wisdom itself abides." Elsewhere he writes, "I do not recall a single day of attentiveness outdoors, in fact, when something unknown, something new, hasn't flared up before me."

Often the word appears in the phrase "pay attention," in which to pay might mean to give. You give your attention and you are paid back with whatever joy and knowledge you receive through that process. He portrayed learning as a holy and exhilarating mission. Perhaps attention is what we owe one another and the world first, and this writer wandered about, paying it out lavishly and writing down what he learned as an exhortation to others to likeways pay attention, not as a duty, not because we are in debt, though of course

---

* It should be noted that while Barry was a careful reviser of his pub- lished work, four of the essays in this collection were still in draft form at the time of his death.

we are in debt to the great complex web of life in which we are situated, but because attention brings epiphanies, orientation, fellowship, insight. Sometimes he was seeking the places to which he himself desired to pay close attention, sometimes he was seeking the people who already did so. Thus scientists and Indigenous people loom large in his work as practitioners in two schools of epistemology, different but not opposed.*

In this book he states a credo: "Perhaps the first rule of everything we endeavor to do is to pay attention. Perhaps the second is to be patient. And perhaps a third is to be attentive to what the body knows." That state of paying full attention is both the prayer and the communion that is the prayer's answer. He pursued it over and over, found it over and over, prayed it, praised it, and urged us all to do the same, over and over. We are his congregation; these are his sermons. In them, loneliness is transmuted into connection, in which some part of what was broken is made whole. He made contact with these rare and vanishing and remote phenomena, like a priest reaching toward the divine, and then sought to share this communion as a writer, to turn it into a communion for us and with us.

---

* It might be worth mentioning that Barry's work talked extensively and respectfully about contemporary Indigenous people when that was unusual in mainstream American writing. Into the 1990s most settler-writers either ignored them or talked about them in the past tense, as people who were no longer part of the conversation, or never had been. If Barry's perspectives there and elsewhere do not always seem of this very moment, the reason may be that while he helped shape the moment we now inhabit, it had yet to come into being while he was writing many of these essays.

Barry often seemed serious, but he had a sly sense of humor in person and a capacity for delight. I met him for the first time when we were both staying in Galisteo, New Mexico, one summer around the turn of the twenty-first century, and an editor who knew both of us introduced us by email. When we met, I told him he should see the life-size bear petroglyph hidden in the hills beyond, and while I knew there were thunderstorms pretty much every afternoon, he insisted on writing mornings, so we set out as the white clouds gathered and began to darken into the color of a great blue heron's wings in flight.

We talked, we walked, he often paused en route to examine a plant or a stone; we admired the bear petroglyph and the others surrounding it, including two great serpents zigzagging like lightning, and then the lightning itself came, and the thunder, and a heavy rain that quickly soaked us to the skin. We crouched under a ledge during the most torrential minutes of the downpour, but it was impossible to stay apart from the rain, and easy on that warm afternoon in an otherwise arid landscape to yield to the delight of being—"baptized" is the word that comes to mind—in the storm. We had walked there on sandy soil, but we walked back on mud that turned our boots into clods.

I wrote, afterward, about something that happened near the petroglyphs:

> I looked down to see he had left one perfect footprint, and in it lay a small potsherd, striped red and black. That the footprint was not a minute old and the fragment in it might have been lying there five hundred

years compressed two kinds of past into one dazzling encounter. The term "walking in someone's footprints" instantly became literal, for this was a writer whose work had long ago suggested to me something of what I might dare to aim for with mine.

I have my own paths now, but Barry helped me find them. Which is what we always want writing to do, and so perhaps I'm just here to say he did it.

The footsteps that are these essays lead in many directions; all of them have older matter embedded in them. Some of you may want to follow them only as far as they go; others may find guidance for the paths you choose yourselves in exploring relationships to land and language, to the quest for meaning.

Rebecca Solnit
November 2021

CONVERSATIONS

Six Thousand Lessons

WHEN I WAS A BOY I WANTED TO SEE THE WORLD. BIT BY BIT IT'S happened. In 1948, when I was three, I left my home in Mamaroneck, just north of New York City, and flew with my mother to a different life in the San Fernando Valley, outside Los Angeles. I spent my adolescent summers at the Grand Canyon and swam in the great Pacific. Later, when my mother married again, we moved to the Murray Hill section of Manhattan. Another sort of canyon. I traveled across Europe by bus when I was seventeen. I went to Mexico. I camped in the desert in Namibia and on the polar plateau, twenty kilometers from the South Pole. I flew to Bangkok and Belém, to Nairobi and Perth, and traveled out into the country beyond.

Over the years I ate many unfamiliar meals, overheard arguments conducted on city streets in Pashto, Afrikaans, Flemish, Cree. I prayed in houses of worship not my own, walked through refugee camps in Lebanon, and crossed impossible mountain passes on the Silk Road. Witness, not achievement, is what I was after. From the beginning, I wanted to understand how very different each stretch of landscape, each boulevard, each cultural aspiration was. The human epistemologies, the six thousand spoken ways of knowing God, are like the six thousand ways a river can run down from high country to low, like the six thousand ways dawn might break over the Atacama, the Tanami, the Gobi, or the Sonoran.

Having seen so much, you could assume, if you are not paying close attention, that you know where you are, succumbing to the heresy of believing one place actually closely resembles another. But this is not true. Each place is itself only, and nowhere repeated. Miss it and it's gone.

Of the six thousand valuable lessons that might be offered a persistent traveler, here is a single one. Over the years in speaking with Indigenous people—Yupik and Inupiat in Alaska and Inuit in Canada—I came to understand that they prefer to lack the way we use collective nouns in the West for a species. Their tendency is not to respond to a question about what it is that "caribou" do, but to say instead what an individual caribou once did in a particular set of circumstances—in that place, at that time of year, in that type of weather, with these other animals around. It is important to understand, they say, that on another, apparently similar occasion, that animal might do something different. All caribou, despite their resemblance to each other, are not only differentiated one from the other but in the end are unpredictable.

In Xian once, where Chinese archaeologists had recently uncovered a marching army of terra-cotta soldiers and horses, and where visitors can view them in long pits in situ, I studied several hundred with a pair of binoculars. The face of each one, men and horses alike, was unique. I've watched herds of impala bounding away from lions on the savanna of Africa and flocks of white corellas roosting at dusk in copses of gum trees in the Great Sandy Desert in Western Australia, and have had no doubt in those moments that with patience and tutoring I could distinguish one animal from another.

It is terrifying for me to consider, now, how television, a kind of cultural nerve gas, has compromised the world's six thousand epistemologies, collapsing them into "what we all know" and "what we all believe." To consider how some yearn for all of us to speak Mandarin or English, "to make life easier." To consider how a stunning photograph of a phantom orchid can be made to stand today for all phantom orchids. To consider how traveling to Vienna can mean for some that you've more or less been to Prague. How, if you're pressed for time, one thing can justifiably take the place of another.

During these years of travel, my understanding of what diversity can mean has evolved. I began with an intuition, that the world was, from place to place and culture to culture, far more different than I had been led to believe. Later, I began to understand that to ignore these differences is not simply insensitive but unjust and perilous. To ignore the differences does not make things better. It creates isolation, pain, fury, despair. Finally, I came to see something profound. Long-term, healthy patterns of social organization, among all social life-forms, it seemed to me, hinged on work that maintained the integrity of the community while at the same

time granting autonomy to its individuals. What made a
society beautiful was some combination of autonomy and
deference that, together, minimized strife.

In my understanding diversity is not, as I had once
thought, a characteristic of life. It is, instead, a condition
necessary *for* life. To eliminate diversity would be like elimi-
nating carbon and expecting life to go on. This, I believe, is
why even a passing acquaintance with endangered languages
or endangered species or endangered cultures brings with it
so much anxiety, so much sadness. We know in our tissues
that the fewer the differences we encounter, wherever it is we
go, the more widespread the kingdom of death has become.

An Intimate Geography

IT WAS NIGHT, BUT NOT THE COLOR OF SKY YOU MIGHT EXPECT. The sun was up in the north, a few fingers above the horizon, and the air itself was bluer than it had been that afternoon, when the light was more golden. A friend and I, on a June "evening," were sitting atop a knoll in the Brooks Range in northern Alaska. We had our spotting scopes trained on a herd of several hundred barren-ground caribou, browsing three miles away in the treeless, U-shaped valley of the Anaktuvuk River. The herd drifted in silence across an immensity of space.

Sitting there, some hundreds of feet above the valley floor, we joked that the air was so transparent you could see all the way to the Anaktuvuk's confluence with the Colville River, ninety miles down the valley. The dustless atmosphere scattered so little light, we facetiously agreed, it was only the curvature of the Earth that kept us from being able to see clear to Franz Josef Land, in the Russian Arctic. I braced the fingers of my left hand against a cobble embedded in the tundra by my hip, to shift my weight and steady my gaze. The orange lichen on the rock blazed in my eye like a cutting torch before I turned back to the spotting scope and the distant caribou.

Years later, at the opposite end of the planet, I was aboard a German ecotourist ship crossing the Drake Passage from the Falkland Islands to South Georgia. The vessel was yawing through forty-foot seas, pitching and rolling in a Beaufort force 11 storm, one category shy of a hurricane. Dressed in storm gear and gripping a leeward rail outside on one of the upper decks, I stood shoulder to shoulder with a colleague. The surface of the gray sea before us had no point of stillness, no transparency. Veils of storm-ripped water ballooned in the air, and the voices of a flock of albatrosses, teetering in incomprehensible flight, cut the roar of the wind rising and collapsing in the ship's superstructure. In the shadowless morning light, beyond the grip of my gloves on the rail, beyond the snap of our parka hoods crumpling in the wind, the surface of the ocean was another earthly immensity, this one more contained, and a little louder, than the one in the Brooks Range.

IN APRIL 1988 I WAS traveling across China in the company of several other writers. In Chongqing, in Sichuan Province, we made arrangements to descend the stretch of the Yangtze River that cuts through the Wushan Mountains, the site of the famed Three Gorges, upriver from Yichang. At that time, years before the completion of the Three Gorges Dam, the Yangtze still moved swiftly through the bottom of this steep-walled canyon, falling, as it did, 519 feet between Chongqing and Yichang.

Despite the occasional set of rapids, the water in the gorges teemed with commerce—shirtless men paddled slender, pirogue-like boats down, up, and across the Yangtze; larger passenger vessels, such as ours, plowed through; and we passed heavily loaded lighters and packets laboring against the current. The air was ripe with the smells of spoiling fish, fresh vegetables, and human waste. The scene, a kind of Third World cliché, didn't fully engage me—until I caught sight, unexpectedly, of great runs of vertical space on the right bank, variegated fields rising straight up, perhaps nine hundred feet, into a blue sky. The terraced slopes were as steep as playground slides, a skein of garden plots and traversing rice paddies, dotted with sheds and houses. These images might be visible between sections of bare cliff for no more than thirty seconds as the ship passed them, but the convergence of cultural and physical geography was spectacular. The boldness of the farming ventures made my heart race. And in that mute, imposing gorge I discovered a different type of seductive earthly immensity. I wanted time to ferret out all the revealing detail in those densely patterned clefts. But our riverboat bore on. I inhaled sharply the damp perfume of human life around me, and gazed instead at the bolus of light shattering endlessly on the turbid water of the bow wave.

LIKE OTHER PERSISTENT TRAVELERS, I have often viewed the surface of the Earth from high-flying aircraft, but those

intangible expanses have rarely had the emotional impact of
the stillness I experienced that night in the Anaktuvuk River
valley or the more circumscribed view I had later of the cha-
otic Southern Ocean, let alone the detail and animation of
the Yangtze River scenes. What's missing in views from high-
flying aircraft is the sensual immediacy of a place. The sound
and the smell of it, the press of tempered air on the skin that
accompanies what one sees. It's the full reach of the landscape that's not apparent, what you could call the authority
of the land. The impression of distance in the valley of the
Anaktuvuk that night was intensified by seeing the brilliance
of a few lichen-covered rocks close to my hand, by being able
to make a connection, in that same instant, between the near
and the far. Also, a ground-level view, unlike the view from a
plane, has both a foreground and a middle ground—my yellow gloves grasping the rail of the ship and the albatrosses
flying between the ship and the horizon. Or the gardens rising from riverbank to canyon crest.

I don't mean to imply that someone can never establish
an intimate connection with the Earth from an airplane,
though this seems to happen only at low altitudes and slow
speeds. Many years ago, when I was doing research for a
book about the Arctic, I flew regularly with a bush pilot
named Duncan Grant. He traveled routinely and widely in a
twelve-passenger Twin Otter across Canada's Queen Eliza-
beth Islands, north of the North American mainland, ferrying scientists and their gear to and from remote summer
campsites. Most bush pilots in that country tended to fly in a
straight line from point A to point B, cruising at an unvarying altitude of three thousand feet. Duncan flew zigzag

courses, like an Arctic fox searching for something to eat, always at an altitude of about three hundred feet. As his passenger, you never quite lost touch with the Earth. He would habitually follow leads in the summer pack ice, hoping for a glimpse of narwhals. He'd throttle the aircraft back nearly to a stalling point so he could pass a flock of snow geese more slowly.

I learned from Duncan, who maintained close visual contact with the varied and active surface of the planet whenever he flew, what Antoine de Saint-Exupéry, Anne Morrow Lindbergh, and other writer-pilots meant by the phrase "the romance of flight." It was not freedom from the Earth they sought as much as a release from the tyranny of distance. And what they discovered, what was genuinely new in their explorations, was a different kind of intimacy with earthly places, both the ones they were already familiar with and those they were seeing for the first time.

Books like Saint-Exupéry's *Wind, Sand and Stars* and Beryl Markham's *West with the Night* held my attention because of the pilots' allegiance to the physical Earth, including their own trackless paths through the atmosphere. Their descriptions revealed more deeply the complex relationships to place that are the hallmark of strong human feelings about geography. They particularized the dull abstractions—the purple plain, the shining river, the amber waves of grain. They enlivened and humanized them.

WHEN I THINK OF MY own attempts to maintain intimacy with the Earth, what first comes to mind is not any arduous

encounter with the terrain or a deliberating hour on my
hands and knees somewhere, but the Paleolithic cave complex at Altamira. In the spring of 1991, the director of the
local museum offered me a private tour of this underground
gallery of early human art, in Cantabrian Spain. Accompanied by a guide and with no limit on my time, I was able to
move through its various sections at my own speed, grateful
for the guide's patience with my slowness. I observed each
tableau of animal life, studiously altering my perspective
before each one, feeling all the while the damp closeness of
the walls and the darkness crowding in. I speculated, like any
visitor, about the meaning of what was before me, but these
intellectual efforts were the least important thing going on.
Surrounded by this vivid, riveting evidence of human imaginations at work, and with the humid silence exaggerating the
paintings' starkness, I felt a tenuous identity with its creators.
In some sense, these people were my Cro-Magnon ancestors.
Holocene history—the domestication of wheat, the codifica-
tion of law under Hammurabi, the emergence of the Chinese dynasties—none of that entered my mind. All I could
see was this glistening testament that Magdalenian hunters
had left behind, and myself standing before it, the staring,
slow-breathing, distant relative.

When I exited the caves on a promontory and looked out
across a Mondrian patchwork of kitchen gardens, corralled
stock, and simple two-story houses at the edge of the town of
Santillana del Mar, I felt a surge of empathy for all humanity,
as if the paintings and the cultivated soil before me had been
created by human beings separated by no more than a few
generations.

INTIMACY WITH THE PHYSICAL EARTH apparently awakens in us, at some wordless level, a primal knowledge of the nature of our emotional as well as our biological attachments to physical landscapes. Based on my own inquiries, my impression is that we experience this primal connection regularly as a diffuse, ineffable pleasure, experience it as the easing of a particular kind of longing.

I recall diving on a nameless seamount in Dixon Entrance, near the southern tip of Prince of Wales Island in British Columbia's coastal waters, a kind of flooded landscape. I was working with a team of ecologists surveying benthic communities in the area. Diving is a highly charged form of human inquiry and many divers become aware of a renewed sense of intense, amorous contact with the Earth almost immediately upon entering the water. A limit on the supply of air you can take along lets you know that your time here will be relatively short. The resistance of the water tells you that you won't be going very far. And the projecting frame of your mask suggests, like a monk's cowl, that much will likely go by you unnoticed. Gravity, however, will clearly not be a restraint on your desire to examine things here, where you are "out of your element." You can swim up and down the face of one-hundred-foot cliff walls, and if you have good neutral buoyancy skills, you can suspend yourself a few inches from a wall and scrutinize every movement a tiny creature makes, minute after minute, while it feeds.

That day, diving at Dixon Entrance, I felt like an astronaut, untethered, on an extravehicular excursion. The seamount, which rose to within sixty feet of the surface and was only about two hundred yards in diameter, fell away into abyssal darkness on every side. While our mother ship, the National Oceanic and Atmospheric Administration vessel *Alpha Helix*, floated overhead in station-keeping mode, the six of us split up to inspect the complicated contours of this isolated formation. Predictably, in these cold, nutrient-rich waters, the mount was thickly covered with sponges, hydrocorals, anemones, tubeworms, basket stars, and brilliantly colored nudibranchs. Crustaceans appeared in nearly every crevice, and one of us saw an octopus. Small fish darted about, larger fish lumbered past. The scene was generally familiar from other cold-water dives I'd made in the Pacific Northwest, until I passed within a few feet of a hole about the size of my fist. The blunt head of an eel protruded from it—an ancient, bald, almost terrifying face. A wolf eel, I realized, and I pulled back sharply. Later, I encountered another wolf eel, this one about three feet long, undulating across the expanse of the seamount in its eerie, limbless way. It triggered the same sudden alarm in my mammalian cerebellum, but the rocky field of bright color over which it moved, pale greens and dark browns, dappled with the shadows of surface waves and accentuated by luminous spots of chartreuse, apricot, carmine, and lavender, gave the eel a kind of innocence and vulnerability with which I identified, suspended there in the open ocean.

I FEEL FORTUNATE TO HAVE been able to experience so much of the physical world directly, to have had time to linger and observe, to ask questions, and to listen while someone explained some subtle characteristic of his local landscape. I have felt pulled since early childhood toward the raw materials of geography and toward its local interpreters, though the pull has not always been toward unpopulated places like those I've been describing here. On a visit to Kabul, in the fall of 2007, my host offered me the services of a Pashtun driver and a battered car, which gave us a lower profile. Over two days the driver and I made our way through virtually every quarter of that blasted, crowded, dust-choked, and heroic landscape. I had told my host that I wanted to see what was actually going on in the streets of his city. What were people really doing in this place?

I watched men in open-air foundries taking infinite care as they hand-peened pieces of scrap metal into parts for cars. I watched a man sell a single pomegranate from a tiny tray of pomegranates, the entirety of his wares. I watched herdsmen moving their goats through reeking heaps of street-corner rubbish—and recalled a dinner conversation I'd had a few days earlier with one of Afghanistan's ministers, a man anxious about plans for his country's economic survival and development. It is from observing the interplay of minute details like these within the larger, overall picture, sensing the tension between the revelatory particular and the general condition, that the written stories we most trust about life begin to take shape. For me, those stories have very often been about human drama in specific places—Herman Melville's Pacific, William Faulkner's Yoknapatawpha County, Saigyō Hōshi's Honshū, Nadine Gordimer's Johannesburg.

Geography, some scholars believe, has subtly but directly influenced the development of our cultures, our languages, our diets, our social organization, and to some degree even our politics. Whenever I travel in remote or in still largely tribal places, I'm often conscious of watching for something modern humans might have misplaced on their way from Altamira to Rome and Tenochtitlán—specifically, the understanding that geography was central to any idea of their destiny. Once, I can easily imagine, we each had a fundamental sense of well-being that grew directly out of our intimacy, our back-and-forth, with the profundity embedded in the places we occupied.

FROM TIME TO TIME I'VE been asked, as a traveler, which landscape I favor most. Would it be, the interviewer inquires, the Tanami Desert in Australia's Northern Territory? The terraced hills of Bali, or perhaps the intracoastal waterway of southern Chile? I always respond in the same way, saying no, it would be my home in western Oregon, where I have lived since the summer of 1970.

The house is situated on a bench above the north bank of the McKenzie River, in mixed old-growth forest. The valley here is too steep for farming, so human settlement has been light. Industrial logging has taken a toll, sweeping the mountain slopes clear of trees in many places. But Chinook salmon still spawn in front of the house and, just glancing out the windows, I've seen bobcat, mink, and black bear. Elk and mountain lion are nearby in the woods, as are coyote, beaver, river otter, and black-tailed deer. I often come upon their tracks. From the river, I regularly hear ospreys and belted kingfishers call; and from the trees, ravens, pileated woodpeckers, and a host of other birds—warblers, tanagers, and thrushes among them.

Douglas firs, cedars, hemlocks, and big-leaf maples surround the house so tightly they take away the horizon. Sometimes, when their crowns sway in the wind, I have the sense that I'm living at the bottom of a kelp forest. The expanse of this montane forest, like the expanse of the Pacific Ocean, is something I feel, and against this volume of space I array the details of life here: the late-night caterwaul of a gray fox, so like the wail of a terrified child; claw marks on the broken boards of an outbuilding, dismantled by a black bear; a rubber boa, pale as the stem of a mushroom, curled up by the kitchen steps one morning; the glint from an obsidian spear point, a broken section of which I unearthed one evening with a trowel while laying a brick walk in the forest.

Over the years I have seen, heard, tasted, palpated, and smelled many remarkable things around the place. I do not recall a single day of attentiveness outdoors, in fact, when something unknown, something new, hasn't flared up before me. I'm kept from the conceit that there is anything remarkable in this, however, by steady streams of weekend tourist traffic that speed past the house, en route to recreation areas in the mountains or to launch points on the river. To most, my landscape, I have to think, must appear innocuous, ordinary.

Still, I'm happy in this undemonstrative, rural place. In my conversations with it I know, once more, who I am. It inundates me continually with mystery, because its nature is too complex to be fully known. If I want the comfort of intimacy with it, of integration and acceptance, my only choice is participation—to learn from it by participating. I imagine my choice here is very like that of Magdalenian cave painters in their time, one of stepping into the physical world as fully as circumstances permit. Of not opting for the expediency of detachment.

Accelerated global climate change, an abstraction around elements of physical geography, has become an inexorable force in the alteration of the Earth's biological fabric. As climatic change begins to affect long-range strategic planning for human survival, as the Earth's stocks of pelagic food fish plummet, as dry-land aquifers are drained, we can easily believe we've been shortsighted in a loss of intimacy with place, in largely ignoring the impact geography has on our daily lives. As humans in Africa and Asia migrate today from their derelict lands in search of ground more habitable—or simply in search of gainful employment—we can even wonder whether, in not providing a central role for geographical awareness in the shaping of our country's domestic and international policies, we've erred fatefully.

THE JACK HILLS IN WESTERN Australia lie about four hundred miles north-northeast of Perth. There, in the 1980s, scientists found a lode of zircon crystals that at the time represented the oldest known bits of the Earth's crust. One of these extremely hard and durable crystals was dated at 4.27 billion years, about 250 million years after the formation of the planet. After reading in *Nature* about the discovery, I felt compelled to see the region. I didn't want to spirit away any specimens. I just wanted, if I could, to become for a moment a part of the flow of time there.

From the regional airport at Meekatharra I drove overland in a rented four-wheel-drive about two hundred kilometers to a sheep station near the site of the find. The next morning, the manager of the station offered to fly me slowly over the section of the Jack Hills I was trying to reach, to help get me oriented in a roadless area. Employing that overview, and using a hand-drawn map given to me by one of the geologists involved in the research, I located by midmorning the dry wash in which the crystals had first been discovered. I parked in a copse of eucalyptus trees and walked slowly uphill, studying the ground closely. Distant, almost mythic events in the Archean Eon came to mind while flocks of small, bright, green-and-yellow budgerigars zoomed close overhead. Galahs and crested cockatiels called from trees in the distance. I sat for a while at the edge of a dry watercourse and, from time to time, studied open sections of the broken, hilly country with a pair of binoculars. Nothing moved. I saw no sheep, no feral cats or goats, only the arid contours of a brittle land with little soil, one that carried few footprints distinct enough for me to read.

By early afternoon I was satisfied that I'd located the precise spot where the crystals had first been noticed. The geological exposure was unequivocal. I lingered there for an hour, viewing all I saw in light of the tiny crystals glittering in the rock formation at my feet.

On my way back to the truck I stopped to focus my binoculars ahead on a small flock of gray-and-pink cockatoos with white crowns—galahs. The late-afternoon light inflamed their pink chests and I could now easily distinguish female galahs, with their red eyes, from brown-eyed males. The heated air buzzed with their raucous calls, erupting from the upper limbs of the eucalypts under which I'd parked. From the upper end of the wash, my line of sight carried out over the crowns of those trees into a plain beyond, a sun-drenched expanse of savanna under a massive, pale blue sky. It was too far off, on the plain, to catch and identify the voice of any bird there, but perhaps, just then, birds unknown to me were announcing themselves in that welter of space.

An Era of Emergencies Is Upon Us
and We Cannot Look Away

WE'VE LIVED FOR GENERATIONS IN AMERICA WITH OUR PROMISING tomorrows waiting for us just up ahead. Despite world wars and ceaseless warfare, despite backbreaking (for some) economic depressions and recessions, despite a history of slavery and genocide and being plagued by regular flare-ups of malfeasance and corruption in government, despite the oceans of filth and poison that hang menacingly in suspension in our air and water, we continue to believe in deliverance. We believe in the eventual triumph of liberal values—the passage and enforcement of equitable laws, comity in all our daily affairs, affordable education, probity from our politicians— the full embrace of which will allow us finally to dismantle entrenched bigotry and injustice.

As I write these words I'm compelled to say that I see no sign of such a salvation on the horizon. This is not to imply that the situation in the United States is hopeless— even considering the wealth gap, widespread environmental degradation, institutionalized cheating in business, the many biological and economic problems associated with advancing climate breakdown, and the social inequity created by, say, male privilege—but only to suggest that we have been kidding ourselves about there being, just up ahead, a clear path to the other side of all this. Our children and grandchildren, seeing how tentative our response has been to global climate disorder and to whatever else might conceivably be coming along—the sudden collapse of an international financial institution like Deutsche Bank or a pandemic for which there is no immediate cure—have framed already their objections: Why did you not prepare? Why were you so profligate while we still had a chance? Where was your wisdom?

Many of the pictures in the 2021 book *American Geography: Photographs of Land Use from 1840 to the Present* speak to questions about our survival as a species. Some reflect our sense of grief about what has happened. In others you can feel the photographer's bewilderment at the same time as his or her wonder. For some viewers, these pictures might prompt feelings of anger and condemnation. If you imagine the project as a whole piece of cloth, you could say that the larger question here is: *What have we done?*

For me, who began my professional life as a photographer as well as a writer more than fifty years ago, the stance *American Geography* takes is one of direct confrontation. The volume dispenses with sentimentality and nostalgia about our once-primal landscapes and is, further, not compromised by iconic photographs of the beautiful. Also, for all of its pictures from the nineteenth and early twentieth centuries, the project is much less about our past than it is about our future. *American Geography* persistently questions the value of the "fruits of progress" (or the lack of them) and also the putative ethical foundation for Manifest Destiny. To go on like this, the photographs suggest—to continue to applaud the individual quest for substantial personal wealth at the expense of others, and to continue to promote the puerile dreams of some to secure positions of social and political advantage over others—would be suicidal.

When the curator Sandra S. Phillips first invited me to discuss the ideas behind this project, I urged her to consider, along with the pictures of cultural imposition she had already located—the boot prints, if you will, of the colonial invader—other, perhaps more welcoming photographs of the enduring biological, geological, and botanical integrity of American landscapes, pictures not marred by clearcuts, toxic settling ponds, transmission towers, contrails, open-pit mines, stalled traffic, sprawling feedlots, and the rest of humanity's infrastructure. These pictures of unmanipulated land, I thought, would contrast sharply with scenes of economic hardship and the heedless marauding that drove the westward movement. They would make the ethical debacle documented in many of these photographs more apparent.

But I came around to her point of view. Crudely put, it is that we can no longer afford to carry on in a prolonged era of polite reflection and ineffective resistance. An Era of Emergencies is bearing down on us. We must now consider, for example, how to organize the last industrial extractions of oil, fresh water, natural gas, timber, metallic ores, and fish in order to ensure our own survival; and we must consider, of course, what comes after that. We must reckon with the Sixth Extinction, which will remove, for example, many of our

pollinators and one day, probably, many of us. We must
invent overnight, figuratively speaking, another kind of civilization, one more cognizant of limits, less greedy, more
compassionate, less bigoted, more inclusive, less exploitive.

It is startling to encounter in some of the earlier photographs in *American Geography* the capacity of women and men,
many decades ago, to recognize and capture on film juxtapo-
sitions that expose the potential for natural and cultural
disaster in what, for so long, we had considered the normal
order of Western progress.

The courage behind curating *American Geography*, for me,
is the decision to address unflinchingly the troubling future, to
prompt a reconsideration of what will work for us now, what
we will freely abandon, and what we will hold on to at any
cost. In contemporary art today, internationally as well as
here in America, I have noticed opposition to entertainment
for its own sake and a burgeoning desire to create art of con-
sequence, art that does not trifle with us or exploit our grief.
More prominent in the arts now than the desire to inform
and to illuminate our predicament, or to indict its causes, is
the desire to probe it, and to identify previously unconsid-
ered approaches to managing it, to offer metaphors that
open out onto workable solutions. With this different kind
of orientation it is then possible to regard the dark underbelly of the Industrial Revolution and understand that that
radical change in social organization, alongside the sheer
scale of industrial production, is now presenting us with a
medical bill for all this change, for the treatment of mesothe-
lioma, black lung, pollution cancers, and the rest. To consider that the honeybee and the wild horse have their own

integrity and perhaps even their own aspirations, and can no longer be viewed as subjects, willing to participate in the construction of a world built to serve the needs and desires of human beings alone.

At the heart of the lifework of many artists I have known is a simple but profound statement: "I object." I have studied what we have done to the planet and I object. I object to the exploitation of, and the lack of respect for, human laborers. I object to the frantic commercialization of the many realms of daily life, I object to the desecration of what is beautiful, to the celebration of what is venal, and to the ethical obtuseness of the king's adoring enablers. I object to society's complacency.

I would ask you not to give in to the temptation to despair, not to retreat into cynicism or settle into disaffection, but to recognize in these photographs the resilience, determination, and concern for the fate of humanity that these photographers possess. And I would ask you further to consider how integral to *American Geography* is the idea of an *ensemble* of work like this. While there is individual genius behind many of these pictures, it is the community of artists, the absence of overbearing individual sentiment, that stands out here.

It was during the Scientific Revolution that Art, as a distinct and enduring form of truth-telling—as important for us to consider as the data sets Science has produced in its own ongoing effort to plot a viable future for humanity—began to lose its stature. Since then we have come to regard the voice of Science as definitive. Now some are saying that we appear to be on the verge of another kind of orientation, resituating Art in a position of authority. We are seeing this in photography, in musical composition, in fiction, in dance and theater, in installation and performance art, and in painting, as artists make our existential predicament more apparent and point us in the direction of radical social change, for which, frighteningly, we have made virtually no preparation.

The photographs in *American Geography* are not an indictment of human enterprise, nor are they a critique of industrialization or a condescending assessment of humanity's failures. If anything, they reveal the artists' sense of implication in whatever they confront with the camera, and in some ways the grief that they share with the viewer. In *American Geography* there is no one to blame. The project is an invitation, instead, to reimagine our future, to identify a different road than the one that the prophets of technological innovation, or global climate change itself, are offering us.

It's the road to our survival.

In Memoriam: Wallace Stegner

I HARDLY KNEW WALLACE STEGNER. WE MET A FEW TIMES and exchanged letters, but it would be misleading to say that I knew him any better than any other close and admiring reader of his work.

The first time we met was at his home in Los Altos Hills, and what I particularly remember about that meeting was the way humility and wisdom came together in the man. As a young writer, I very much needed to pay my respects, and he let me do that without trying to cut me off, without trying to deny his own worth—which would have been like telling me I didn't know what I was talking about. In that most concrete way I learned something about how a writer should conduct himself or herself. Over the years I came to greatly admire that quality in him, his behavior as a writer. In our era of celebrities, he would have none of it. In an era of self-promotion he just walked away. In an era of obsession with personal goals, he wanted to know how he could help the community.

Stegner saw a continuum, I think, in which writers were part of the human community, with obligations and responsibilities—which might or might not turn out to have a political expression. A separate continuum linked writers, a more or less loosely knit group of men and women intent on telling stories and feeling various degrees of professionalism and spiritual allegiance toward each other. It was in that context, I believe, that Stegner heard me out that afternoon on his deck in Los Altos Hills.

When I had spoken my piece, he said some kind things about my work and put his hand on my shoulder, as if to convey his feeling that we stood on the same floor together—which was not true but, rather, kind and generous, and one might say constructive, because he was demonstrating a way to share.

Years later I was sitting with the writer Wendell Berry in Wendell's kitchen in Kentucky. We came around to talking about Stegner and I told Wendell some of the things that Wally had written me about my work. And we agreed that he was the only person either of us knew who could pay you a compliment in such a way that you felt you had to continue, and maybe do better just to live up to the implied expectation.

One of the most astonishing things about him was reiterated for Wendell and me in that moment—Stegner found, or made, time for other people. He encouraged people and assisted them. I think he truly believed the world, or at least the West, could become a better place if people were generous with what they had—if they gave away their time, for example, to a vision larger than any vision they themselves had or could entirely appreciate. In a way this flew in the face of a tradition of hostility in the West, range wars between settlers and cattlemen a hundred-some years ago and now contention between logging and mining interests and conservationists. Wally was saying: We must find a way to trust in our neighbors, to invest in them.

I don't mean to suggest, either naïvely or with the admiration for another that distills so readily after death, that Stegner was flawless. I have no doubt but that he was human, that he stumbled and fell with the rest of us. And I feel no shred of a need to know the particulars of such things. What I want to know, what I look for as a writer, is what good was a person capable of, how did love flourish around him or her? How did what they do help?

News that a person parted his hair in the wrong place or committed some ordinary indiscretion is no news. The news is: How did a person love? That's the news we're eager to hear. That is what we want to know.

So here is this person whom I knew but slightly, who in our first meeting found a way to say, with such integrity, I love you. And he knew what sort of effect that might have, and he meant for that to happen. And that is admirable. I feel as an American writer a responsibility to imitate, for example, Stegner's scrupulous attention to history; but I also feel an obligation to try to conduct myself, as well as I can, with the same kindness and generosity he showed me that day on his deck.

We are all going to die, of course. And deaths remind us to live our lives fully, to take advantage of every opportunity to love and to be loved. And deaths as large as Stegner's—

a first-rate novelist and essayist, a model historian, a man who took citizenship seriously—remind us how poorly we often do, meaning to love each other.

I don't know that Wallace Stegner ever meant to teach that particular lesson; it's in our way of life that we often teach best what we're not conscious of, by the example of our lives. But I will always remember this about him, what he encouraged. It is a good idea to love each other, and to love the Earth. It is the only way we can make children. It is the only way we can have a place to abide. And by those two things perpetuate ourselves. No one knows what human destiny is, but surely it must be our hope that it is something good, that it is striving toward what we call God. And we know that it is love and all that love contains—passion, awe, allegiance, ecstasy, respect, selflessness—that carries us in that direction.

If love is to discover and rediscover life, to encourage and protect it, to marvel at it and serve it, that lesson is scripted on the rock walls of Arnhem Land and Cantabria; it has been passed down in Aramaic and Shona, in Gaelic and Mandarin and Chinook; and it comes round to us again in the memories of *Wolf Willow*, the admiring prose of *Beyond the Hundredth Meridian*, the virtue of *Crossing to Safety*. It is the best we can do for each other, to remember, to say it all again. And in this instance of Wallace Stegner, the best he could do was very much enough.

Out West

I. THE MASSACRES

In the early 1970s I began to take an interest in the Nez Perce retreat, an effort by this Oregon band of Sahaptin people to reach political asylum in Canada in the summer of 1877. Before they were cornered at an abbreviated range of low hills in north-central Montana, north of the Bears Paw Mountains, an emotionally exhausted and spiritually devastated group of families—they'd left their ancestral lands in the Wallowa Mountains three months earlier—the Nez Perce had fought off a pursuing U.S. Cavalry force in several skirmishes. As frequently occurs when I begin researching such a subject, I developed a keen interest in visiting some of those sites. Even the most meticulous history of such events, I had found, tends to be deskbound; the why and wherefore of what occurred often becomes more obvious (and less confabulated) when the real ground, the actual location, becomes a part of what one knows.

Accordingly, on June 17, 1973, I began at White Bird
Canyon in western Idaho, the site of the first lethal encounter of the retreat. (Despite the Nez Perce's intent to leave the
United States peacefully, historians routinely refer to what
happened as the Nez Perce War.) My plan was to camp at
this and subsequent sites—at Camas Meadows and Clearwater in Idaho and at Big Hole in Montana—during the
same hours of the solar year in which the killings had taken
place. I would begin at White Bird Canyon, visit the others
in the coming years as I could, then travel to the Bears Paws
in 1977, planning to arrive on October 4, the centennial eve
of the last killings and the Nez Perce surrender.

Readers of nineteenth-century Native American history
would rightly regard this as a quick sketch presented from the
Nez Perce, or Nimíipuu, point of view, and know I was passing over contradictions and complexities. My interest here,
though, is not history so much as it is those who write the histories upon which we so often stake our political and spiritual
lives. (Irritating to many historians today is the charge that
when it comes to defining such encounters, Native American
versions are routinely dismissed by scholars as "unorthodox.")
My further interest—and what would compel other visits to
fatal-encounter sites in the United States in the years after
this—is the role the land itself played in these histories. I don't
mean solely issues of tactics, weather conditions, or the position and angle of the sun on a particular day, but what might
be learned from a people forced to unravel from their home
land, to abandon an integration with place that would strike
many of us in the United States in the twenty-first century as
bizarre, were we not so concerned with being respectful.

One further thing was always on my mind during the days I made my visits: the intractable problem of what one remembers. Who now recalls what happened during those years of warfare? And how does forgetfulness work in the service of illusions of national destiny?

I was recently in Germany. In Berlin I visited three times in one week a work by Peter Eisenman, his *Memorial to the Murdered Jews of Europe*—an entire city block turned into something approaching a Dantean ring of Hell, an architecture that simultaneously evokes the Warsaw Ghetto, a morgue, and George Orwell's *1984*. Like many compelling three-dimensional works, the monument is simple to the point of being reductive, but it draws very strongly on the fourth dimension, on time, the multifaceted antecedents that we call history; it cannot be entirely fathomed, in fact, without the aid of memory. What one has read, whatever one might have seen around the world of the iconography and tools of genocide, whatever images of madness and cruelty one has encountered in a museum—Francisco de Goya, Käthe Kollwitz, Leon Golub—come into play. Because it is a work of genius, however, at least in my mind, memory merely intensifies, to an almost unbearable degree, what such a monument already conveys with its lines, its volumes, its textures, its absence of color.

I thought about Eisenman's work for weeks afterward, what it is doing for the German people by way of catharsis. There is, of course, no such public work to memorialize what happened to Native Americans in the United States. We have built a Holocaust museum in Washington, D.C., but no monument to acknowledge responsibility for actions many

American citizens today might be distressed, or even out-
raged, to hear called an American genocide.

For the majority of citizens in the United States the
Native American has vanished. Or, to use a euphemism of
the twentieth century, the Indian has been assimilated, an
idea that would raise a few eyebrows in 2006 at Oraibi, at
Huslia, Tsaile, and Onondaga. The nation, firm in the conviction that Indigenous people have disappeared, that this is
all in the past and requires no review, remains steadfastly
focused on "moving forward."

I grew up steeped in works of fine art set out for the edification and appreciation of visitors to the Metropolitan
Museum of Art, the Museum of Modern Art, the Frick Collection, the Cloisters, and New York's other museums. Sanc-
tuaries, temples of meaning, portals of history—I've not
known a diminishment of the adolescent enthusiasm I first
brought to those places and with which, each time, I walked
away. It's simply a more refined reverence now, I hope. (In all
the countries I've been able to travel to it's been my custom
not only to try to visit that culture's museums, the obscure
along with the touted, but to carry with me afterward post-
card reproductions of the work on display—images of what
others have preserved as beautiful or inspiring.) Over the
years, of course, the display of art and the popularity of
styles in America have changed. Under the influence of
modernism's and then postmodernism's protocols, some
things I had come to trust in art—the concept of place, for
example, that inapprehensible and profound sensation of
being present at one spot only—were marginalized. Though
I had read, and for a brief time even studied, enough

quantum mechanics to be wary of absolutes, of categorical assertions, I also rued the diminished importance of empiricism in modern art. Postmodernism, as I understood the school, preferred the imagination to the senses and took modernism's mistrust of the past, its argument with Western tradition, a step further, finally coming to trust only the tradition of the self.

My personal misgivings about modernism's evaluations and its influence count, certainly, for very little. I've no elaborated theory, no reevaluated social history with which to pose an argument with modernism. I have, for my purposes here, however, two relevant thoughts. What kind of governance is apt to arise among us as a people if specificity of place is unimportant, and if empirical witness is no more to be trusted than a flight of imagination?

IN THE DECADES AFTER THAT October night I spent asleep on the Nez Perce encounter ground north of the Bears Paws in Montana, I visited, whenever the opportunity arose, many of the Western battle and massacre sites of the American Indian wars (injustices that, like the Punic Wars, for instance, came to be named for a menace "rightfully" defeated). The battle sites—Beecher Island (1868), Lava Beds (1873), Little Bighorn (1876)—were fewer than the massacre sites: Bear River (1863), Sand Creek (1864), Washita (1868), Tule Canyon (1874), Wounded Knee (1890). At Tule Canyon, Texas, having burned the homes, winter food stores, and clothing of hundreds of Southern Cheyenne, Kiowa, and Comanche people wintering at nearby Palo Duro Canyon, Colonel

Ranald Mackenzie ordered his troopers to shoot 1,100 tribal horses and mules he'd captured and cordoned off in a box canyon. Some of the tightly bunched animals took days to die. For sixty-two years they lay where they fell that September morning. At Sand Creek, Colorado, a Methodist minister, Colonel John Chivington, led a similar raid at dawn against another group of unsuspecting people, mostly Southern Cheyenne, who, in addition to having raised a thirty-five-star American flag, were camped under a white flag of truce. What happened at Bear River, Idaho, on January 29, 1863, is the least publicized and, for the number of human beings killed, the greatest of the Western massacres. A freelancing group of California Volunteers, thwarted in their attempt to join in the Civil War, attacked a winter village of Northern Shoshone and without cause killed more than three hundred people. Their leader, Colonel Patrick Edward Connor, wrote in his official report of the essential need generally to "chastise" these people for their way of life.

Where is the art to help us deal with these actions and with the long silence that persists? Is what has been offered so far, mostly by Native American artists, so offensive to the nation's sense of self, so inconsequential when put up against the mythology of a chosen people, that it can't be accommodated? The Mexican novelist Carlos Fuentes once wrote that it was impossible for his country and the United States to have a productive conversation. Mexico, he said, is so burdened by its past it cannot easily imagine a future. The United States, he said, is so intent on imagining its future it isn't troubled by rewriting its past to serve that future.

What of the present? What is there in contemporary art

for those who, offered destiny's Eden, cannot relax their suspicions about its foundations?

Standing or walking the slaughter grounds I traveled
to—astonishing, really, how infrequently I encountered
another human being at these places—I could not quite
make the leap to a resolution from the horror of what had
happened. All my life, to be free of dejection and pessimism
about the imperfections of my own culture, I've read poets
of the past and of my own generation, listened to Bach's
Mass in B minor and his cello suites, and recalled Vermeers
in the Frick Collection, but the distance from Tule Canyon
and Bear River to Bach's Leipzig or Zagajewski's Paris is
very great.

As a longtime resident of the rural West, I can easily
imagine that a concern about the killing of Native people,
let alone a disturbance of this old and suppurating wound,
might be viewed as a regional, even an unseemly, affliction.
But in this celebratory year of the Corps of Discovery's journey west and back, one is compelled to come face-to-face
with the violent ghost history of Manifest Destiny, the kind
of nineteenth-century assertions of rightful ownership and
of racial and cultural superiority that would lead an unrepen-
tant Connor to take pride in his chastisements. The haunting
figure in that 1803–1806 expedition, because the memory of
him will not completely quit the national conscience, no matter how often he is written off—a drunk, a manic-depressive,
a man done in by the burden of responsibility—is Meri-
wether Lewis. Expedition enthusiasts who seek to explain
his violent death usually choose one of two competing theories. When he died in his room at an isolated inn on the

Natchez Trace, fifty-some miles from Nashville, Tennessee, on October 11, 1809, he was the victim of either murder or suicide. Murdered, one theory goes, because he was traveling to Washington with papers that would have compromised people in the federal government jockeying to profit personally from 828,000 square miles of Western real estate, the windfall of the Louisiana Purchase; a suicide, others propose, because he could not drink himself sufficiently into oblivion over the contradictions in Mr. Jefferson's dreams of democracy. (Lewis, who had served Jefferson as his chief of staff for eighteen months, was in thrall to his interpretation of Enlightenment ideals.)

In support of the latter argument, one might imagine the blow Lewis sustained when he came to realize that the peoples he had encountered, as different in their epistemologies as the landscapes in which he found them, were not to be included in Mr. Jefferson's democracy, that the Mandan, the Assiniboine, the Nez Perce, the Cayuse, and the Chinook were to be swept away, like the Yamasee, the Mahican, the Nanticoke, and the Powhatan before them. As governor of the Upper Louisiana Territory, meeting daily with his constituents in St. Louis, he was familiar with the nature of the first wave of citizens who wished to take over for the Lakota in the Black Hills, for the Pawnee on the Platte. They were a class of men most American historians, until recently, have worked tirelessly to clean up but who have come down to us looking as feverish and ruthless in pursuit of wealth as the conquistadores, men largely unmodulated by family life and lawless where the law was an inconvenience.

It is easy to imagine that in the three years between his

return from the Pacific and that October night at Grinder's Inn, Lewis lost faith with the ideals of the Republic, and that Jefferson, by then, couldn't afford, or didn't want, to hear his complaint.

ONE DAY LATE IN THE spring of 2005 I walked the Cheyenne massacre site on the Washita River in western Oklahoma. On the morning of November 27, 1868, Lieutenant Colonel George Armstrong Custer led four cavalry battalions in a surprise attack on a small encampment of Southern Cheyenne overwintering in the Washita bottoms (from *owa*, big, and *chito*, hunt, two Choctaw words, also anglicized as Ouachita). The isolated village of about fifty lodges was the farthest west outlier of a gathering of some four to six thousand Cheyenne, Arapahoe, Kiowa, Comanche, and Plains Apache settled farther downstream. Custer's men killed the Cheyenne chief Black Kettle that morning (it was from a lodgepole of this man's tepee that the white flag had flown four years earlier at Sand Creek), also twelve other men, sixteen women, and nine children. In a hurry to depart with his force of eight hundred soldiers before the downstream camps were alerted, Custer still took time to savage the Cheyenne horses and mules in accordance with a military objective of the time, to deprive the enemy of mobility. His troopers shot and cut the throats of about 875 animals and fled.

As I walked that afternoon—a child could pitch a stone to the far bank of the river, a man wade across without wetting his waist—I imagined no scene of redress, did not even think of blame. I was overcome by the immediacy of the place, the cemetery peace. Even though I would later come to feel that an understanding of the particulars of incidents like this was crucial to the nation's sense of identity, early on even I, curious and earnest as I was, knew little of Washita, even its whereabouts.

Walking the bottomlands, I came upon badger holes and coyote scat, stopped to gaze at bright yellow patches of prairie coneflower and clusters of white blooms on plains yucca stalks rocking and nodding in a light wind. Overhead, two Mississippi kites courted. Away on the hills to the north black Angus grazed. A few fair-weather clouds drifted in a milk-blue sky. The calls of male bobwhites pierced the warm air lying over the wooded flats.

If someone were to paint this place as it stands today, or to paint the history of that morning in this place, were to translate the acuity of his own senses, the emotional currents these sensations released in conversation with these very coneflowers, the discovered fate of Black Kettle, the silt-burdened Washita, the stray chips of horse bone still lying dull in the sunlight, would we turn our backs because it struck us as too representational, too sentimental, too Western?

II. THE COUNTRY IN WINTER

When I was in my twenties and thirties, I regularly drove thousands of sojourning miles across the western United States. I slept in my truck or, if the weather was good, on the ground. I believed if I could actually see a location such as Teapot Dome, Wyoming, or drive the east–west intergrade between shortgrass prairie and tallgrass prairie in Kansas, I would be a better reader of the literature of the West, not to say its history. (Teapot Dome, thirty miles north of Casper, was the site of an oilfield leased without competitive bidding by Warren Harding's corrupt secretary of the interior, Albert Fall, to an equally corrupt oil operator, Harry Sinclair, in 1922.) Among the books I was thinking about were Ole Rølvaag's *Giants in the Earth*, Frank Waters's *The Man Who Killed the Deer*, Wallace Stegner's *Angle of Repose*, Willa Cather's *My Ántonia*, and Ken Kesey's *Sometimes a Great Notion*. I carried them with me like another set of road maps, reading them in the evening along with works of history and anthropology.

In 1979 John Unruh published a landmark work of revisionist Western history, *The Plains Across: The Overland Emigrants and the Trans-Mississippi West, 1840–60*, carefully dismantling the foundations for an entrenched American belief in God-blessed pioneers besieged by rapacious Natives during the westward movement, a folklore imposed on the West later by Hollywood and by many writers of pulp Westerns. Unruh's work opened the door for writers as diverse as Annette Kolodny (*The Lay of the Land*) and Cormac McCarthy (*Blood Meridian*) to elucidate Western history from perspectives less romantic, less racist, less colonial. I felt as if I were living through a period of revolt in those years, one almost unheralded, a time when geography was making its way back into history, and when the genocidal origins of the nation might be brought up in conversation without apprehension. And when corporate attempts to gain control over the West's natural resources—timber, water, grazing land, and minerals—might actually be addressed on ethical as well as economic grounds. The novelist and historian Wallace Stegner, mentor at Stanford to a remarkable group of writers—Wendell Berry, Larry McMurtry, Robert Stone, Tillie Olsen, Ken Kesey—was a major force in this revisionist movement, a broad-based effort by writers, artists, and humanists to throw off definitions long imposed on it by outsiders and to propose in their stead another set of definitions, ones truer to the actual place. (In the only area of the visual arts with which I have more than a passing acquaintance—photography—I saw the sensibility emerge early in the work of Robert Adams [*To Make It Home*] and continue through people like Richard Misrach [*Bravo 20: The Bombing of the American West*] and Mary Peck [*Away Out Over Everything*].)

When I learned that an exhibition called *The Modern West: American Landscapes, 1890–1950* was being organized at the Museum of Fine Arts in Houston, and received a letter from its curator, Emily Ballew Neff, asking for some thoughts about the show, I was eager right away to look at what she was bringing together. Also somewhat nonplussed. I'd no credentials as a Western historian (let alone an art historian), no expertise, as I saw it, to offer. I had enthusiasm, respect. Wonder. A longtime interest in the work of such people as Laura Gilpin, Maynard Dixon, Ansel Adams, and Alexandre Hogue, partly because their kinds of realism had gotten such a cold reception from critics who thought that Western realism was too illustrative, in general, to be considered fine art. (In that way, Dixon and Hogue seemed to share the fate of Rockwell Kent.)

I knew very little, really, about what Ms. Neff was trying to say with the show, or about the West that was her West, but when I saw the paintings and photographs she had assembled, I recognized in the groupings many of my own concerns about Western art, particularly the struggle in the nineteenth century to impose lines on volumes of space unfamiliar to the European imagination, the conceptual and technical effort it took to bring together the very far away and the intimate nearby when they were not connected by conventional human culture, by farming and roads. I saw the weird shimmer, too, of *toujours une étrangère*, the artist-observer's deepening awareness that he or she was not a resident of what he or she depicted; the geography of a place initiates misgivings about belonging. These misgivings are intensified by a growing awareness that the mythos most of us were born to, the early gyroscope of our cultural psyche, does not fit here, and, further, that those myths that do fit have nearly been eradicated by cultural and religious zealotry. I also recognized in Ms. Neff's selections the ruptured bosom of the Western Earth—in Hogue and Thomas Hart Benton, in Dorothea Lange and Arthur Rothstein—all of them forcing the irritating question that those politicians compulsively traveling on a folklore of unique American genius and rectitude would rather not see raised: Is this what we want? Is there something deeper in Lange's and Hogue's images than failed husbandry?

The culminating images in the show brought a new perception into focus for me. It was one thing to find in Western painting and photography from this period a reading of the West's contours, a rendering of its geography that suggested an alternative to urban blight and haste, a refuge from wheedling advertising and commerce, a dream world of Rousseauian ideals. It was another to see in these images a lament, the kind of lament that lies within the foundation of Rainer

Maria Rilke's *Duino Elegies*, that we are still so far from where we wish to be as a people. The approach taken to our dilemma in this exhibition, it seemed to me, made the following assumption: In order to serve Progress, it's been necessary for us actively to refute the assertion of Indigenous North American cultures that the land is sentient. The artists' recognition in *The Modern West*, then, of a spiritual dimension to Western space leads us to consider that this refutation might be perilous. If place is stripped of geography, and if geography is stripped of spirit, any destructive scheme for profit will fly. The ghost towns, tailings piles, clearcuts, emptied lakes, bomb craters, and devastated working lives of the West tell us this is so.

When I stepped away from the first sight of Ms. Neff's images, my thoughts were far more vaporous than this observation suggests. The ideas foremost in my mind then were about the West's all but incomprehensible spaciousness, and the suggestions in some of the paintings of places I thought I recognized. The paintings and photographs made me want to return to the road, to travel again as I had years earlier, to drive across the West and refamiliarize myself with it. With little more thought than that, I decided to go. I wrote a few particulars into my plan: I wanted to see Georgia O'Keeffe's White Place and her Black Place; El Morro National Monument (the site of Timothy O'Sullivan's Inscription Rock photograph, the most literal image in the show); Carson Sink in Nevada; and the convergence of the Comanche, Rita Blanca, and Kiowa National Grasslands in panhandle Texas, southeastern Colorado, panhandle Oklahoma, and northeastern New Mexico. I'd never seen these places. And I wanted to return to some geographies that had long been touchstones—Jackson Hole, Wyoming; Taos, New Mexico; Canyon de Chelly ("canyon of the canyon"—*chelly* is a French corruption of the Navajo for canyon, *tsegi*).

I got out some books to refresh my mind. Stephen Pyne's *How the Canyon Became Grand*, his story of how that Colorado River canyon got its adjective, and Gary Witherspoon's *Language and Art in the Navajo Universe*. Witherspoon says that the aim of all Navajo art is the creation, maintenance, and restoration of *hózhó*, which he translates as "beauty," and that for the Navajo, beauty is not about perception, is not in the eye of the beholder, but is the outcome of the artist's relationship to the world. The creation of beauty is simultaneously intellectual (the creation, maintenance, and restoration of order), emotional (of happiness), moral (of good), aesthetic (of balance and harmony), and biological (of health). Art is integral to life, and *hózhó*, distinctly different from Aristotle's "beauty," is the goal of art—and life. Witherspoon's long effort has been to comprehend "the frame of meaning in which other people move." Another anthropologist who has done this brilliantly among the Western Apache is Keith Basso, whose *Wisdom Sits in Places*, a cultural and spiritual geography, I had long wanted an opportunity to read.

As important to me as any of this remembering and self-tutoring was choosing to make the journey in winter. I wanted to see the land obscured by weather, see it covered over with snow, its colors muted, its edges rounded, its plants quiescent. Watching someone you love asleep is what I thought.

I drove for several weeks, speaking to no one but

strangers. I had laid out a general route that I knew winter storms would force me to change. What I wanted more than meaning was experience. I wanted to sense the magic within the real in the untenanted West, where on a day's drive one might easily see from the public roads a hundred times as many wild animals as people—jackrabbits, coyotes, golden eagles rising in thermals, herds of pronghorn antelope, flocks of juncos and other small birds fleeing the roadside, wild horses grazing bunchgrasses, porcupines ambling.

I made notes daily, not toward any particular goal but because, like others, I forget the details of experience. I retain only a general impression, which contributes to a general sense of placelessness, which itself seems to have become part of the nature of reality for us. I remember, then, noting more than a hundred pieces of abandoned farm machinery; walking the still-unmarked massacre site at Sand Creek, listening to killdeer and coyotes; and walking away from FM (farm to market) 296 in Dallam County, Texas, a mile across the shortgrass prairie, the wind whistling and booming against the sheaves of it, a sound like tin roofing lifting and dropping. And in southeastern Nevada using the map dividers to determine that a two-lane highway stretching away from me to a spot where it pinched out in a climbing turn at the foot of a mountain, a road straight as laborers could make it, was 15.2 miles long, the end of it no wider than the pencil point I was holding up.

Winter subdued every landscape. Near Deer Lodge, Montana, and later east of Quemado, New Mexico, I could barely hold the road in snowstorms I had to give up fighting; the weather, for that season, was mostly fine, though. The bitterness of the wind on my bare ears at some points—at White Place, at Sand Creek—sharpened the melancholy. Traffic, in a geography thick with tourists in summer, was largely absent. The land was still and bloomless, skeletal but not dead. Not empty.

I found O'Keeffe's (and Eliot Porter's) Black Place along a stretch of U.S. 550 east of Counselor, New Mexico. I don't know what I expected—preservation of some sort. An honoring. But like White Place, a few miles from Ghost Ranch, it, too, is an abused place, crowded with a consumptive culture's jetsam: empty beer cans, plastic ice bags, cigarette filters, tire rinds, candy wrappers, fast-food cartons, torn medicine packets, broken electronic gadgets, spent matches, empty water bottles. (Around White Place, not so hard by a paved road, visitors have left various large and small targets demolished by gunfire, the derelict carcasses of house furniture set on fire, drained whiskey bottles, and scraps of clothing.)

Though I was able to locate it, I could not *see* the place Porter photographed in 1945 and that O'Keeffe had painted the year before. It is half a fool's errand trying to match even highly representational art to a particular place; art's purpose in the cultural West has been to create *symbols* of emotion and thought. You cannot, in this narrow sense, lament the demise of the model. And, after all, many of the paintings in *The Modern West* are composites—Frederic Remington's *Fight for the Water Hole*, N. C. Wyeth's *Moving Camp*, and a dozen others. But somewhere in the filaments that bind place to art it is disturbing to note the passing of an empirical authority—the actual thing—that, once the artist became

intimate with it (or afterward with the memory of it), compelled the work of art.

BEFORE LEAVING ON MY ORIENTATION trip, I'd written down
some notes about coal-fired power plants in the West. In
seeking out the atmosphere, literally, that might have engen-
dered some of the images in the show, I knew I no longer had
available to me the same "open curtains," the same transparency. The Grand Canyon is periodically shrouded in Los
Angeles's pallid air; the Four Corners country is blighted by
exhaust from a coal-fired energy complex nearby. In the
winter of 2004–2005, new coal-fired power plants, thirty-
two of them, were on the drawing boards in nine of the
eleven western states. (Oregon and Washington had none.
If you included the tier of states adjacent to the east, from
North Dakota to Texas, the total number of plants was
forty-eight.)

    I tried to break my travels each day by hiking away from
the truck, down into the draws, up the arroyos, into the foothills, across the playas, into the gallery forests of Frémont's
cottonwoods along the creeks, the bird-sheltering bosques. I
would bring my binoculars, find a place out of the wind, and
pick over the land, acre by acre, watching for movement.
The creation of a painting or museum-quality photographic
print requires an analogous kind of concentration, unusual
in our lives now. To consider this is to see how diminished the
longer rhythms of human life have become in the cultural
West, and to renew a perception of how art, itself a record
of human concentration, can restore an awareness of those

rhythms. We've become, it seems to me, a chronically distracted people, yearning to be relieved of the misgivings and anxiety we feel, thinking we no longer have time to go deep. We doubt the relief claimed for the manufactured products we're told will help. In some basic way, we've come to doubt our culture.

When I caught movement through my binoculars, animation suddenly mixed into the pastels of a sage flat or across the chiaroscuro of snow-patch-and-basalt scree, I responded with a quickening of the blood, like any animal. Concentration eventually reveals what at first was not apparent. It is as though the act of concentration itself draws out something latent, or, if time becomes a dimension like width, something that was there all along.

The country in winter, like a painting hung on a wall in a museum's quietest room, invites participation in the artist's concentration, which can take you as deep as you feel safe to go into a "frame of meaning" in which another person moves, someone with whom you share a heritage and the pursuit of a cultural identity.

On leaving some of the isolated landscapes I tried so hard to observe, I often sharply sensed that I remained a stranger there, and that I would always. Still, I'd leave with the stranger's ardent wish after experiencing such numinous events, the traveler's insistent plea: Don't forget me.

III. The Museum Room, Houston, Texas

I did not want the trip to be over, so on what I knew to be my last day I drove north from Nevada into Oregon through a front of snow squalls moving away to the southeast, crossed the Malheur Basin, came around the north flank of the Sheepshead Mountains and through the town of Burns, and a few miles farther west turned north on the road to the Bureau of Land Management's wild-horse corrals.

The storm was distant in the south by then; the snowless skies here were decked gray and grayer with cumulonimbus, like sheets of construction paper torn across the grain. It was midmorning, a January Sunday. Two cowboys were haying and graining horses from the back of a pickup moving through a warren of abutted corrals, the horses separated according to sex. They were feral and never-ridden beings of every color and genetic background, the majority of them sorrels, browns, grays, roans, and claybanks. A few showed the characteristics of Spanish mustangs; other bloodlines included saddle horses, Thoroughbreds, and draft horses. Two feet of snow on the ground, the ground hard, the snow packed hard in the corrals. They had recently been brought in off open ranges in eastern Oregon, from some of the BLM's federal Herd Management Areas: Paisley Desert, Stinkingwater, Palomino Buttes, Murderer's Creek. When I climbed the fence boards to get a better look across the checkerboard of corrals and let my head clear the last of the close-set rails, the horses, their nostrils flaring, spooked, bolted, and halted. We were a long ways here from *haute école*.

I watched the bewildered hundred fifty of them, mestizo creatures, their lower lips newly tattooed with purple numbers, their future no longer their own, their meaning no longer theirs to define, until I was too cold to sit the fences and the cowboys were ready to be gone.

The last leg of the journey, crossing the high desert for

the Cascade Range and home, I thought how, between those beachhead days at Plymouth Rock and Jamestown and now, we'd lost a sense of geographical vastness, of the unique and inaccessible, the too far. What was once vast we have now reduced to patterns of swift movement so ingrained, so routine, that much of the land's guiding specificity has fallen away. We move quickly now, through a country very different from the one that William Henry Jackson saw, that Marsden Hartley painted, that D. H. Lawrence wrote about, and one as different from the country known to Bear's Heart, Pylen Hanaweaka, Julian Martinez, and Riley Sunrise as the Carolinas are from the Dakotas.

ALEXANDRE HOGUE IS PERHAPS BEST known for his *Erosion* series of paintings, one of which, *Erosions No. 2, Mother Earth Laid Bare*, is included in this exhibition. According to Lea Rosson DeLong in her biography of the artist, *Nature's Forms/ Nature's Forces: The Art of Alexandre Hogue*, he "has wrongfully been identified with the Midwestern Regionalists who idealized the agrarian life and values and viewed rural America as the repository of the best American values." Something powerful, it had long seemed to me, even bridging, was at work in some of Hogue's images. He painted like a man at once intimately familiar with the literalness of machinery— employing a draftsman's eye—and also driven by second sight. The spiritual dimensions of landscape clearly were evident to him.

Curious about the history of *Erosions No. 2, Mother Earth Laid Bare*, I went one day to the Philbrook Museum of Art, in

Tulsa, Oklahoma, to look at the charcoal and pencil sketches
he'd made in 1926, 1928, and 1930, leading up to the oil
painting of 1938. The sketches show a progression. From
a spectral presence in 1926, the woman in the painting
becomes increasingly more apparent, a bolder, starker being.
The sketches recall two statements DeLong makes in her
biography. Hogue, she writes, was imbued from childhood
with the sense of "a great female figure under the ground
everywhere." And "Hogue believed the understanding of
nature and the understanding of art go hand in hand."

When set against the reveries of some twentieth-century
Western landscapes, Hogue's paintings, like those of Grant
Wood and Benton, bring us up short with their visions of
forsaken machines and consuming and corrosive technologies. In *Pulliam Bluffs, Chisos Mountains*, however, a painting
from his Big Bend series, Hogue uses fractal scaling to integrate reeling geographic space; he also creates a resonant
middle ground, absent in many Western landscape paintings. All his earlier work is here a palimpsest. It's a painting
eerie in its parallels with the landscape painting of traditional
Native Americans trained later in life to a Western style, people coming at geography from another direction. In all this
work the land is alive, unclaimed.

Hogue walked off the abused Texas landscape of his
youth into some other, wholly different country, the habitat
of his adult years.

THE FIRST TIME I SAW a set of color reproductions of the art-
work assembled for this exhibition was in a windowless room

in the Museum of Fine Arts, Houston. The images were pinned to two opposing walls, grouped according to the six sections Ms. Neff had devised to structure the show. As I walked around the room, I noticed how many of the images were informed by crosses, from the ones on Lange's Western churches to those in Ansel Adams's *Moonrise, Hernandez, New Mexico*, from William Henry Jackson's *Mountain of the Holy Cross* to Morris Graves's *Memorial Day Wild Flower Bouquet in the Cemetery of an Abandoned Western Mining Town*. It could not have escaped the imagination of Native Americans coerced into one or another of the Christian religions that it was this very symbol of the church's authority (bearing, in this instance, copper wires) that brought to their world the lightning-fast communications that were to stymie their last attempts to stay free of confinement, and that would later bring power to the industries that would desecrate the space upon which they had founded their own guiding and sustaining mythologies.

I marked, in that room that day, the terrifying communication between earth and sky I saw in Edward Weston's *White Sands, New Mexico*, the clouds racing, the sand abiding. Also the dead end in Dixon's *No Place to Go*. And how placeness disappears in abstract expressionism. How pervasive, deep, and unconscious, I thought that day, looking at all those images, is a cultural understanding of place, of geography. And how strikingly, how almost necessarily, is Western space broken by a vertical line—the strange pole in Paul Strand's *The Dark Mountain, New Mexico*, the poles in Henry F. Farny's *The Song of the Talking Wire*, the woman in Laura Gilpin's *The Prairie*.

The last of these thoughts lingered for weeks, unfinished. Where it finally took me as I drove day after day across the West was to a realization of how deeply Europe's sense of identity was affected by the development of cathedral architecture, how profoundly this architecture had shifted a European understanding of interior space. Here in the West, I had now come to believe, was a long-running experiment in how to depict exterior space, to render a vast geography that, since the survey photographers first went west in the 1860s, had not been so much plumbed as skirted. A new geography, made apparent in modern landscape art by incorporating duration of time, would mean a new American politics, at the least.

The work Emily Ballew Neff selected for the show seemed, during those first hours of my exposure, taken in the aggregate, like a chrysalis. What might we gain as a people if we were to reimagine what was, at one point, too vast either to imagine or render? It was with that thought that I turned out the lights in the windowless room and pulled the door shut behind me.

A True Naturalist

IT SEEMS APPROPRIATE TO ME TO REFLECT FIRST ON THE undistinguished chair I'm sitting in as I try to put together a few words about my friend Richard Nelson. I bought the chair long ago in a secondhand store in Springfield, Oregon. I've had to repair it occasionally to ensure its sturdiness. Two worn-out seat cushions, one atop another, make it easier to occupy for hours at a time. Two newel posts brace a tapered backrest of wooden spindles. The caps of the newel posts gleam from the rub of human hands over the decades.

I've written seventeen books while sitting in this chair, and I hope to complete a couple more in the years ahead. In the early 1980s, because I sensed that resting my back against a pair of cured black-tailed deer hides from Richard's hunts would put me in a more respectful frame of mind when I wrote, and that they might induce in me the proper perspectives about life, I wrote him and asked for his help. Would he honor our friendship by sending me a couple of black-tailed deer hides? These were from deer he'd been given as a

subsistence hunter (as he understood that relationship with
them) in the woods near his home. In my experience, no
other nonnative hunter's ethical approach to the archetypal
form of fatal encounter was as honorable as Richard's. He
hunted to feed his family, imitating the way his Inupiaq,
Koyukon, and Gwich'in teachers had taught him to hunt,
through the example of their own behavior in engagements
with wild animals—humbly, gratefully, respectfully. I felt the
hides might care for me as I stumbled my way through life,
in the same way our friendship with each other would take
care of both of us in the years ahead.

So, this morning, I am sitting in front of my old typewriter
with my back against those soft hides, and I want to say a few
things about a book in which Hank Lentfer introduces us to
this extraordinary man, Richard K. Nelson, most of whose
friends called him simply Nels. I think of him as remarkable
among Western anthropologists who have apprenticed themselves to traditional people because, as a young man, he took
on with fierce dedication under discouraging circumstances a
journey that few people have ever had the opportunity to
experience, and he pursued that journey with great attentiveness and care for more than fifty years. He listened to his
teachers, immersed himself in their landscapes as a naturalist,
and became, without intending to, a great teacher himself.
What Nels modeled was a way of knowing the world, an
epistemology different from the one most of us have unconsciously accepted and sworn ourselves to. It led him to recon-
sider what in his own life was to be valued over human
exceptionalism: for example, progress for the sake of progress, or the manic accumulation of material wealth.

Lentfer's thoroughly researched chapters describe a man who dedicated himself to an unending personal task—self-education. A man who became, because of that, to use Lentfer's unusual but apt term, a kind of monk. He didn't pursue life alone in a cave, staying out of touch with others and the physical world, but became instead a carrier of wisdom from traditions he had known nothing about as a young university student. This is to say the wisdom of marginalized and vanishing hunter-gatherer cultures in remote parts of North America. He came to understand, through decades of intimacy, applied study, and life practice, a frame of mind he was once innocent of, one based much more firmly on enduring human values like thinking respectfully about wild animals. As Nels wrote about this perspective in books and articles, and as he began to speak publicly about other ways of knowing, he developed the aura of a person shaped by something on the far side of pedestrian reality. A monk then.

A key to understanding Lentfer's pages is to recognize how often illumination came to Richard Nelson in the company of other people, to see the social dimension of the wisdom he offered to share with us. Over time, Nels slowly became someone more intent on listening than in advancing himself as a speaker. Inupiaq people in the 1960s saw that this outlander from Wisconsin was willing to listen attentively and to work hard in order to acquire knowledge and field skills. By the time he arrived among the Koyukon in Huslia and Hughes in the seventies, he had learned to present himself as a listener, quintessentially, not a cultural anthropologist. As a result, the breadth of his learning widened and deepened. By the time he was camping in Glacier Bay with

Lentfer in 2016, he was listening to the world around him so closely he could differentiate between the seemingly identical calls of two fox sparrows in the same thicket. He could tell from the anxious behavior of a gray whale in a protected bay that orcas were swimming nearby, unseen. He understood that his professional position in life had moved beyond anthropology, good as he was at that, to a level of attentiveness to the nonhuman world that one of his Koyukon teachers, Lavine Williams, alluded to when he informed Nels one day in Hughes that "every animal knows way more than you do."

The truth of Lavine's remark was both allegorical and factual. To be patient, to pay attention to the world that is not yourself, is the first step in the neophyte's discovery of the larger world outside the self, the landscape in which wisdom itself abides. Other residents of the world, Lavine was telling him, know more than we do about how to survive whatever is coming. Their investment is not in progress but in stability. Nels's life became the passing on of this deceptively simple message about human survival. It was this message that he lived.

Landscapes of the Shamans

I RECENTLY SPENT A FEW WEEKS AT THE PENLAND SCHOOL OF Crafts, in the Blue Ridge Mountains of North Carolina. The artists and artisans who secure residencies to pursue their work here are among the best in the country, visionary people producing museum-quality work in glass, steel, clay, wood, and other materials. Most are in mid- or early career and I found them at work in their studios—in front of coal forges, at jewelers' tables, easels, and lathes—at every hour of the day and night.

It was here that I first encountered the creations of Sylvie Rosenthal. The piece that initially drew me in was a large black wooden rabbit. The fore- and hindquarters were carved and finished realistically; connecting the two was a loggia, an airy, furnitureless, roofed corridor suggesting an isthmus.

Ms. Rosenthal showed me photographs of some of her other large works—a baleen whale, a giraffe—in which she'd combined realism and invention to suggest both the animal's underlying nature and its possibilities in a world where, for many, wild animals are little more than opaque objects.

A couple of years before this encounter, I received a set of images in the mail from an acquaintance, the photographer Lukas Felzmann. They were selections from his *Gull Juju* archive, showing the remarkable range of objects he'd removed from the entrails of seagulls washed up on the Northern California coast: toy soldiers, used syringes, tampon applicators, golf tees. I assumed many, or perhaps all, of these gulls had been killed by ingesting these things they had mistaken for food. Mr. Felzmann's arrangement of these objects on a piece of cloth suggested both human indifference and ethical complexity.

Another, much less alarming set of photographs, made by Wayne Levin, was sent to me at about the same time by a mutual friend. Mr. Levin had been photographing aggregations of akule (bigeye scad) in the waters of Kealakekua Bay, on the leeward coast of the island of Hawai'i. In a comment on the back of *Akule*, a book of these photographs, I wrote that Levin's work revealed a genuine appreciation of akule life, and that he had reopened "the door to a world that much of humanity long ago turned its back on in order to pursue forms of wealth far more perishable, less elegant, and more banal." For me, some of the power behind his photographs came from the way he invoked clouds of interstellar gas in the cosmos and the yearning that many people have to live in a community that can cooperate.

For a decade or more I have been looking at the work of another artist intent on pushing deep into the borderland between the human and the nonhuman, the painter Tom

Uttech, who lives in Wisconsin. Consider *Mamakadjidgan*, a recent 91-by-103-inch oil painting on linen, in which Uttech takes up what is for him a familiar theme. We're looking into a section of the North Woods, a remnant forest of tall, spindly evergreens, all of which seem to be dying. A black bear sits on a log in the foreground, amid a crosshatching of subdivision roads. His back is to us. This melancholy scene, with its suggestions of abuse and domestication, is brilliantly relieved, however—and counterbalanced—by loose flocks of a dozen or so species of birds flying through. The birds might have passed this way days before, or even months ago, but Uttech has gathered them together in a single moment.

Among the many contemporary artists exploring the nature of animals, our perceptions of them, and our own animal natures, I'm also thinking just now of the South African installation artist Jane Alexander. For a recent show at the SCAD Museum of Art, in Savannah, Georgia, she mounted *Infantry*, a brigade of men with the heads of African hunting dogs, marching during the days of apartheid, their heads cocked sharply to the right, a troop of jackbooted Schutzstaffel passing a reviewing stand.

I've selected these artists—Rosenthal, Felzmann, Levin, Uttech, and Alexander—as being broadly representative of an emerging sensibility in contemporary art about animals, about the nature of our sensory and philosophical perceptions of them, and about our being related to them. I began thinking about this new way of looking at animals in the late 1960s, when I came upon a series of portraits of large African cats made by John Dominis for *Life*, in 1967. Sometime in the 1970s I was given a set of photographs of zoo animals

taken by an artist named Ilya, work commissioned by *Life*, I
was told, but which it declined to publish because the animals appeared deracinated and impounded in the pictures,
like patients in a mental hospital. Around that same time I
read John Berger's seminal essay "Why Look at Animals?"

How we imagine wild animals today, during the Sixth
Extinction, came more sharply into focus for me in the 1980s
when I became familiar with the photographs of Frans Lanting
and, later, Michio Hoshino, and when I became acquainted, in
the early 1990s, with the collaborative work of Susan Middleton and David Liittschwager. Lanting and Hoshino, it seemed
to me, gave wild animals back their dignity and mystery, obviat-
ing years of wildlife photography that was merely decorative,
reductively iconic, or "family friendly." Middleton and Liittschwager, by exploring animals' complex morphologies and
pointing to their vulnerability, pushed us deeper into a consid-
eration of their differing personalities and their tenuousness.

IT'S NEITHER MY PLACE NOR my wish to speculate about what
Ms. Rosenthal or Mr. Uttech is really up to, and I want no
part of identifying a formal movement that confines artists
like them to a "school," or which collapses their unique
visions into a similar meaning. It does seem to me, though,
that there are legitimate, unifying threads in all this work,
that each of these artists is hostile to the idea of the animal
as an object and is suggesting that we are in deeper water
than we think when we dream of animals, attempt to cast
them as exemplars, set out to describe their unsettling or disruptive behavior, or refuse any longer to eat their flesh.

As I visit galleries today or find myself on a studio tour with a painter like Walton Ford—someone at the forefront of reimagining what is animal, what is human, and what is real—I'm struck by the variety of approaches and the range of provocation in this work. An art critic might say that it's all part of contemporary artists' ongoing rejection of scientific reductionism, the deadening of the human imagination that came with the despiritualization of nature. But it's enough, surely, to put it more simply, to say that artists, too, are highly attuned to endangered species lists, habitat destruction, episodes of human barbarism glibly described as "bestial" by television commentators, and to qualities of "the marvelous" inherent within "the real," the foundation of magical realism in literature.

What animals signify, and how our perceptions of them shape our relations with them, have long lain at the core of human art, from at least the time of the cave paintings at Chauvet. Native American artists especially have continued this ancient tradition, and its foundational imagery is now apparent in a bewildering range of modern expression. It's a species of art characterized by a keen awareness of the many crossover points at which human and nonhuman nature merge. To my mind, contemporary Native American art calls out to artists to explore the nonhuman further, to work the boundary between animals and humans, and to promote discussion of which ethics now apply here, in this liminal landscape of the shaman. Among the many inspiring contemporary Native American artists conceptualizing in this area, I think right away of the Wiyot painter and carver Rick Bartow, whose massive sculpture poles were recently installed

at the entrance to the Smithsonian National Museum of the
American Indian, in Washington, D.C.

PERHAPS IT'S NECESSARY TO EMPHASIZE that works of art are
not generally intended to function as political or social statements. Many artists, however, are reacting to social and
political realities when they're creating, so their work often
informs us though it sets out no agenda. During the time I
spent interviewing artists at the Penland community, I found
deeply affecting the degree to which artistic excellence, not
political or social comment, was the primary focus. How a
particular work might later be interpreted seemed not to be
much on anyone's mind.

    Those who devise the social and economic policies we're
all asked to support and abide by encounter little or no art in
their deliberations. This is an unenlightened, not to say coun-
terproductive, approach to solving human dilemmas like the
collapse of near-shore fisheries, the pollution of groundwater
with synthetic hormones, and the desperate drive to profit
financially at any cost, which is behind, for example, the mar-
keting of oil from Alberta's tar sands. The thinking that artists
provoke in us, about the meaning of life or what constitutes
reality, about the inutility of war or the venality of a longing
for material wealth, are crucial to our understanding of, and
our planning effectively for, a viable future.

    If we learn to listen to the artist as attentively as we listen
to the spellbinding orator, how can we not help but become
a wiser country?

The Invitation

WHEN I WAS YOUNG, AND JUST BEGINNING TO TRAVEL WITH them, I imagined that Indigenous people saw more and heard more, that they were overall simply more aware than I was. They were more aware, and did see and hear more than I did. The absence of spoken conversation whenever I was traveling with them, however, should have provided me with a clue about why this might be true, but it didn't, not for a while. It's this: When an observer doesn't immediately turn what his senses convey to him into language, into the vocabulary and syntactical framework we all employ when trying to define our experiences, there's a much greater opportunity for minor details, which might at first seem unimportant, to remain alive in the foreground of an impression, where, later, they might deepen the meaning of an experience.

If my companions and I, for example, encountered a grizzly bear feeding on a caribou carcass, I would tend to focus almost exclusively on the bear. My companions would focus on the part of the world of which, at that moment, the bear was only a fragment. The bear here might be compared with a bonfire, a kind of incandescence that throws light on everything around it. My companions would glance off into the outer reaches of that light, then look back to the fire, back and forth. They would repeatedly situate the smaller thing within the larger thing, back and forth. As they noticed trace odors in the air, or listened for birdsong or the sound of brittle brush rattling, they in effect extended the moment of encounter with the bear backward and forward in time. Their framework for the phenomenon, one that I might later shorten just to "meeting the bear," was more voluminous than mine; and where my temporal boundaries for the event would normally consist of little more than the moments of the encounter with the bear, theirs included the time before we arrived, as well as the time after we left. For me, the bear was a noun, the subject of a sentence; for them, it was a verb, the gerund "bearing."

Over the years traveling cross-country with Indigenous people I absorbed two lessons about how to be more fully present in an encounter with a wild animal. First, I needed to understand that I was entering the event as it was *unfolding*. It started before I arrived and would continue unfolding after I departed. Second, the event itself—let's say we didn't disturb the grizzly bear as he or she fed but only took in what the bear was doing and then slipped away—could not be completely defined by referring solely to the physical geography around us in those moments. For example, I might not recall something we'd all seen a half hour earlier, a caribou hoof print in soft ground at the edge of a creek, say; but my companions would remember that. And a while after our encounter with the bear, say a half mile farther on, they would notice something else—a few grizzly-bear guard hairs snagged in scales of tree bark—and they would relate it to some detail they'd observed during those moments when we were watching the bear. The event I was cataloging in my mind as "encounter with a tundra grizzly" they were experiencing as a sudden immersion in the current of a river. They were swimming in it, feeling its pull, noting the temperature of the water, the back eddies, and where the side streams entered. My approach, in contrast, was mostly to take note of objects in the scene—the bear, the caribou, the tundra vegetation. A series of dots, which I would try to make sense of by connecting them all with a single line. My friends had situated themselves within a dynamic event. Also, unlike me, they felt no immediate need to resolve it into meaning. Their approach was to let it continue to unfold. To notice everything and to let whatever significance was there emerge in its own time.

The lesson to be learned here was not just for me to pay closer attention to what was going on around me, if I hoped to have a deeper understanding of the event, but to remain in a state of suspended mental analysis while observing all that was happening—resisting the urge to define or summarize. To step away from the familiar compulsion to understand. Further, I had to incorporate a quintessential characteristic of the way Indigenous people observe: They pay more attention to *patterns* in what they encounter than to isolated objects. When they saw the bear, they right away began searching for a pattern that was resolving itself before them as "a bear feeding on a carcass." They began gathering various pieces together that might later self-assemble

into an event larger than "a bear feeding." These uninte-
grated pieces they took in as we traveled—the nature of the
sonic landscape that permeated this particular physical landscape; the presence or absence of wind, and the direction
from which it was coming or had shifted; a piece of speckled
eggshell under a tree; leaves missing from the stems of a species of brush; a hole freshly dug in the ground—might indi-
vidually convey very little. Allowed to slowly resolve into a
pattern, however, they might become revelatory. They might
illuminate the land further.

If the first lesson in learning how to see more deeply into
a landscape was to be continuously attentive, and to stifle the
urge to stand *outside* the event, to instead stay *within* the event,
leaving its significance to be resolved later, the second lesson,
for me, was to notice how often I asked my body to defer to
the dictates of my mind, how my body's extraordinary ability to discern textures and perfumes, to discriminate among
tones and colors in the world outside itself, was dismissed by
the rational mind.

As much as I believed I was fully present in the physical
worlds I was traveling through, I understood over time that I
was not. More often I was only *thinking* about the place I was
in. Initially awed by an event, the screech of a gray fox in the
night woods, say, or the surfacing of a large whale, I too often
moved straight to analysis. On occasion I would become so
wedded to my thoughts, to some cascade of ideas, that I
actually lost touch with the details that my body was *still gathering* from a place. The ear heard the song of a vesper sparrow, and then heard the song again, and knew that the second
time it was a different vesper sparrow singing. The mind,

pleased with itself for identifying those notes as the song of a vesper sparrow, was too preoccupied with its summary to notice what the ear was still offering. The mind was making no use of the body's ability to be discerning about sounds. And so the mind's knowledge of the place remained superficial.

Many people have written about how, generally speaking, Indigenous people seem to pick up more information traversing a landscape than an outsider, someone from a culture that no longer highly values physical intimacy with a place, that regards this sort of sensitivity as a "primitive" attribute, something a visitor from an "advanced" culture would be comfortable believing he had actually outgrown. Such a dismissive view, as I have come to understand it, ignores the great intangible value that achieving physical intimacy with a place might provide. I'm inclined to point out to someone who condescends to such a desire for intimacy, although it might seem rude, that it is not possible for human beings to outgrow loneliness. Nor can someone from a culture that condescends to nature easily escape the haunting thought that one's life is meaningless.

Existential loneliness and a sense that one's life is inconsequential, both of which are hallmarks of modern civilizations, seem to me to derive in part from our abandoning a belief in the therapeutic dimensions of a relationship with place. A continually refreshed sense of the endless complexity of patterns in the natural world, patterns that are ever present and discernible, and which incorporate the observer, undermines the feeling that one is alone in the world, or meaningless in it. The effort to know a place deeply is,

ultimately, an expression of the human desire to belong, to fit
somewhere.

The determination to know a particular place, in my
experience, is consistently rewarded. And every natural
place, to my mind, is open to being known. And somewhere
in this process a person begins to sense that they *themselves* are
becoming known, so that when they are absent from that
place they know that place misses them. And this reciprocity,
to know and be known, reinforces a sense that one is necessary in the world.

PERHAPS THE FIRST RULE OF everything we endeavor to do is
to pay attention. Perhaps the second is to be patient. And
perhaps a third is to be attentive to what the body knows.
Individual Indigenous people are not necessarily more aware
than people who've grown up in the modern culture I grew
up in (and Indigenous cultures, of course, are as replete with
inattentive, lazy, and undiscerning individuals as "advanced"
cultures). But they tend to value more highly the importance
of intimacy with a place. When you travel with them, you're
acutely aware that theirs is a fundamentally different praxis
from your own. They're more attentive, more patient, less
willing to say what they know, to collapse mystery into
language.

When I was young, and one of my companions would
make some stunningly insightful remark about the place we
were traveling through, I would sometimes feel envious, a
feeling related not so much to a desire to possess that same
depth of knowledge but a desire to so obviously *belong* to a

particular place. To so clearly be an integral part of the place one is standing in.

A grizzly bear stripping fruit from blackberry vines in a thicket is more than a bear stripping fruit from blackberry vines in a thicket. It is a point of entry into a world most of us would have turned our backs on in an effort to go somewhere else, believing we'll be better off just *thinking* about a grizzly bear stripping fruit from blackberry vines in a thicket.

The moment is an invitation, and the bear's invitation to participate is offered, without prejudice, to anyone passing by.

An Afterword

For Bob Stephenson

IN THE FALL OF 1975 I READ A SCIENTIFIC REPORT THAT MADE me sit up straight in my chair. It was entitled "The Eskimo Hunter's View of Wolf Ecology and Behavior" and appeared in a peer-reviewed volume of technical papers called *The Wild Canids*, edited by Michael Fox. At the time I was in the middle of researching a book about wolves, so I read carefully every paper in Fox's book. The one I regarded as a watershed statement was co-authored by Bob Stephenson and a Nunamiut hunter from the central Brooks Range named Bob Ahgook.

In the early 1970s, the notion that Indigenous peoples had anything of substance to offer Western science about wild animals, any important contribution to make to the overall study of wildlife, was either scoffed at by professionals in wildlife science or gently dismissed because the Indigenous information, purportedly, "lacked rigor." The report by

Stephenson and Ahgook flew directly in the face of this idea. In my mind, their observations on wolf behavior were far and away the most interesting in Fox's volume, though few recognized the revolutionary nature of this piece back then.

From the beginning of the colonization of the New World, Western science has had an ingrained, cultural prejudice against the validity of what Indigenous people know about wild animals, about what they have learned during their centuries of living with them in the same environment. Their observations on social dynamics, cooperative hunting, ecology, neonatal behavior, and diet were considered "contaminated" by folk belief or to have been based too often on anecdotal evidence alone.

IMMEDIATELY AFTER READING STEPHENSON AND Ahgook's paper I wrote to Stephenson, a wolf biologist with the Alaska Department of Fish and Game (ADF&G), and asked if I could fly up to Fairbanks to speak with him. I'd not yet come across his perspective in the literature on wolves but very much wanted to listen to what he had to say, both about wolves and about his interactions with the Nunamiut. I arrived in Fairbanks in March 1976, which was late winter in interior Alaska. Bob picked me up at the airport and offered me a bed at his cabin outside the city, in Goldstream Valley. Three days later I was sitting next to him in the back seat of a Bell 206 JetRanger, a four-passenger helicopter, flying across Nelchina Basin, in the drainage of the Susitna River south of the Alaska Range. We were looking for wolves to radio-collar.

This was a mind-boggling excursion for me, to find myself so suddenly on the front lines of wolf research. I was nearly speechless with appreciation at Bob's invitation to go into the field with him, and for his trust that I would be capable as an assistant working alongside him. In the days that followed, I came to marvel at the breadth of his knowledge of wolf anatomy, morphology, and social behavior.

After that first meeting, and after I finished the book I was working on, *Of Wolves and Men*, Bob and I traveled together extensively across central and northern Alaska. We canoed up the Yukon River to explore the Charley River, which had just gained protection as a part of Yukon–Charley Rivers National Preserve; we flew out to St. Lawrence Island in the northern Bering Sea during walrus-hunting time there; and we camped at several places in the central Brooks Range (all of them now part of Gates of the Arctic National Park and Preserve). Our intent on these trips, for the most part, was simply to watch animals together.

It wasn't until decades later that I was able to look back on those trips and comprehend how deeply the major themes of my professional writing life were informed by these excursions with Bob. My gratitude for his company and expertise, for his introduction to other wildlife biologists, and for his hospitality whenever I came to visit knows no bounds.

IN JUNE 1979, BOB AND I journeyed up to Anaktuvuk Pass—a village of just 110 people back then—where I finally met Bob Ahgook, Justus Mekiana, and some of the other hunters Bob had worked with in the early seventies. The afternoon our plane landed, nearly every woman in the village rushed down to the airstrip to greet Bob. Some years before this, after Bob started living sporadically at Anaktuvuk in a sod house he purchased from Justus, a flu swept through the settlement. Bob nursed dozens of people through this epidemic, emptying honey buckets, changing and washing bed linen, and cooking meals. The senior women in particular never forgot his courtesy and allegiance.

I listened in on his conversations with the hunters during our time in Anaktuvuk as they caught up with each other's lives. The regard in which they held Bob was obvious. Relations between ADF&G personnel and Indigenous hunters in many of the villages back then were less than friendly. Bob, however, had not originally come to the village to lecture people about adhering to state hunting regulations; he'd come to hear what the local hunters had to say. He was eager to get their insights into the nature of *amaguk*, the wolf, especially about the parts of its life that had not yet made it into the professional journals. No wonder, when he initially approached them about it, they had welcomed him to travel with them as they set out in early summer to look for wolf dens.

Beyond his own empathetic personality, his obvious lack of racial prejudice, and his respect for people with backgrounds very different from his own, Bob had a sharp sense of humor. One day when we were all sitting around telling stories, especially about wolverines, as I remember, Bob told a story about an arrogant man and his humiliating comeuppance. The Nunamiut men roared at the well-delivered punch line. One leaned so far sideways on his stool he fell over. Another man nearly spit out his dentures.

Bob helped pioneer something new and unprecedented in Western wildlife science—the inclusion of traditional Indigenous knowledge in peer-reviewed wildlife publications. (There were a few others in Fairbanks at the time who sought out Indigenous knowledge and gave it equal standing with Western-based knowledge. I think immediately of two marine mammalogists, John Burns and Bud Fay, and of Kathy Frost and Lloyd Lowry, both of whom I worked with later when I was researching another book, *Arctic Dreams*. But the road to advancing mutual cultural respect in Alaska was to be long and hard.)

ON THAT FIRST TRIP WITH Bob, to radio-collar wolves in Nelchina Basin, I saw firsthand an exhibition of the knowledge he had acquired by choosing to turn first to the Nunamiut instead of investing his allotted ADF&G funds in flying aerial surveys. (He had been charged by ADF&G with learning how the Alyeska pipeline might be affecting the lives of wolves. He believed he'd learn much more by traveling with Nunamiut hunters first, questioning them about wolf behavior in general, before setting off to study wolves along the pipeline corridor.) One day we spotted a wolf trail in Nelchina Basin—seven wolves walking single file across a frozen, snow-covered lake. They were more than a mile ahead of us when we sighted them nearing the edge of the taiga; when they heard the helicopter approaching, they bolted. We caught up with a group of three. Bob was able to dart two, one of whom entered a dense copse of trees before going down. As we got out of the helicopter in knee-deep snow, Bob said,

"Female. Maybe six or seven." In my naïve way I jokingly said, "Oh, come on. You can't sex and age that animal at this distance."

"Well," he answered, "that's what those guys taught me to do, anyway."

We followed the wolf's tracks into the trees and found it lying on its right side, its eyes fully dilated. I lifted its left rear leg. Female. I eased her lip up to reveal her premolars and the left canine. Her teeth were blunt and worn down, to the degree you'd expect in an older wolf. When we prepared to carry her back to the helicopter, I ran my bare hand up through the fur where her shoulder blades came together. I felt a distinct layer of fat there, and in that moment I understood what knowledgeable people meant when they referred to the wolf as a "social animal." Though she was probably too old to hunt efficiently, she was still in excellent physical condition for late winter, usually the leanest time of year for wolves.

We moved her out of the trees to where the other wolf lay sedated on an open stretch of tundra. Bob said it would be less traumatic for them if they woke up near each other. He cut spruce branches to build a platform for the wolves, to keep their heads from going nose-down in the snow while they were immobilized. He placed cloths over each wolf's dilated eyes to shield them from the bright light of the sun and began his field exam. We weighed them and then put the radio collars on.

I recalled this particular moment several years later when Justus told me that sometimes when wolves approach a junction where two valleys meet, you can see them making a decision about which valley would be the one most likely to provide them with food. The female lying at my feet that time in Nelchina Basin, I thought, might very well have been a decision-maker. Too old to hunt effectively, probably, but maybe she had something else to offer the pack: the experience needed to ensure that all of them would make it through the winter. She would know which of the two valleys was more promising.

AFTER A COUPLE OF DAYS spent hiking around Anaktuvuk Pass and talking with residents on that 1979 trip, Bob and I flew west, paralleling the north flank of the Brooks Range, to arrive at a field camp on the Utukok River. A half dozen or more biologists were using the site for summer wildlife research. A large wall tent, set amid eight or so individual tents, served as a mess hall, radio room, and field lab. A landing strip had been smoothed out on an old gravel bar near the river.

The charter flight that had brought Bob and me there loaded up quickly with a couple of scientists and their gear and roared off for Kotzebue. After we pitched our tent and squared away our things, Bob began introducing me to people who were conducting research on caribou, tundra grizzly, arctic fox, wolverine, and, now that Bob was here, wolves. A JetRanger, a Super Cub, and a Helio Courier sat on the runway. The latter could fly very slowly, staying aloft at speeds other aircraft couldn't maintain without stalling. A good plane from which to survey caribou herds.

On any given day, these biologists might be ferried up

into the foothills of the western Brooks Range or out onto the adjacent coastal plain. There they would set up spike camps and observe animals in the area for a week or so before returning to the base camp. One morning I joined one of the pilots in a Super Cub to search for bears. (It's more economical to look for bears in a small plane and, having found one, to radio the base camp with coordinates, than it is to use much more expensive helicopter time to do the searching. The biologist can then fly directly to the area where you found the bear.) About ten miles south and west of the base camp, we came upon a lone adult grizzly chasing a herd of about fifty caribou. The herd began running up a tundra slope and quartering away from the bear below and behind them. Instead of slowing down, the grizzly charged furiously up the slope, cutting across the radius of the turn the caribou were making. It hit one of the galloping animals hard in the shoulder and took it to the ground. The speed with which the bear ran up the hill was astonishing.

After spending another day or two with people at the base camp, Bob and I helicoptered south, up into the De Long Mountains. We set our camp up on a bench partway up the side of Ilingnorak Ridge, several hundred feet above the floodplain of the Utukok. Bob had heard about an active wolf den nearby, three-quarters of a mile west of us in a cutbank above the river.

The conditions were perfect for observing animals. After we set up the tent and put our food and gear in order, we began watching the wolves with forty-power spotting scopes—three adults, a pair of yearlings, and four frisky pups, whom we then studied continuously for a week. The vast, rolling countryside surrounding us was treeless and the air was eerily transparent—at one point we were observing a herd of caribou that was six miles away according to our topographic map. The weather was clear and the summer sun never set. From the elevation of our camp we could look straight across and slightly down to the entrance of the den.

Our regular routine was to sleep for four or five hours when we felt the need, but otherwise to watch the wolves and other animals, unless we were taking a few minutes to cook and eat, or to stretch our legs. If we both were going to sleep at the same time, we left a spotting scope on a tripod in the doorway of the tent, focused on the den. If either of us woke for some reason, he checked the scope. If anything was going on, he woke the other guy up. One day we saw members of the pack create an ambush a hundred yards from the den and surprise a herd of caribou. It worked and they made a halfhearted chase before giving up. "Practice," Bob observed. Once when the adults and one of the yearlings were away hunting, we watched a single female yearling hold off an adult grizzly trying to get into the den, where the cubs were. Another time, I was sitting near our tent, steadily glassing the hillside beyond the den for any movement. Bob was asleep. I sensed something to my left and turned. There, thirty feet away, was a yearling wolf, sitting its haunches and watching me. I knew it was a yearling because its body hadn't yet filled out fully and because, by then, I had absorbed from Bob a little bit of what the Nunamiut had taught him about sexing and aging wolves. When the yearling got up, she walked off at a steady pace, heading straight for the den, weaving her way through tussock mounds on the mesic tundra. Two jaegers harassed her, diving at her head. She leapt up several times to try to snatch one of them out of the air, behavior, I now knew, an adult wolf would never have wasted its time with.

IN OCTOBER 2016, BOB STEPHENSON passed away in his cabin outside Fairbanks. His work with wolves, and later with lynx and wood bison, was groundbreaking. His field methods were sometimes unorthodox, involving, for example, tracking lynx in an ultralight he built and flew. He jokingly referred to his methods as "commando biology," exploring the lives of wild animals in other-than-standard ways. Because he rarely said much about himself, never pursued fame or notoriety, never traded on his close relationships with the Nunamiut, and published little, he was not as widely known in his field as he might have been. What he cared most deeply about was the fate of the animals he studied. He wanted them to fare well in the world that was coming for them, which world, he believed, maintained a certain prejudice toward them and accorded them little of the protection they needed to pursue lives of their own.

THRESHOLDS

On the Border

ONE EVENING IN THE AUSTRAL WINTER OF 1992 I ASKED THE captain of the ship I was traveling on if I could step overboard and take a walk. The *Nathaniel B. Palmer*, a 308-foot icebreaking research vessel, was docked that night in a large ice floe in the Weddell Sea in Antarctica, wedged bow-first in an ice slip it had created for itself on the floe's perimeter.

There are two theories of design in the building of icebreakers. With what some call the Russian approach, you put a ton of nuclear power behind an iron fist and never take your foot off the accelerator, even if the ice is heavy and visibility is limited. The other way to go—the design used for the *Palmer*, and one that provides an environmentally kinder way to proceed—is to reduce the power needed and finesse your way through, with a lighter, more maneuverable vessel. This doesn't mean a vessel of the latter design lacks for critical power: the *Palmer* could still make a steady three knots in three feet of level ice, but the fuel burn for this kind of progress can be terrific. Where the *Palmer* was on that particular night, amidst close pack ice at 67° S, far inside the Weddell Sea and many days from the nearest fuel depot in Ushuaia, Argentina, the bullish choice would have been profligate. Also unwise. In such high latitudes in winter, the short days take away, early in the afternoon, an ice master's ability to navigate visually. He can no longer see weaknesses in the ice cover to exploit. At that point in the day it's better to force the ship into the edge of an extensive ice floe, where the hull is less vulnerable to pressure from the shifting pack, and to halt for the dark hours. With the return of twilight in the morning, the ice master can once again spot favorable leads of open water and read the mute surface of the ice for thinness and cracks.

I went overboard on those evenings and walked off across the hard rind of the sea. Needless to say, no one else but the ship's complement was in sight. The world's southernmost shipping lanes hug Cape Horn, eight hundred miles north and far to the west of where we were; and transpolar air routes don't exist at this end of the planet—nor, at that time, did satellite orbits cross Antarctica. The *Palmer* was, strangely enough, headed for "neighbors" a hundred or so miles farther south: We were the winter resupply and crew swap-out mission for two dozen Russian and American scientists living in shelters on an ice floe where they'd been dropped off a couple of months earlier by a Russian breaker, in high summer. But Ice Station Weddell was still several days of hard travel ahead of us.

THE WEDDELL SEA IS ABOUT the size of the Mediterranean. Nevertheless, few people can place it geographically. By comparison with the Mediterranean's human history, the Weddell lacks story and stature, but it holds its own among the world's seas by functioning, according to oceanographers, as the planet's main engine for global weather. Cold bottom water flows north from there into the South Atlantic, maintaining currents and temperature gradients that, in conjunction with solar radiation, bring warm winters, foggy days, rain, clear weather, and the occasional hurricane to Africa, Europe, and the Caribbean, all of which affect weather worldwide.

In that southern winter of 1992 I embarked on a routine of evening strolls because I wanted to stride across the frozen membrane of that isolated planetary heartbeat, so far from anything man-made except the ship; there, docked at night, came the opportunity to walk that pellicle, beneath a vault of starlight so intense you could read your shadow in the snow.

To meet the captain's expectations for safety, I regularly asked among the crew members for two companions to join me. We hardly spoke as we strolled. That wordless hour, and the starkness of the Weddell's chromatic geography—a white plain stretching outward, everywhere, to a flat horizon, from which rose a blue-black dome of sky with its needle points of light—strengthened an impression I had that, for that brief while, we were not of this Earth. We seemed to be tramping instead across squeaky patches of thin, wind-packed snow on the ice apron of some far-off, intergalactic way station.

We were out of sync, in that place, with every one of the Earth's human centers—Delhi, New York, São Paulo. Even the ship was far from home, 7,500 crow-fly miles from Bayou Lafourche, Louisiana, where it was built, and 1,030 miles in a straight line from our last landfall, at Staten Island, just east of Tierra del Fuego. Still, I wanted the experience of moving even farther out. So after dinner each evening for a week, the sun long since having dropped below the northern horizon, a couple of acquaintances and I would dress against the enervating cold and drop over the side.

MY ADULT JOURNEYS AS A writer, if they can be said to have had a rationale, have usually been efforts to move away from civilization's conservative social centers, to leave everyday life behind. My intention has not been always to arrive at the far edges of the world, but often that's what's happened. In the Tanami Desert in the Northern Territory in Australia, or in the Namib Desert on the southwest coast of Africa, or up north on Ellesmere Island in the Canadian High Arctic is where I've felt the most heightened sense of relief and clarity about human culture, the deepest sense of empathy with other humans. Or so it seems, recalling moments in those places when everything idle or petty in my thoughts appeared to drain away.

Those evenings on the sea ice, years ago, I had suspected could be clarifying. I'd sought out such situations before, and that one looked just as promising. Each night the hike out over the ice revitalized me—and then the three of us reached a point where, simultaneously, apprehension rose up—too far from the ship!—and we turned in unison, like a small flock of birds, and began circling back.

As we approached the *Palmer*, it took on for me the appearance of a deep-space freighter, dwarfed by the firmament of bright constellations above. With every one of its exterior search, navigation, and work lights ablaze, the ship's entire superstructure—bristling with thin masts and bulbous electronic gear—glowed in a rondure of brightness. The percussive murmur of its four idling diesels came to us heavy on the dense air, and steam from its ventilation and exhaust ports billowed skyward in the frigid atmosphere. (The temperature was frequently −20° or −25°F, but the wind all that week was "inclinable to calm," as nineteenth-century sailing-vessel mariners once put it. Even if a Beaufort force 10 storm *had* blown in on us, we were so deep in the ice, so far from open water, that such a disturbance would have created no more than a ground blizzard, swirling across a dead-calm plain.)

Given an opportunity, I've usually opted for venues like that one from which to report—remote, elementary, harsh, the scenery experienced in the company of just a few people. The biological and cultural complexities of jungles and cities, for me, have been more difficult terrain. Whatever insight I am groping for as a writer—that unpremeditated comprehension lying just beyond the obvious events and circumstances of a particular journey—has become more apparent to me when I am at some distance from the cultural center. The challenge of finding a path to what I would call the periphery, even if I fail at it, is a task that I at least can understand. In a Venezuelan jungle, or inside Chicago's Loop, I feel overwhelmed by too many options. Such places require a different kind of discernment than I have, a different sort of patience with what lies hidden, a greater tolerance for tight quarters.

I can say this in spite of the fact that I grew up, quite happily, on the outskirts of Los Angeles and lived through my adolescence in the Murray Hill section of Manhattan. I have cherished memories, too, of exhilarating days in Paris and Tokyo, in Istanbul, Santiago, and a dozen other densely populated places. Still, something in me has long been drawn almost exclusively to the classic lines of a desert, to the open ocean and the receding tundra plain—something almost genetic in me, which grows restive in the baroque mazes of a city or in a jungle.

Social historians and evolutionary biologists might easily define this urge more clearly than I can. Like so much of what makes each of us tick, trying to figure out what compels our professional lives often creates an excess of self-consciousness—and little illumination for the road ahead. I have rarely considered why I seek out isolated places, only pondering the matter when someone asks, "Why did you travel to Broome [an unassuming town at the northern end of Eighty Mile Beach in Western Australia] when you could have gone to Alice Springs or Sydney? *That's* where you'll find the real Australian zeitgeist, not in Broome!"

Fair enough. But social historians and evolutionary biologists tell us things change over the centuries. And changes in the social organization of human societies, argue the historians, rarely seem to come from the centers of cultural, financial, or political power. More often, the changes come from a society's outlying districts. The biologists argue, in a similar vein, that a species' most genetically diverse expressions are not to be found at the center of its range but at its periphery.

Certainly it's good to question why anyone would choose to place his professional compass out there on the edge. Put your working life on the periphery and you risk missing all that's happening at the cultural center. You'll miss the debut of, and familiarity with, everything deemed new in the arts, in literature, in fashion, in pop culture. For some reason—perhaps those privileged teenage years of upper-middle-class life in Manhattan—staying current has never registered as a pressing need. The urgency for me is always on the horizon, is always something inchoate, perhaps even a warning that I'm looking for. Many times I've found myself staring intently across a high desert plain or grassland steppe. Occasionally I bring a pair of binoculars to my eyes, to fix upon some small anomaly in those geographies, some sudden tiny movement in the planes of color. Then I lower my glasses, and go on watching. I am not discouraged by the lack of an answer, of a resolution.

When I was growing up in Southern California I spent time around horses. I followed the adventures of all the TV cowboys of the day—Hopalong Cassidy, Roy Rogers, the Cisco Kid. When I look at scrapbooks from my childhood now, collections of images I put together at the age of five or six—the years, psychologists tell us, when you're too young to deceive yourself about your longings—I find pictures that sometimes capture with eerie precision the landscape and circumstances of my later life. For example, caught in illustrations of Western cattle drives are the figures of departing or returning outriders, scouts going ahead to look for water. I identified strongly, then, with those men. Theirs was work I would have chosen.

MAKING OUR WAY BACK TO the *Palmer* on those nights, my companions and I would sometimes stop and consciously try to take in the whole scene: the space, the stillness, the cold. Like middle schoolers we were reluctant to return to the classroom after recess. We dawdled on the ice, stepping more cautiously over frozen cracks than was necessary. We turned around momentarily, away from the ship, to verify our footprints in a skim of crusted snow beneath the starlight. I would often feel an urge to reverse course just then, and go even farther out. One night I deliberately let the others get well ahead of me, two dark, hunkered figures walking the frosted sea, nearing the ship without me.

SOME MONTHS AFTER THE DECEMBER 2004 Boxing Day tsunami overwhelmed Aceh province in northern Sumatra, I stood in the gallery atop a minaret attached to a mosque in the city of Banda Aceh. From that height I could view most of the suburbs in the metropolitan area's southwestern quarter. Between me and the ocean, a thousand yards of land had been shorn of most everything that had once stood there—fruit trees, fish ponds and kitchen gardens, goat pens, fences, motorbikes. A few concrete house slabs were all that remained—those and derelict scraps: a pair of undershorts, a buckled dog collar on a shred of rope. The devastation rolled on in the opposite direction as well, eastward to the base of some hills.

The untoppled white mosque was as revealing an object

there as was the stripped ground. A wall of water over eighty feet high had hit it at about sixty miles per hour, fracturing walls and blowing out its windows and doors, but the edifice had stood. The afternoon I was there its walls glowed in the sun like the sheer faces of a talc quarry, a serene and eminent house of worship. It was as if every building in the Department of Eure-et-Loir in France had been leveled in an earthquake, leaving only the great cathedral at Chartres standing.

I remained awhile at the top of the minaret, studying details of the catastrophe. The tsunami had heaved the ocean's near-shore mud and sand hundreds of yards inland, leaving a sharp, dark line of demarcation. Signs of the city's recovery—cerulean-blue plastic tarps flapping here and there in a light breeze—were apparent in every direction, except in the flats between the mosque and the ocean. In this reach of land, perhaps every person but the fishermen in these families had been killed. The fishermen, bobbing several miles offshore that Sunday morning, might have detected the tsunami as it passed, a wave no more than a foot high, moving so swiftly under them they would have been hard-pressed to credit its having been there at all. In that same moment, someone standing at the top of the minaret would have seen a breaker rising suddenly to a phenomenal height above the beach, as the shock wave from an earthquake below the Indian Ocean came into contact with the coastal shallows. But seconds later he, too, would have been part of the mass drowning, his shouted warnings buried with him.

IT HAS LONG BEEN MY thought—a conceit, probably—that
we live now in a special time, one in which the scale of
commonplace accidents—a leak in an industrial pipe (Bho-
pal), a ship running aground (*Exxon Valdez*), a viral outbreak
in Africa (HIV)—routinely reaches the level of disaster. Few
of the cultural and scientific sentries we assign to our figura-
tive walls can see such things coming, apparently. And the
rest of us seem largely indifferent to frightening news from
the forward observation posts.

I do not think of myself as a forward observer, working
in a dangerous time. I have no romantic infatuation with
heroism. But, having been drawn to the outer edges, I've
recently been trying to understand why. My journal entries
from those winter weeks as a supernumerary journalist
aboard the *Palmer* indicate a prolonged period of confusion
about my motives for making such a long journey—sixty-
eight days in all. Going over the notes, I see that I addressed
that persistent doubt—why make this journey?—even as I
concentrated each day on one task after another. I learned
to weld. I stood watch in the bow. I pored over blueprints
for the 3,300-horsepower Caterpillar diesels driving us across
the face of the planet.

I remember I descended the stairs of the minaret that
day at Banda Aceh with a feeling of great tenderness toward
every human being. So many were swept to their deaths
without warning—without reason, we sometimes say.

DRAWING NEAR TO THE *PALMER* on the evening when my companions went on ahead of me, I stopped to focus my

binoculars on the Magellanic Clouds, two closely set stellar objects not visible from the Northern Hemisphere. I'd once assumed both were part of our galaxy, but each, actually, is a galaxy unto itself, twin cauldrons of gas and young stars. Through the glasses, they had the appearance of wispy cirrostratus, of Portuguese men-of-war adrift in a depthless ocean.

Closer to the ship, I could see the second mate on the bridge, keeping watch and monitoring the life systems of his immensely complex vessel. I heard more emphatically through my parka hood the rhythmic, sonorous dreaming of the diesels, keeping us wedged safely in the floe.

The *Palmer*'s stern deck lay close to the water, a design that facilitated the work of scientists who had to swing cumbersome, deep-sea research gear overboard on cranes. Only an eight-foot climb up a Jacob's ladder and I was back on board.

A scientist was relaxing at the aft rail that evening, despite the intense cold. I admired very much what these unheralded shipboard oceanographers and marine biologists and geologists were doing. Probing the surface of the Earth, they hoped to tease out some meaning to guide us, to inform us about where we are and where we might be headed. I admired as well certain members of the crew, whose knowledge of seamanship and machinery outstripped mine at nearly every turn, and whose holding forth on the design of the research ship's propulsion system and its station-keeping thrusters, as well as arcane aspects of pelagic navigation, I looked forward to hearing every day.

Most of my thoughts, though, especially after that evening foray, I kept to myself. I could have easily gotten a conversation going, back then, about what was looming for us as human beings, if it was to talk only about global climate change. Or the modern disturbances of the formerly self-contained viral ecologies that had brought us the hantavirus, the Lassa and Marburg fevers. Or the desolate expanses of plastic already beginning to gyrate in the Pacific and Indian oceans, material that won't degrade. By now, of course, the need for level-headed, selfless global planning is acute, the need for unusually well-informed strategies obvious to almost everyone. But I had too much unconsolidated speculation in my head to seek out conversation that night.

When I stepped inside from the open deck, I secured the bulkhead door behind me and began stripping off my weather gear in the thick air, the damp heat, of the passage-way. I was mostly anticipating the comfort of my bunk at that point, but thought I might have enough acuity of mind left to tackle one more tedious research paper on the biology of epontic algae—creatures living on the underside of the sea ice, for whom at that moment the *Palmer* was little more than a trembling steel wedge, an intruder beyond comprehension.

Fourteen Aspects of Power

I.

Suddenly there is shouting in the wadi, around the bend up ahead. Three Kamba men have reversed direction and are racing toward Kamoya and me. "*Ikuuwa, ikuuwa!*" they shout. There's a dugway in the stream bank to the left up which we all scramble. From the top of it the five of us watch the snake's approach. It moves briskly, a thin stream of gleaming water nine feet long, gliding through brush on the far side of the wadi a foot off the ground. It carries enough neurotoxins and hemotoxins to kill ten humans. When it disappears downwadi, we reenter the dry streambed and continue our search for fossils emerging from the eroding wall of the cutbank. The mamba seemed to pay us no mind.

II.

My friend Will and I have stepped outside onto a deck three above the main deck of the ship we are traveling in. A storm is churning the ocean into a crosswise confusion of forty-foot seas. The winds, fairly steady at over fifty-five knots, rip spume from the ocean's crests and howl through the ship's uppermost deck. The bow of the 403-foot ship buries itself in the wall of a wave and water geysers through the hawse-holes, bursting against the windows of the bridge. We shout to hear each other, gripping the hand rail next to a companionway in the lee of the ship's superstructure. I can feel the shudder of the vessel's hull in my thighs as the stern lifts, its props breaking the surface of the water, and then the prow rises through and over the crest of another wave, exposing the forward section of the keel, and the stern buries itself again in the ship's wake. A flock of black-browed albatrosses off the port side holds a course parallel to ours as the ship careers on. Six or seven of them. We can see their eyes swiveling in their heads as they take the two of us in, maintaining a speed identical to ours. Their four-foot wings micro-adjust to the ferocity of the inconstant wind. There's rarely a wing beat.

III.

In Kalamazoo, two men kill a gas-station attendant with a .22-caliber weapon, empty the cash register, and drive off in a 1956 pink-and-white Chrysler sedan. A witness says one of the men looked "Mexican." I'm on U.S. 27, twenty miles south of Lansing, driving a 1956 pink-and-white Chrysler sedan, when I see the first state trooper speeding up on us in the rearview mirror. He pulls alongside and gestures sharply with a rigid index finger for me to pull over. Immediately. I've hardly rolled to a stop before two more cruisers arrive, pin-

ning me in on three sides on the shoulder. My college roommate and I, spread-eagled on the hood, are shouted into
silence. They find a .22-caliber rifle in the trunk. We're hand-
cuffed and put in separate cars. The driver of the cruiser I'm
in pulls a shotgun out from under the seat before we leave,
puts the tip of the barrel in my abdomen, the trigger housing
in his lap, and tells me not to move. At the police barracks in
Lansing we're fingerprinted and photographed. They talk to
us in separate rooms. They do not believe we're students at
Notre Dame. The questioning is aggressive, disorienting. No
phone calls allowed. I'm left alone in an empty room with a
three-page confession to sign. A ground-floor window without a screen has been left open behind me. After a while a
detective enters and explains, like a sympathetic friend, how
this will go much better if I just sign the papers. It will get
worse if I don't, he says. They've taken my belt, my shoe-
laces, my pocketknife. The ballistics test on the rifle comes
back. It's negative. The Indiana State Police have ransacked
our dormitory room at Notre Dame. No evidence found.
We're told we can leave. We've been here nine hours. The
car seats have been yanked out, the fabric slit open, our luggage opened, the upended contents flung back in the trunk
with the bags.

We'd been headed for southern Ontario. We could go
back to Notre Dame and try to explain why we were arrested.
Instead, we decide to just keep going.

IV.

I'm in the kitchen making a sandwich when I hear the bird's
wings flicking at the glass in the mudroom. Frantic. A winter

wren. I cup her gently against the windowpane with both hands and carry her through the open door by which she entered. She's so still in my palms I have to concentrate to detect the pinprick points of her claws on my skin. Away from the house, so she'll have space enough to maneuver if she chooses to head in that direction, I open my hands. She doesn't move. Nor do I. I blink and she's forty feet away, disappearing into groundcover beneath the soaring trees. Good for her. I close the mudroom door and return to the sandwich. It occurs to me darkly that I might have killed her, out of curiosity, crushed her paper-thin skull with my fingers like a grape.

V.

I reach for the small notebook next to my sleeping bag and try to write down the few scraps of knowledge I possess about these sounds, words other than "howl" and "scream," though I mark them down, too. I write "caterwaul" and "shriek" and "moan" but not "bay." A banshee wind. Its swift jabs against the tent fabric aggravate more than "buffet." The shrillness rises an octave, reaching a pitch like the highest note from an oboe. The suction of it sags the tent, then the tent slowly inflates and the walls pop. The aluminum poles bend and shiver. The whining hunter wants in.

We're 161 miles from the South Pole. Minus seven degrees Fahrenheit outside. Windchills in the minus forties and this is the fourth day of this. We read, make dinner, play pinochle. A flagged rope guides us to the latrine. This katabatic wind is why we anchor the tent so securely, burying its wide skirts in a foot of snow. It's also why we go outside to refuel the stoves. A slight spill of fuel inside might catch fire as I strike a match to light the stove. If the flame jumps to a tent wall with this wind, our only shelter would be gone in seconds. The wind is why our ears ache. It's the only predator on the polar plateau. It goes for days without sleep.

VI.

I'm headed out to my studio to begin the day's work when I see five or six Roosevelt elk in the trees, lined out behind a large cow. Still as posts. I stop to stare. A few more emerge. I count twelve now. The lead cow has fixed her eyes on me. The other eleven—four cows, a few yearlings, three calves— look to her. When she cocks her head farther sideways to appraise me, I can see the bare white of her large left eye. She holds me and takes in the others, standing hesitant behind her. I can feel the soft texture of the wood-chip path I'm on through the soles of my slippers and see the branch tips of a red cedar limb barely gyrating above her head. Her inquiry, which fills this opening in the forest where we have encountered each other, is very much larger, I think, than, Who are you? It's closer to, What are you planning to do, now that it's come to this? One of the calves turns in to her mother's flank as if to begin nursing. The lead cow continues to stand like someone straining to hear a faint sound. And then she moves and the others follow, drifting like smoke into the trees.

VII.

I step from the taxi in a rainstorm on Central Park South well after midnight and am quickly soaked getting my

luggage out of the trunk, a task the cabbie has waved off as a
nuisance. I step into the club, my baggage dripping on the
marble floor where I pause to get oriented. An attendant at
the lobby desk says, "Sir, you are not properly attired to enter
the lobby of the club."

I acknowledge that I am certainly not, but counter that
I've dressed for the storm, hoping to make light of the protocol. I have a reservation, I say. While he checks I thumb
through my last few hours. The delayed flight, the haphaz-
ard piles of late luggage at LaGuardia, the surly cab driver.

"You have no reservation, sir. Are you a member?"

I say I am not, that my father is, a life member, and that
he has made a reservation for me for two weeks, starting
today. He looks in his records.

"Starting tomorrow, sir."

I offer that my father was probably confused about the
dates when he made the reservation. I gesture at my soaked
clothes, the heavy bags.

"We look forward to seeing you tomorrow evening, sir."

I ask to speak with the manager on duty. I ask the manager for some understanding, given the late hour and the
weather. He says I have a reservation starting the next day,
not tonight. I decide to play the strongest card I have. I tell
him my grandfather, a founding member, once owned the
land this club is now sitting on, and that he sold it to the club
for exactly what he originally paid for it. The manager, with a
Bronx accent, says, "That don't cut no ice with me."

I step out from under the shelter of the New York Athletic Club's awning with my luggage, having waited twenty
minutes for a cab with no luck, and meet the bite and force

of the rain. I don't recall ever having heard that line, except from an actor.

VIII.

In the basement of Building Eleven, the guide shows me an enclosure, a kind of concrete closet with a crawl-in entrance hole at floor level that looks like a port for a dog. Six workers, he says, were forced to crawl through this entry at the end of every day, too many for anyone to be able to lie down, too few for them to lean comfortably against each other for the night. Upstairs I see a monochromatic pile of three thousand empty shoes pressing against the glass wall of a display case and, next to it, loose bales of human hair. When my eyes adjust to the dimness of the gas chamber, with the guide urging us to please move right along, not linger, I see the gouges from fingernails in the plaster walls. At the Holocaust museum in Berlin I will study sheets of corporate letterhead placed side by side in a viewing case. The sequence depicts the design of a new type of convection furnace, one in which the dead, arranged like vented cordwood, can be employed as fuel to incinerate additional bodies moving through on a steel conveyor belt, a process which, once set in motion, eliminates the need for, and the expense of, commercial fuels.

IX.

Riding into Seoul in the cockpit of a 747-400, I page through the tissue-thin pages of the copilot's *Jeppesen Airway Manual*, reading a long list of warnings about attempting a landing here, so close to the DMZ. The warnings are terse, the wording about the inherent dangers blunt. With the plane docking at its gate in the terminal, a squad of South Korean soldiers, automatic weapons at the ready, feeds toward the plane's vulnerable points—the baggage bays, the passenger egress door, the wheel wells. They challenge an approaching refueling truck and two galley vans.

I remain behind in the cockpit, after the crew and the passengers leave. I'll be traveling on to Taipei with a different crew.

The new copilot is the first crew member aboard. He checks my papers quickly and finds them in order. We've met before on another flight. I accompany him on his walk-around, a preflight inspection of the plane's undercarriage— tires, hydraulic brake lines, the alignment of the plane's ailerons with its flaps. I have no official airline employee ID so have made one up. Clipped to my jacket pocket is a clear plastic badge bearing the logo of the Boeing Company. It holds my state driver's license with an embedded photo of me. The copilot nods at the ruse, gives me a thumbs-up. While I follow behind him on inspection, a South Korean soldier approaches, giving me the "And you are . . . ?" look. He underscores the authority behind his query for me by resetting his hands on the stock and barrel of his gun. The copilot intervenes in the same moment that I gesture toward my badge. The soldier examines it closely, comparing my face to the photo on my driver's license. He's familiar with the Boeing logo. He gives me a thumbs-up.

X.

The Yupik people call them *angeyeghaq*, a rogue walrus, almost always a male. A meat-eater. He will make eye contact with you and come off the ice floe he's resting on to go straight for your boat. If you do not depart quickly, or are prevented from escaping by the closeness of pack ice, the walrus will rise in the water and hook its tusks over the gunwale. You have to lift the walrus by its tusks and push him off to make a getaway. If you kill him, the sudden dead weight of his body on the gunwale will flip the boat.

We're subsistence hunting in Russian waters, forty miles west-northwest of the village of Gambell, one of two towns on St. Lawrence Island in the northern Bering Sea. I'm scanning the pack ice for *angeyeghaq*. I've never watched hunters kill an animal this big. I know they must, to keep life in Gambell as they know it going, but the sound of the big .30-06s firing, the creature's death, the massive bleed-out, butchering the animal on the ice—I'm never completely at ease with it. This is not my culture.

I'm the guest. I help with the butchering, as they expect.

XI.

I'm boarding a plane for Denver at the municipal airport in Amarillo, following a recent upgrade of TSA security rules. One of the inspectors questions the bottle of ink.

"It's ink. For a fountain pen," I say. "Less than three ounces."

He knits his brows and waves a colleague over.

This young man's approach is a slow, self-conscious swagger. "Ink," the man tells him. The second man appears to feel that his uniform and his bearing radiate authority. The men share a look of amused disbelief. The new fellow, standing a little too close, displays a ballpoint pen for me. He says that, in the future, I should consider traveling with something like this, that a fountain pen is not an appropriate item for air travel.

"Are we all right now, sir?" he says. It's a taunt.

I don't respond. He says the words again, louder, closer. I can feel his spittle on my cheek. He has me wedged against a steel inspection table.

"Ready to go now, sir? Can we offer you any additional help?" These are jeers. He's crowding very close but not actually touching me. I pick up my hand luggage and turn toward him, waiting for him to give way, which he delays in doing. As I walk off he says, "Have a good trip, sir."

XII.

It's long ago in Nelchina Basin, south of the Alaska Range. I'm helping Bob Stephenson anesthetize wolves and place radio collars on them. A part of me is uncomfortable doing this, but I know that without this data, about their movements and their territorial boundaries, the chance of getting an enforceable legal ruling to relieve hunting pressure on wolves in this state will be almost impossible. The law as it currently stands privileges the hunter.

We dart the wolves with a tranquilizer gun from a helicopter, land, perform a physical exam, and fit each of them with a collar. If we've darted two or three from the same pack, we gather them up where they've gone down, sedated by the drug, and ferry them all to a spot where they'll be examined together. We arrange their heads to keep their noses out of the snow and face them away from the sun, because the drug we're using dilates their pupils. As if it

would make a difference, or as though they could understand, I apologize to them. I explain what we're doing in a
few sentences. That morning a wolf not fully sedated had
snapped at my friend, opening a gash and producing a hema-
toma half the size of his right forearm. When I commiserate,
he says, "Wouldn't you do the same? If you were him?"

We're ferrying one of the wolves to a rendezvous point
where we already have two others from his pack. He's draped
unconscious across my thighs. Then he lifts his head. He
turns to face me, opens his mouth, the lips drawing back.
Without hesitating I fling him sideways out of the helicopter.
He falls fifty feet into deep powder snow. My friend convulses
with laughter. We swing back, find him, and dart him again
with a syringe on the end of a pole, a smaller dose this time.
We check to see that there are no obvious injuries. The next
day we find him with a scanner tuned to the frequency of his
radio collar. He's traveling with the other two, bounding
away from us through deep powder.

XIII.

I've just dropped my girlfriend off at her apartment on East
77th and turned south onto Park Avenue. I'm driving my
father's new Chrysler Imperial. It's after 2 A.M. There's
hardly any traffic and I know I can make ten blocks on a
green light on Park without really pushing the speed limit.
I'm just about to enter the bypass around Grand Central
Station when I see the red lights flashing behind me and pull
over.

The officer asks for my driver's license and registration.
I tell him it's my father's car, not mine, but point out that

the address on the registration, in my father's name, and the address on my driver's license are the same: 105 East 35th Street. And we have the same last name. He asks me where I've been. He asks me what I've been doing. He asks if I am aware of the speed limit on Park Avenue.

"Twenty-five," I say.

"Right. And you were doing forty."

I make a gesture with my hand, as much to say, "Well, there we are then."

He walks back to his car with the license and registration. I'm surprised by how casual I am about the infraction. I've never gotten a ticket. As I begin to imagine the ramifications and the consequences I get out of the car and, keeping my hands clearly visible, approach him and his partner to plead my case. I have a slight limp from a sports injury and am wearing a Notre Dame soccer club letter jacket. He asks about the limp. I explain the injury. He wants to know how the Fighting Irish of Notre Dame are doing this fall. I say we're two-and-three but getting better, and we almost beat St. Louis, the top-rated Billikens. He wants to know if I'm going to the Garden on Sunday to watch the Knicks against the Pistons. I say no, it's Thanksgiving vacation. I have to fly back to school.

"I'm going to let you off with this, but I'm telling you to watch the speeding. Otherwise, next time, a drunk comes out of one of these side streets, it might be way worse than that bum knee. All right?"

I describe the stop the next morning to my father. He shrugs. "An Irish cop," he says.

XIV.

Years after we collared the wolves in Nelchina Basin, I'm with the same friend, Bob Stephenson, on the upper Yukon River. It's late spring, just after breakup. Ice floes have gouged and shaved the cutbanks and the flooding river has uprooted large spruce trees. One afternoon we spot a natural break in the riverside forest and decide to paddle ashore and take a walk in the clearing there. We tie the canoe to the root wad of a beached spruce tree and climb the cutbank to the edge of the clearing. It's a clear, sun-beaten day. We can smell the perfumes of wildflowers in the air and hear the bumblebees hovering. After a while we suddenly both feel that we should leave. On the way back to the canoe we come upon a dead caribou bull. A fresh kill. The neck is broken, the inert head twisted backward over the scapulae. The right flank has been torn open and blood glistens there in the sunlight. We do not run but we move quickly now toward the canoe. I soak myself pushing off hard from the shore.

Love in a Time of Terror

This world is just a little place, just the red in the
sky, before the sun rises, so let us keep fast hold
of hands, that when the birds begin, none of us
be missing.

—EMILY DICKINSON, in a letter, 1860

SOME YEARS BEFORE THINGS WENT BAD, I ARRIVED IN AN
Aboriginal settlement called Willowra, in Australia's Northern Territory. A small village, it's haphazardly situated on
the east bank of the Lander River, a dry watercourse. I'd
driven into the area several days earlier with a small team
of restoration biologists. They were intent on reintroducing
a small marsupial in the vicinity, the rufous hare-wallaby, or
mala in the local language (*Lagorchestes hirsutus*). The animal
had been eliminated locally by feral house cats, domestic
pets left behind decades earlier by white settlers. When I
arrived in Willowra, I was introduced to several Warlpiri

people by a friend of mine, an anthropologist named Petro-
nella Vaarzon-Morel. She'd been working for some years
around Willowra, and when the biologists dropped me
off—Petra's work now completed—she helped move me
into a residence in the settlement, a guesthouse where she
had been living. She then returned to her home in Alice
Springs and I was on my own.

Before she left, Petra had pointed out numerous places in
the countryside nearby that I should neither approach nor
show any interest in. These were mostly innocuous-looking
spots to my eye—rocks, trees, small sand hills—but they were
important elements in the Dreamtime narratives that form
the foundation of Warlpiri identity. Many of these sites were
close to the Lander.

When I asked my hosts, then, if I might walk out into the
desert a few miles, in the direction that I was indicating, and
then return along roughly the same track, the man I was
speaking to pointed in a slightly different direction and said
simply, "Maybe better."

I set off that afternoon on a walk north and west of the
village, across a rolling spinifex plain that stretched away to
hills on the horizon in almost every direction. The flow of
the bland, uniform colors of the countryside was broken up
only by an occasional tree or a copse of trees.

This universe of traditional Warlpiri land was completely
new to me. I had no anxiety, however, about getting lost out
there. At a distance of several miles, the settlement and the
Lander, with its tall gallery forest of gum trees growing along
its banks, remained prominent, in a land that displayed to
my cultural eyes no other real prominences.

It was midday when I left, so if I happened to walk too far to the west (on what would soon be a moonless night in June) darkness might conceivably force me to lie down and wait for dawn. (I could easily have strayed unawares into some broad, shallow depression on that plain, from which all horizons would appear identical.) But getting lost seemed most unlikely. Starlight alone, in this sparsely populated country lying on the southern border of another, much more stark, challenging, and enormous desert, the Tanami, would be enough to guide me home.

My goal that day was intimacy—the tactile, olfactory, visual, and sonic details of what, to most people in my culture, would appear to be a wasteland. This simple technique of awareness had long been my way to open a conversation with any unfamiliar landscape. Who are you? I would ask. How do I say your name? May I sit down? Should I go now? Over the years I'd found this way of approaching whatever was new to me consistently useful: establish mutual trust, become vulnerable to the place, then hope for some reciprocity and perhaps even intimacy. You might choose to handle an encounter with a stranger you wanted to get to know better in the same way. Each person, I think, finds their own way into an unknown world like this spinifex plain; we're all by definition naïve about the new, but unless you intend to end up alone in your life, it seems to me you must find some way in a new place—or with a new person—to break free of the notion that you can be certain of what or whom you've actually encountered. You must, at the very least, establish a truce with realities not your own, whether you're speaking about the innate truth and aura of a landscape or a person.

I've felt for a long time that the great political questions of our time—about violent prejudice, global climate change, venal greed, fear of the Other—could be addressed in illuminating ways by considering models in the natural world. Some consider it unsophisticated to explore the nonhuman world for clues to solving human dilemmas, and wisdom's oldest tool, metaphor, is often regarded with wariness, or even suspicion, in my culture. But abandoning metaphor entirely only paves the way to the rigidity of fundamentalism. To my way of thinking, to prefer to live a metaphorical life—that is, to think abstract problems through on several planes at the same time, to stay alert for symbolic and allegorical meanings, to appreciate the utility of nuance—as opposed to living a literal life, where most things mean in only one way, is the norm among traditional people like the Warlpiri. In listening to negotiations, for example, between representatives of industrialized societies and representatives of traditional societies, it has always seemed that the latter presentation is meant to be more open to interpretation (in order not to become trapped in literalness), while the former presentation too often defaults to logic and "impressive" data sets, but, again, perhaps this is only me.

The goal in these conversations, from a traditional point of view, is to put off for a good while arriving at any conclusion, to continue to follow, instead, several avenues of approach until a door no one had initially seen suddenly opens. My own culture—I don't mean to be overly critical here—tends to assume that while such conversations should remain respectful, the outcome must conform to what my culture considers "reality."

My point here is that walking off into what was for me anonymous territory, one winter afternoon in north-central Australia, was not so much an exercise in trying to improve myself as a naturalist as it was an effort to divest myself of the familiar categories and hierarchies that otherwise might guide my thoughts and impressions of the place.

I wanted to open myself up as fully as I could to the possibility of loving this place, in some way; but to approach that goal, I had first to come to know it. As is sometimes the case with other types of acquaintanceships, to suddenly love without really knowing is to opt for romance, not commitment and obligation.

The evening before I went off to explore the desert around Willowra, I finished a book called *The Last of the Nomads* by William John Peasley, published in 1983. Peasley recounts a journey he made into the Gibson Desert in Western Australia with four other white men in the winter of 1977. They were accompanied by an Aboriginal man named Mudjon. The group was looking for two people believed to be the last of the Mandildjara living in the bush. Mudjon, a Mandildjara elder living at the time in a settlement on the western edge of the Gibson called Wiluna, had known for decades both of the people they were searching for— a hunter, Warri Kyango, and his wife, Yatungka Kyango. These two had refused to "come in" to Wiluna with the last of the Mandildjara people during a prolonged drought in the seventies. Mudjon respected their effort to continue living a traditional life under these very formidable circumstances but he feared that at their ages—Warri was sixty-nine, Yatungka sixty-one—they were getting too old to make their way successfully in the outback without the help of other, younger people.

The search for this couple, across hundreds of square miles of parched, trackless country, interrupted in various places by areas of barren sand hills, culminated with the party's finding the couple, together with their dingoes, at a place called Ngarinarri. (The dingoes helped them hunt and huddled up close with them on cold nights to share their warmth.) A few palmfuls of muddy water every day from a seep, and a small store of fruit from a nearby stand of quandong trees, was all that was sustaining them. Warri was injured and sick, and they were both emaciated.

An argument later ensued in Wiluna and then spread far and wide about the insistence of the rescue party that the couple travel with them back to Wiluna instead of leaving them there to die at Ngarinarri, which it seemed they preferred to "civilized" life in Wiluna.

I wasn't party to this, of course, so can offer no judgment, but this is an old story, characterizing many encounters over the years between "civilized" and traditional styles of living in the Australian bush. Like many readers, I brooded over the fate of these people for days after reading the book. (They both passed away within a year of their arrival in Wiluna, despite the availability there of food, water, and medical treatment.) This is a story of injustice, of course, and, too, a tragedy that virtually anyone can understand. What really stuck in my mind, though, was how love dramatized this narrative, a narrative as profound in its way as the other narrative, the one about colonial indifference and enduring harm.

Because Warri and Yatungka were both born into the same moiety among the Mandildjara, they were prevented by social custom from marrying. When they defied this custom and married anyway, their lives from then on, after their formal banishment, became far more difficult. They knew if they attempted to return to the society of their own people, they risked being physically punished. So they chose a life on their own. Even when they learned, years later, that they had been forgiven, and that their Mandildjara culture was unraveling further in the face of colonial intrusion, and even though they learned that a terrible period of widespread drought had brought most all of the "desert tribes" into white settlements like Wiluna, they continued to choose their marriage and their intimately known traditional country.

Warri and Yatungka looked after each other over all that time, and they took care of their beloved country according to the prescriptions and proscriptions in the Dreamtime stories, observing their obligations to it. They also knew, I have to think, that the watering places their people had traditionally depended on for generations had now withered and dried up or, in the case of the animals they regularly hunted, their food had simply departed the country. And yet they refused to succumb, even at what you might call the point of their natural end. It would be arrogant and certainly perilous to subscribe to any theory of what the two of them might have been thinking at the end, at Ngarinarri. What stood out for me as obvious, however, was their fierce allegiance—to their Mandildjara country and to each other. Death in this case was not for them tragic but inevitable, onerous but acceptable; and death in this place was preferable to lives lived out in Wiluna.

But, of course, this is not for me to determine.

The day I walked out into the desert in the direction I was pointed, I was intent on immersing myself in the vastness of something I didn't know. I carried in my backpack a few books about recognizing and preparing "bush tucker," the desert plants and small creatures that could sustain Aboriginal people; a dependable bird book; and some notes about marsupials and poisonous snakes. In terms of what governed the line of my footsteps, my many changes of direction, my pauses, my squattings down, it was primarily my desire to pursue immersion—letting the place overwhelm me.

Drifting through my mind all the while, however, was the story of Warri and Yatungka, or at least the version of it that was written up and that I had read.

At some point late that day, I came upon several dozen acres of land more truly empty than the desert landscape I'd been walking through for hours. It consisted of an expanse of bare ground and coarse sand with shattered bits of dark volcanic rock scattered about. I walked as carefully here as I might have through an abandoned cemetery. Silence rose from every corner of the place, and the utter lack of life drew heavily on my heart. As I walked on, I saw no track of any animal, no windblown leaf from a mulga tree, no dormant seed waiting for rain. Other images of bleakness came to mind: bomb-shattered rubble that buried the streets of Kabul; a small island in Cumberland Sound, a part of Baffin Island in Nunavut, Canada, where dozens of large whale skeletons lay inert in acres of tawny sea grass rolling in the wind like horses' manes; the remains of a nineteenth-century whaling station; tiers of empty sleeping platforms, each bunk designed to hold four men, rising to the ceiling in a derelict barracks at Birkenau, where every night exhausted men lay in darkness, waiting to be carted off in wheelbarrows to the nearby ovens and burned on the day they could no longer wield their tools.

I had halted with these images pushing through my mind and in the moment was toeing a stone the size of my fist when another thought burst in: that most of the trouble that afflicts human beings in their lives can be traced to the failure to love.

In the summer of 1979, I traveled to a Nunamiut village in the central Brooks Range in Alaska to visit my friend Bob Stephenson, who had a sod home in this settlement of 110 Nunamiut people, and in the days following our arrival we spent many hours listening to stories about local animals: wolverines and snowy owls, red foxes and caribou. The Nunamiut were enthusiastically interested in their lives, as were we. We spent a few days, too, hunting for active wolf dens in the upper reaches of the Anaktuvuk River. Then we flew several hundred miles west to the drainage of the Utukok River. We stayed a few days at a temporary summer camp there on the Utukok, where Bob and other field biologists could regularly observe tundra grizzlies, caribou, wolves, gyrfalcons, wolverines, and other creatures during the summer months. Bob and I then helicoptered south to a place in the De Long Mountains farther up the Utukok called Ilingnorak Ridge.

We camped there for a week, watching a wolf den across the river from us—five adults and five pups.

Whenever I'm asked what I love, I think of the aggregate of relationships in that place that summer. Twenty-four hours of sunshine every day at 68° N latitude. Cloudless skies, save for fair-weather cumulus. Light breezes. No schedule for our work but our own. Large animals present to us at almost every moment of the day. And, this far north of the treeline, looking through a gin-clear atmosphere with forty-power spotting scopes, we enjoyed unobstructed views of their behavior, even when they were two or three miles away. I had daily conversations with Bob about the varied and unpredictable behavior of wild animals (or, as I later came to think of them, free animals, those still undisturbed by human interference). We reminisced about other trips we'd made together in the years before this, on the upper Yukon River and out to St. Lawrence Island, in the northern Bering Sea.

The mood in our camp was serene, unhurried. We were excited about being alive, about our growing friendship, about this opportunity to watch free animals in good weather, and about the timelessness of our simple daily existence. I loved the intensity of our vigil. Every day we watched what was for us—probably for anyone—the most spectacular things: wolves chasing caribou; a grizzly trying to break into the wolf den, being fought off by a single young wolf; thirty caribou galloping through shallow water in the Utukok, backed by the late-evening sun, thousands of flung diamonds sparkling in the air around them; an arctic fox sitting its haunches ten yards from the tent, watching us intently for twenty minutes.

When we returned to base camp, we enjoyed meals with the other scientists and talked endlessly with them about incidents of intriguing behavior among the animals we all watched every day. One afternoon someone brought in a mammoth tusk she had dug out of a gravel bank close by. Somehow, we no longer felt we were living in the century from which we had arrived.

During those days we all resided at the heart of incomprehensible privilege.

Evidence of the failure to love is everywhere around us. To contemplate what it is to love today brings us up against reefs of darkness and walls of despair. If we are to manage the havoc—ocean acidification, corporate malfeasance and government corruption, endless war—we have to reimagine what it means to live lives that matter, or we will only continue to push on with the unwarranted hope that things will work out. We need to step into a deeper conversation about enchantment and agape, and to actively explore a greater capacity to love other humans. The old ideas—the crushing immorality of maintaining the nation-state, the life-destroying belief that to care for others is to be weak and that to be generous is to be foolish—can have no future with us.

It is more important now to be in love than to be in power. It is more important to bring E. O. Wilson's biophilia into our daily conversations than it is to remain compliant in a time of extinction, ethnic cleansing, and rising seas. It is more important to live for the possibilities that lie ahead than to die in despair over what has been lost.

Only an ignoramus can imagine now that pollinating insects, migratory birds, and pelagic fish can depart our company and that we will survive because we know how to make tools. Only the misled can insist that heaven awaits the righteous while they watch the fires on Earth consume the only heaven we have ever known.

The day of illumination I had in the plain west of Willowra, about a world generated by the failure to love, which was itself kindled by the story of the lovers Warri and Yatungka, grew out of my certain knowledge that, years before, I had experienced what it meant to love, on those summer days with friends in the Brooks Range. The experience delivered me into the central project of my adult life as a writer, which is to know and love what we have been given, and to urge others to do the same.

In this trembling moment, with light armor under several flags rolling across northern Syria, with civilians beaten to death in the streets of Occupied Palestine, with fires roaring across the vineyards of California and forests being felled to ensure more space for development, with student loans from profiteers breaking the backs of the young, and with Niagaras of water falling into the oceans from every sector of Greenland, in this moment, is it still possible to face the gathering darkness and say to the physical Earth, and to all its creatures, including ourselves, fiercely and without embarrassment, I love you, and to embrace fearlessly the burning world?

Southern Navigation

I'VE ALWAYS BEEN FEARFUL OF BIG SEAS FAR FROM SHORE. IN making ready for a voyage to Antarctica, this was the disturbed dog lurking in a dark alley. As much as I hoped to step ashore at South Georgia, Elephant Island, and the other markers of Sir Ernest Shackleton's famously desperate journey, as curious as I was about the Edenic spectacle of the Lemaire Channel and natural hot spring pools on Deception Island—both destinations well known, now, to Antarctic travelers—I dreaded the approach across "the Drake."

The Drake Passage, separating Antarctica from South America, stretches east several hundred miles from Cape Horn into the Scotia Sea. An open-ocean passage here makes for one of the riskiest crossings on the planet (the Gulf of Alaska, where winds coming unimpeded from Japan have tremendous fetch, is as dangerous, as are waters in the "Furious Fifties" between Australia and Antarctica, though ships rarely visit there).

Our 403-foot German cruise vessel, the *Hanseatic*, is

designed for passenger comfort, with well-appointed rooms, a beauty salon, observation and bar lounges, and the usual immaculate trio of Jacuzzi, sauna, and gym. Its restaurants serve credible five-star meals and, in warmer weather than we would experience, passengers can enjoy an outdoor pool and mixed drinks served at deck chairs while they tan. The *Hanseatic*, however, is canted toward adventure cruising: Its complement of passengers is small (180), and its observation deck is stacked not with chairs but with black Zodiacs—inflatable outboard-powered boats designed for beach landings and shallow-water excursions. Also, shipboard lectures on the region's cultural history, its fauna and (limited) flora, on icebergs and the whaling industry, fill out the hours that on other cruise vessels might be given over to shuffleboard tournaments or cabaret evenings. The *Hanseatic* strikes an earnest note with its ice-reinforced hull, bow thruster, and twin propellers, which help it maneuver through floes and narrow channels. It also has retractable stabilizers to dampen its roll in large seas.

On the first day of our three-week Antarctic journey, one day out of the Falkland Islands and crossing the Drake Passage, the *Hanseatic* enters a Beaufort force 11 storm— technically a "severe storm." Our course is east-southeast for the coast of South Georgia; the storm is blowing from the west-southwest, hammering the ship's starboard side. The heavy seas seem riotously confused at first glance, but when I study them closely, I see a wave pattern bearing off east-northeast, underneath sheets of wind-whipped spindrift, hydra-headed whitecaps, and the sudden surface detonation of water caused by ferocious downdrafts of air.

On the *Hanseatic*'s bridge, gripping console railings, I am able to read our instruments as clearly as the officer on watch: winds, steady at about forty knots, peaking at sixty; angle of roll, approaching fifteen degrees. Headway, six to seven knots. The window wipers forward are buried regularly by the tongues of broken waves, lunging up from the ocean forty feet below. The window glass is wiped clear so often that the seas off the bow go continuously in and out of focus.

Retreating from the bridge in foul-weather gear, I turn down a passageway and exit the corridor on the ship's lee-ward (protected) side. Here, the wind comes fitfully from every direction at once, but in short bursts like jabs. I climb an open steel stairway from the bridge deck to the observation deck and continue to the uppermost deck, the—though not just now—sundeck. With my gloved grip tight on the ship's rail and my back bent under the wind, I try to appreciate the great ocean from this precise, infinitesimal spot on the surface of the globe: 53°03.17′ S and 49°19.86′ W.

These seas are running (the officer below has told me) at about thirty-five feet, meaning someone standing three stories above the ship's waterline is looking straight at the crests of waves as they approach. But the waves come, actually, in uneven sets of four or five: twenty-five feet, thirty-seven feet, twenty-eight feet, forty-one feet. Just after I leave this spot, a fifty-foot wave will slam into our starboard side, washing over the deck below me.

From my vantage point at the railing, I feel as though I am examining some sort of animal. Far from here, on the beaches of Cancún, say, or up in the Maldives, this same ocean may be as disinclined to stir as a sunning cat—just an occasional rise of the tip of the tail. And somewhere else,

surely, it is even more terrifying than here. What I am wit-
nessing in the protracted dusk of an austral summer, under a
field of incandescent light cast from searchlight stanchions
on this deck, is a surface with no shape the eye can hold. The
ocean mounds into ridges, collapses into valleys, falls backward from its direction of movement, bellies out beneath
blasts of wind (which peen its surface into geometric patterns
that repeat like quilt designs), and surges like a reptile up the
side of the ship.

Three decks below and forward, the ocean geysers
through a two-foot hawsehole as the *Hanseatic* plunges into a
trough and buries its bows in the base of a wave. Occasionally this waterspout reaches the bridge intact before the wind
makes it a column of exploding marble. It is impossible to
tell, here, whether it is raining or whether I am enveloped in
spray thrown about by the wind. Like the waves, the wind
can be felt as a force from a generalized direction (west-
southwest), but it is made up of long shrieks and bursts, plo-
sions of air filling irregular vacuums. The high pitch of its
race through an antenna farm above my head and through
wires guying the searchlight stanchions rises and drops like a
shift in the intensity of a victim's anxiety. It thrums on a different pitch altogether as it blows past the rotating arm of
the radar mast and around the white globe of the Inmarsat
satellite-telephone antenna.

The ship's port bow shoulders into a trough and rises so
fast I float in vertigo. It plunges into the next trough and as it
comes back I feel my intestines flatten out in the bowl of my
pelvis. It rolls sideways off the steep flank of another wave,
and I pin my hip harder to the railing to absorb the sudden

lurch of its recovery. My toes bear into my rubber boots to drive my feet more solidly into the deck sheathing.

I do not know why I am out here. It does not occur to me that I'm not as afraid as I thought I would be. The unruliness of the storm is as captivating, as attractive, as any scene or event I have ever known in nature. Something in me craves a link with it. I want a knowledge of this storm in my tissues, a memory to draw on the next time I lay my towel out under a tropical sun, feel the air light over my bare shoulders, and hear the soft plash of the ocean on the sand.

For almost an hour I watch the *Hanseatic* burst, career, and shudder through the Scotia Sea. Aft, the stern of the vessel cocks itself sideways forty feet at a time. It drops beneath the horizon and then lifts entirely above it, a silhouette sweeping the low-slung sky. The ship pivots on its three axes like a lugubrious gyroscope, its wake shredded immediately by the wind and the heaving run of the sea. Heat exiting the ship's funnel turns to steam, a white banner instantly unraveled and gone. My balance is threatened and restored continuously as the ship accelerates and as suddenly decelerates on its track through the immediacy of the storm.

I'm aware that this nameless weather is significant; most passengers have returned to their rooms, seasick or terrified. I do not know why I am not among them. It is exhaustion, not loss of interest—a diminished sense of proprioception, which means I am no longer critically alert—that finally takes me below. Chilled and damp, I descend three decks on the leeward side, take a last look at the convolutions of the sea, and enter the windless quiet of the ship's interior. Ahead in the passageway I see a man holding a whiskey tumbler aloft. He is running downhill, away from me, then struggling uphill as the *Hanseatic* surges ahead, his body swaying beneath the glass as if it defined a ceiling strap from which he hung.

IN MY DARKENED CABIN I find my young companion asleep. She stirs at my whisper, assuring me that she feels fine, and goes under again. She is determined not to be sick, and sleeps with a four-point grip on the mattress. She has never been to sea.

I hang my storm gear to drain in the tub and undress in the bathroom. In my pajamas, I try to make some notes at a table, but cannot keep my pencil on the paper. The edge of a wave occasionally slides across the room's single large window. I do not know why I am not seasick, or why, gripping the sides of my own mattress later with the arches of my feet to keep from being thrown to the floor, I am not afraid. The best I can say is that the ship has in these seas, for me, the authority of a locomotive on steel rails.

Some passengers, I'll learn later, are entirely done in by the storm. Others will denounce the weather as an impertinent nuisance, a disruption of the trip's advertised itinerary (as if the ship were a golf cart forced, by some unforeseen delay, to have to scurry through its stops in a shopping mall to beat closing time). Most, though, will fight off headaches and upset stomachs the next morning to take pictures of half a dozen black-browed albatrosses, swooping the ship's flanks on four-foot wings, and gliding the crests and troughs of thirty-foot waves with an aplomb native to their realm.

As I fall off to sleep, I picture the layout of cabins in the ship, glad we were offered one amidships, where the pitching is not so severe. Officially, my responsibility here is to deliver several shipboard lectures. I am as eager, however, as any of my companions to experience parts of Antarctica I've not seen before. I also want to renew my friendship with another lecturer, the photographer Galen Rowell, and his wife, Barbara. My overriding concern here, though, is the welfare of my twenty-two-year-old companion, Amanda, the eldest of my wife's four daughters. All this—Antarctica, the amenities of a cruise ship, a photo workshop with Galen—is new to her, akin to a child's first snowfall.

AMANDA AND I ARE WITH the second party to land on Albatross Island and then be guided up to a muddy plateau where, with twenty other passengers, we form part of a crescent of observers, silently studying three incubating wandering albatrosses. They nest annually on this and other nearby islands within the Bay of Isles, off the northwest coast of South Georgia. A light wind brings the cries of fur seal pups up from a narrow stone beach on a spit a hundred feet below. To the south, the mainland of South Georgia rises under low clouds, its alpine slopes sheathed in glaciers that terminate as blunt ice walls in the blue-green water.

Of the twenty, only I and the two naturalist-guides are without cameras. For me, the incessant click of shutters disturbs the primordial air, which otherwise carries only the cries of the pups, the mewing of gulls over kelp beds near the shore, the call notes of brown pipits flicking across the tussock grass, the buzz of air through the feathers of giant petrels as they pass close over the photographers, and, overwhelming it all, a continual stream of honks, warbles, chitter murmur, flatus, and clatter horn belches from adolescent and mature fur seals on the plateau.

Each of the three albatrosses incubates an egg on a nest the size of a small café table, built atop a tump of tussock grass. In a bog field of perhaps twenty such tumps, they nest apart but parallel, each with its stout buff-yellow six-inch bill pointing into a southwest wind. Wandering albatrosses, though not the heaviest of birds, are among the world's largest, their wing spans approaching twelve feet. (Royal albatrosses are as large; Andean condors weigh more.) At sea, it's difficult to appreciate their size, seeing them against the water or the sky; when you see them close at hand, motionless on a nest, it's clear why nineteenth-century sailors once referred to these (mostly white) birds as "cape sheep."

For many, myself included, standing before them is a Grail experience, an encounter with one remnant of the cloth of creation. It is not merely the great size of the creatures, their far-gone roaming lives, or the geographical remoteness of their nesting ground that casts a spell; it's their seeming indifference to our presence. Gazing past and through us, they appear so self-possessed as to make our fumbling with lenses and wrestling with tripods seem primitive by comparison.

Observing the birds with the others, I feel some frustration. Given a choice, I would rather not see them this way, as one of the group of twenty people here for only fifteen minutes, on the heels of another group of twenty just departed, and pressed by a third group eager for us to be on our way. But this is how a cruise ship schedule works—and I'm happy for the fifteen minutes. I can shut out from the sphere of my concentration all but the sonic landscape of fur seal yap and the wind's mutter and pop. Inside that cocoon I scrutinize the albatrosses, note how they face the same way into the wind, how they rotate the eggs they're sitting, the manner in which they preen, how the nesting ground is sited above a cliff face, which allows these huge soarers simply to drop off and become airborne.

I cannot unpack the scene enough, though, in my allotted time. What is the temperature here? Where, at this moment, are the mates of these monogamous birds? How large is the egg? Can they differentiate among the sounds they hear us make? One of the naturalist-guides, Don Walsh, pilot of the bathyscaphe *Trieste* when it became the first submersible to reach the bottom of the Mariana Trench in 1960, gives me a subtle signal. Stay. Go back with the third group. I reopen my notebook.

FROM SOUTH GEORGIA, THE PLAN is to turn southwest for the South Orkneys, then the South Shetlands (including Elephant Island); to visit several historic sites along the Antarctic Peninsula; to cross the Drake again to Cape Horn; and then to disembark at Ushuaia in Argentine Tierra del Fuego. On earlier trips to Antarctica, I've benefited from an unusual range of experience: diving under the sea ice in McMurdo Sound; camping for several weeks on three separate occasions in the Transantarctic Mountains and on the polar plateau near the South Pole; and a stretch of time spent in scientific camps in the McMurdo Dry Valleys. I was also fortunate enough to be aboard the *Nathaniel B. Palmer* in April 1992, when it became the first ship to enter the Weddell pack ice in winter since Shackleton's *Endurance* was crushed there in 1915.

It is with this background that I present lectures and socialize with the passengers, but this field experience is also the basis for the exemption Walsh gives me in that moment on Albatross Island. I watch Amanda pack up her camera gear and depart with the others, feeling self-conscious about my privilege. She returns my perplexed glance with the look of the fully satisfied.

I have felt a peculiar species of joy watching Amanda respond to the sudden warning lunges of beached elephant seals or trying to take in the welter of prions, shearwaters, petrels, gulls, and other oceanic birds, the cacophony of a penguin rookery or the spartan walls of tidewater glaciers. It's a sensation akin to what I feel sitting in the tussock grass now, watching the wandering albatrosses: a widening of the heart.

I'm alert to opportunities in our itinerary for my daughter to photograph (she's majoring in photography and environmental studies in college), and at the same time, I'm trying to prepare engaging lectures on Antarctic meteorites and ice-core drilling. I'm trying to read relevant sections of Robert Cushman Murphy's classic two-volume work *Oceanic Birds of South America*. (The mates of the albatrosses we saw are fishing off the coast of Brazil. The egg averages twenty-seven cubic inches, nearly half a quart.) I'm also trying to attend the presentations of the other five lecturers, and endeavoring to stay clear of some of the *Hanseatic*'s time-sink seductions (mostly the sauna and Jacuzzi) long enough to maintain regular contact with the physical world, the one we've all come so many thousands of miles to see.

I want, too, some private hours with Galen and Barbara, and with Will Steger, the great polar explorer and adventurer of my generation and a new friend.

In the end, I put away thoughts of how I might win more time ashore with the albatrosses and penguins on our daily excursions. Instead, I watch over Amanda, solicitously but from a distance. I concentrate on preparing my lectures—and manage to submerge my own earnestness long enough to become something of an evening habitué of the sauna. I rise before dawn nearly every day to get out on deck alone, before breakfast when the obligation to socialize presses in. I search tabular icebergs the size of Manhattan with binoculars, see humpback whales breach and pods of gentoo, king, and chinstrap penguins porpoise past, while light wells slowly over the water and glints in the vastness.

It strikes me often on our journey that a distracted life, a life strung between competing desires, has now become ordinary life for many people in Western cultures. Conscientious devotion to a single task such as Murphy's to the study of oceanic birds not only seems tedious to many, it's even disparaged now as obsessive. Who cares for the refinements that differentiate among populations of wandering albatrosses, let alone the metaphysics behind their peregrinations? And an unplotted hour, when the ordinary world might go inside out, is a source of apprehension, a crow in the garden. Our cruise is predicated on an assumption that people want to know what's *next*—that passengers are most comfortable with the opportunity to do many things, and no one thing for too long. It proceeds with the tacit understanding that the real world is the ship, with its impeccably served six-course dinners, its always-fresh linens, its au courant boutique. The landscape through which we pass, with its great compass of wild animals, its unscheduled weather, its ghosts of Shackleton and Otto Nordenskjöld, its smoldering volcanoes, is enthralling, but it also lies eerily outside the rhythms and confines of modernity.

Antarctica can be understood as something one might turn off for a few hours—or even a few days if you choose movies and room service for a week, as several did. Like Fedallah and the rest of Ahab's stowaway crew, some passengers emerged only after the journey was well under way. They seemed indifferent to what lay outside the ship, showing up only for trips ashore at Port Lockroy, which has a small souvenir shop; at Neko Harbor, the only place they could actually set foot on the Antarctic continent; and, if it wasn't windy or wet, at one or two other destinations.

It's taking a risk—and is presumptuous, of course—to judge anyone's behavior aboard a cruise ship, to make assumptions about the tour operator's day plan or even the purpose behind maintaining the *Hanseatic*'s patrician atmosphere. Hardly a sybaritic dinner passes, however, when I do not glance out the long window rows of the Marco Polo Restaurant at the evening sea or the glacier-cracked land and think of the enduring privation, despair, and death that impinged on everyday life for the first sailors to explore here. As I consume my elegant dinner, the possibility for detachment is scary.

Sometimes at night I sat in a deck chair in the dark in my wind pants and parka, watching the ocean and the less familiar constellations of the Southern Hemisphere. I'd recall the weeks of harsh, flesh-deadening cold I had accepted as a necessary price on expeditions at both ends of the Earth. I could not completely integrate myself into the ship. Privately I began to think of it as the planet *Hanseatic*. Its comforts, against the assertiveness of our environment, were not so much surreal, a potential source of amusement, as foreboding, a source of trepidation.

Maybe the reason I was not afraid in the storm was that the *Hanseatic*'s authority never seemed seriously compromised. In its way, it approached the supremacy of the albatross in this clime, and so I'd allowed myself to be taken in by a sense of security, one that the ship's captain, among others, knew to be naïve. The vessel could have been rolled abruptly on its side as the result of a steering error or shoved under like a Popsicle stick while we were in the Drake. I was grateful, always, for the grand ship, its comfortable quarters and protection, but I longed for the opportunity to engage more often, more completely and for longer periods of time, with what lay beyond the orbit of the ship.

IN THE CEMETERY AT GRYTVIKEN, an abandoned Norwegian whaling station on the north-central coast of South Georgia, the gravestone of Sir Ernest Henry Shackleton, prominent even from a distance, seemed to be a kind of anchor. We stood around it on a sunny, almost balmy afternoon, having our pictures taken while sipping champagne.

I lingered for half an hour after the others left.

Much has been made of "the Boss" in recent years, and

truly it is hard to exaggerate the good points of the man's character, his devotion to his men, his bull courage and pure daring. Robert Falcon Scott pales beside him as a hero of the Edwardian era. There was nothing of noblesse oblige about Shackleton, as there was with Scott, and no prize was worth death, his own or anyone else's. He chose to quit when he was within 111 statute miles of the South Pole on January 9, 1909. Better to be a live donkey than a dead lion, he mused. He was shrewdly cautious, brash, egalitarian, impatient, and charismatic—altogether a healthier mix of flaws and strengths than the morose and neglectful Scott possessed.

Shackleton died of a heart attack at Grytviken on January 5, 1922—age forty-seven—at the start of his fourth Antarctic expedition. It occurred to me as I watched passengers posing next to Shackleton's gravestone, a seven-foot granite stele, that only one of us, really—the polar adventurer Steger—was in a class to stand with Shackleton. It was an uncharitable thought, and Steger waved it away the moment I mentioned it. He came and went among us like smoke, restless and soft-spoken. A few minutes, and he was several hillsides away.

Grytviken, though the evoking of the imagery offends some, is a death camp. Its rendering factory and whale-oil storage tanks, torn open by the wind and scorched by fire, are now rusted a dozen shades of mahogany, from roan through umber to café noir. The grounds are littered with shards of glass, crushed brick, broken screws, bent nails, and shanks of twisted wire and cable. In its heyday the station processed many hundreds of whales every year, a ruthless appropriation that emptied the local seas, an exploitation from which the whale populations have never recovered. Because the station had no village infrastructure—roads out of town, civic buildings, agricultural fields—it sits now on the shore of King Edward Cove, Cumberland East Bay, like a shipwreck: foundered, derelict, haunted. Nearby, between the factory buildings and the cemetery, a hydro powerhouse, used as a target by commandos during the Falklands War in 1982, stands riddled and stove-in by automatic-weapons fire. A few hundred yards from there, burned to the waterline, is the carcass of the *Louise*, until recently one of the best-preserved down-easters, a class of American deepwater sailing vessel, this one built in Maine in 1869. The ship was ignited by an errant flare during a war-games exercise.

It is a narrow focus, of course, that finds only catastrophe at Grytviken. The northern periphery of this forsaken station is occupied by several refurbished and well-tended buildings, among them a church and a museum. In either building it is possible to reflect on the meaning of plunder and human violence, of which the dilapidated, bullet-punched factory is emblematic. Among the bravest and loneliest of jobs, I thought on leaving, were those of Grytviken's four caretakers, working to preserve this memorial for the edification of passengers disembarking in greater numbers every year from cruise ships.

DURING OUR DAYS IN THE vicinity of South Georgia, we also put ashore at Gold Harbor, there to amble through a king penguin colony, twenty thousand or so birds standing for a quarter mile along a curving beach; at Godthul Harbor, where we watched eighty-knot winds tear a waterfall in half, sending the top portion of it back up the cliff face; and at Stromness, a now abandoned and collapsing whaling station on the north-central coast where, on May 20, 1916, Shackleton emerged at the end of his epic journey. (Setting out from a bleak shingle beach eight hundred miles to the west on April 24, Shackleton and five other men had sailed a twenty-foot boat through heavy seas to the shelter of King Haakon Bay on South Georgia's southwest coast. From there, he and two others had crossed the island's heavily glaciated and mountainous spine—a stupendous alpine feat, given their state of exhaustion and lack of equipment—and stumbled into the manager's office at Stromness.)

Amanda, I, and others wanted to retrace the last leg of Shackleton's journey. From the station we hiked up a melt-water river valley about a mile to reach Shackleton's last obstacle, a waterfall. Two dozen of us climbed up to a flat spot several hundred feet above the foot of the fall. From there we could see the last thousand yards or so of Shackleton's route down off the Fortuna Glacier and, to the east, a glittering sheet of water in Stromness Bay, backed by snow-covered peaks and blue-white glaciers. It was not difficult to suppose how salvific the whaling station must have seemed to them on that May day.

The afternoon was so warm, Amanda and I lay jacket-less on our backs on the tundra and talked about men like Shackleton and Scott, shifting stems of native grass from one corner of our mouths to the other as we did so.

———

THE DAY FOLLOWING OUR DEPARTURE from South Georgia we arrived at Laurie Island in the South Orkneys, at an Argentine research station called Orcadas. Here, as in so many places in historic Antarctica, white crosses memorialize the coffinless graves of those who drowned and were lost, who drifted away on ice floes, or who disappeared in a storm in this indifferent country. Standing on the stony beach that day, waiting for a Zodiac to convey some of us back to the ship, I became preoccupied with thoughts of death. It was not entirely an effect of the ten small crosses in the Orcadas cemetery (the most recent of them honor three men who rowed off in a small boat on March 31, 1998; an inscription reads *Sus presencias están por siempre en estos hielos*—the memory of them will stand forever in these ice fields). It was also the seventy-eight chinstrap penguin carcasses I'd counted along the shore, each one turned inside out by a predatory leopard seal. Their black-and-white bodies marked the high-tide line. Without such death, there can be no life. Or so we say in our lectures.

We have yet to see a leopard seal.

The next morning, having by now crossed the southern perimeter of the Scotia Sea, we came up on the north coast of Elephant Island. We caught a glimpse of Cape Valentine on the east end, where Shackleton and his twenty-seven men came ashore for the first time after sixteen months on the ice and at sea (briefly) in their three boats. Six miles farther on, the ship hove to at Point Wild, where Shackleton's party made its permanent camp on April 17, 1916.

The seas were running in six- to eight-foot swells, but in consultation with the captain, our expedition leader Christine Lampe decided we would take to the Zodiacs. There was no possibility of a landing, but with care we might cruise both sides of the spit and so examine the place from fifty feet offshore.

Like many aboard, I'd read a lot about this site, the camp where twenty-one men under Frank Wild had waited 128 days for Shackleton to return, not knowing whether he'd ever made it to South Georgia. I was not prepared, however, for the degree of exposure here. It's easy enough for a reader to picture the heavy surf, the buffeting wind, the damp and cold these men faced in those months. What I had never appreciated before was how confined, how isolated they were. The narrow spit, open to the sea on both sides, juts from a sheer cliff of metamorphic rock, its heights buried in cloud the day I saw them. The spit runs but a dozen yards or so before it terminates in a massive rock-head. The cliff face continues as precipitous to the east, dropping straight into the ocean. To the west it curves away quickly into an embankment and ends against the snout of a tidewater glacier. There's nowhere for a person to stand but on the spit, and only three or four strides of level ground are to be had there. I could not remember, either, having read any pointed description of the stench. The spit is seasonally occupied by colonies of chinstrap and gentoo penguins. The fetor from the muck of guano was so acrid it induced tears when it reached us.

For shelter, Wild and his men had two overturned boats and some canvas sailcloth. They slept in the guano, burned seal and penguin blubber for heat, ate seaweed boiled in seawater, adapted to storm surges that flooded their camp, and worked diligently to keep one another's humor up.

Shackleton finally reached them on August 30, 1916,

aboard the *Yelcho*, a 150-ton Chilean lighthouse tender sailing from Punta Arenas on the Strait of Magellan, seven hundred miles to the northwest. The indefatigable Shackleton and the irrepressible Wild, through all this tribulation, did not lose a single member of the expedition.

EACH DAY OF TRAVEL BRINGS us something we've not yet seen. To our list of five penguin species, Amanda and I now add, at Snow Island, Adélie and emperor penguins. To our list of southern elephant seal and Antarctic fur seal we append Weddell, leopard, and crabeater, all associated with the ice. We opt out of "soaking" in a shin-deep geothermal pool hastily dug in the black beach sands of Whalers Bay, part of the flooded caldera that forms Deception Island, with its narrow (that is, "deceptive") entry from the open ocean. Instead, we take a photographic and reconnoitering hike through the ruins of an old Norwegian whaling station, and through the more recent ruins of a station formerly manned by British scientists, until they were driven off by volcanic eruptions in 1967 and 1970.

Twenty-four hours later, on a brilliant, chilly day of fair-weather clouds, the *Hanseatic* pushes through light ice around Splitwind Island and into the northeast end of a seven-mile-long corridor named the Lemaire Channel. It's confined on each side by enormous mountain walls. To the northwest is the steep, craggy rise of Booth Island; to the southeast, the retreating peaks and hanging glaciers of Graham Land, a part of the Antarctic Peninsula. The topographic relief is so dwarfing, so insistent, so without precedent for most of us, that we can't agree on any landscape to compare. It is prodigiously lit, extensively silent. The closest anyone comes to anchoring a definition is to say it looks like one of the Himalayan ranges above twenty thousand feet: remote, untrodden, seemingly impenetrable. Of course, we are at sea: It's as though we were sailing a few hundred feet off the flanks of the Himalayas in a dirigible.

People on the decks—many of them so entranced they're oblivious of the cold wind—turn repeatedly to each other in speechless wonder, as if to affirm that, to a Western eye, this represents the most intense iteration of the sublime anyone might ever know.

That evening our journey reaches another significant moment at Neko Harbor, an embayment off the Gerlache Strait. We put ashore as usual in our flotilla of Zodiacs—the *Roald Amundsen*, the *Alexander Humboldt*, the *Charles Darwin*, the *Vitus Bering*. The photographers inch up as close as the guides will permit to three Weddell seals resting on the snow, and to a small colony of gentoo penguins, its members mildly curious. Others inspect a crudely preserved survival hut and take in the disintegrating hulks of icebergs grounded in the shallows.

Brash ice from nearby glaciers crackles on the surface of the water as the air in it effervesces, a melting effect of the relatively warmer sea. To the east, Deville Glacier calves into Andvord Bay with a desultory series of thunderous claps. Pods of crabeater seals swim past, staring at us. (The crabeater is one of Earth's most numerous large wild mammals, its population thought to be about fifteen million. Because they live through dark winters in a frigid environment difficult to access, in and around shifting pack ice, it's very hard to study crabeaters—which do not eat crabs—for any length of time. It's a lifeway only sketchily known.)

The polar sun is setting on a long slant over this scene and, our trip nearly over, I am thinking of conversations I still want to have, especially with Will Steger, and also with David Fletcher, one of the naturalist-guides, an energetic storyteller and a man well informed about Antarctica, especially its history. Fletcher traveled long stretches of the Antarctic Peninsula with dog teams in the 1970s, before he became a station manager and then a field operations manager for the British Antarctic Survey, and he maintains dog teams of his own in Greenland to this day. His enthusiasm for what he cares about is considered, historically referenced, and set forth with practiced skill. Like his dinner-table conversation, his stories are self-effacing but crowded with personal anecdote. That evening at Neko Harbor he will tell me he feels driven by a love of polar regions, but he is compelled, too, by a desire to make these landscapes memorable.

In those moments of storytelling about the exhilaration of dog travel, I cannot separate my affection for such dogs, with which I've had some experience, from my affection for David, from my affection for the evening light on Andvord Bay, from my affection for Amanda. She is at the far end of a thin strip of beach exposed between snow and water, writing out some private message in the coarse sand with her finger.

WE MAKE FOR CAPE HORN the next night, a straight run of about five hundred miles across the Drake Passage. We arrive

the second morning, early and in a heavy fog. Isla Hornos—
the southernmost of this island's several headlands constitutes the actual Cape—is unmistakable on the radar screen,
but we can't make anything out through the fog. Finally, six
hundred yards off the starboard bow, we see surf breaking
white over rocks at the foot of a cliff.

The *Hanseatic*, sailing beyond the Cape and then motor-
ing back to the east, technically passes from the Pacific
Ocean into the Atlantic. The captain anchors on the leeward
side of the headland just to the east of Cabo de Hornos. We
go ashore in a light rain and climb a jerry-built wood staircase of some 130 steps, up to a windblown plateau where a
Chilean soldier, his wife and son, and their two dogs maintain a meteorological watch in a few small buildings near a
lighthouse. (The soldier is also there, and not incidentally,
because the Chileans do not trust that the Argentinians won't
attempt to take over the Cape if it's not guarded; during the
Malvinas—Falkland Islands—War, the Chileans seeded part
of the plateau with land mines.)

A long slender boardwalk leads to the soldier's quarters,
where souvenirs are for sale. A muddy footpath continues to
the lighthouse and a small unheated chapel. Just short of this
cluster of buildings, a second boardwalk bears off across the
plateau. The undulating moor of Fuegian heath plants,
blanketed this morning by a rolling fog and girt by a steep
palisade of sea cliffs, is profoundly affecting, or so I find it in
the moment. The boardwalk leads to Cape Horn's monument, a stylized cast-aluminum sculpture erected in 1992 to
honor the thousands of sailors who have perished in these
seas. Nearly fifteen feet tall, it consists of a horizontal stone

base holding aloft, side by side, two solid isosceles triangles, their vertical bases nearly touching. Along the vertical, the artist has cut a cursive line into each triangle, creating between the two the silhouette of an albatross in a sharply banked turn.

On the approach to the monument, carved in marble, is a poem by Sara Vial, written in the voice of the albatross. The bird tells us that these sailors did not really perish in these raging seas (*no murieron / En las furiosas olas*); they soar now on my wings (*vuelan en mis alas*) toward eternity, in the last rift of these Antarctic winds (*En la última grieta / De los vientos antárticos*).

I pull back the hood of my parka and remove my hat. To offer prayers here in the rain and wind is inevitable. The monument memorializes venal and magnanimous men alike. It honors the inevitability of death and the great dignity of the human soul, which, in the belief system of most Chileans, God alone can abolish. It seeks for the dead an eternal association with life, transcending the implacable wind and waves.

The poignancy of the monument in this inclement weather, and my feeling close here to an understanding of why for so long I've had such a visceral fear of ocean storms, leads me to sit down for a while on a bench to wait out the thought. The fog lifts and for a few moments I actually see Cape Horn, just past the monument.

Since the completion of the Panama Canal in 1914, many fewer ships have tried to round this cape—cruise ships, the largest oil tankers, research vessels, and racing and pleasure yachts. From the decks of them all, as from this promontory, you can gaze away south into the *mysterium tremendum* of Antarctica, a land no one owns, a continent larger than Australia, one defined more by the laws of physics and chemistry than by those of the planet's late developer, biology. Though its coasts teem with life, they have known great devastation from the whalers and sealers of the last and the previous centuries. In 1991, the Antarctic Treaty nations approved a fifty-year moratorium on mineral exploration in and around the continent, but no power of enforcement can halt the continual violation of its rich fishing grounds by nonsignatory, rogue, or (presumably) treaty nations alike.

It is a quaint belief that today's ships can weather any sea, as it is a quaint belief that a human economy can subjugate any natural economy to achieve its ends, that ebb and flow of sunlight, nutrients, minerals, water, and creatures that loosely define an ecosystem. Yet the monument here enshrines daring and quest, what at bottom we most admire about Shackleton, the derring-do and the peculiarly Western tradition of Herculean striving for the Grail, in any one of all its pedestrian and sacred guises.

While I sit on the bench with my peculiar longing for deeper meaning, my apprehension about humanity's nuclear-armed vanity, its ignorance, greed, and inattention, I see Amanda kneeling in the heath. She is adjusting her tripod in the blowing fog to frame a portrait of a yellow buttercup, a pinprick star in the dark green firmament of sedges, dwarf shrubs, and stunted trees that marks this extreme southern reach of the Western Hemisphere.

Maybe she is the reason, all those days ago, that I was not afraid.

Our Frail Planet in Cold, Clear View

WAS IT EVENING IN ANTARCTICA? NOTHING ABOUT THE SKY would have told you so. No twilight lingered, no star rose. Local time, I believe, was a little after seven in the morning, Buenos Aires time; we were keeping New Zealand time—a little after ten at night. However one might decide it (we took for our time the time of the people who waited to hear from us each day by radio), the crush of meridians at this spot, the absence of any event even approaching a sunset, made the issue of determining the hour only a vaguely foreboding curiosity.

It was thirty below zero. I stood face to the sun, my eyes shut. A light wind burned my cheeks but it did not disturb my vespers. We were by now, the four of us, used to the chill, and these moments of surcease with the sun at day's end I had come to look forward to.

We were camped deep in the Antarctic interior, at an altitude of 9,300 feet on the polar plateau, our view unimpeded, pelagic, uninhabited. The waist of the sky was a pale

lapis; the sun circled in it at an unvarying elevation, nineteen
degrees above the horizon. High over the shoulders of the
sky, the last thin wisps of mare's tail cirrostratus hung in dis-
array. Below the sun, a dense cloud the shape of a hornet's
nest glowed spectrally, the white of the moon.

In those silent moments before turning to bed I would
stare at the snow's wind-riven crust and careened slabs
and know, lifting my eyes to the horizon, I was as much at
a loss for scale here as for time. No dark stone, none but
the faintest shifts of color, no gradation of form, separated
the damask plain from itself. I could imagine the location
precisely—89°42′ S, some 2,400 miles south of Cape Horn,
3,900 miles south of Cape Town and Sydney—but I could
not imagine it as a place. I felt as if I had fallen overboard in
the night.

Our immediate and daily struggle was with the cold and
a wind that drove the temperature even deeper. (In winter, it
is sometimes colder here than it is on the surface of Mars:
−120°F. Our temperatures, those of the austral summer,
were by comparison mild: −28°F, −31°F, −30°F.) But in the
evening, under the pouring rays of the sun, another dark
undercurrent would emerge. It was not strong enough to
penetrate weariness at the end of the day nor ever to disrupt
completely the rejuvenating effect of the light; but one evening I saw clearly what troubled me: To either side of that
spectral glow beneath the sun the sky deepened, a flaring out
like the wall of a trumpet's mouth. Staring at it through the
rinsed and immaculate air, you could easily imagine that
what lay beyond was not more snow, nor even the near
reaches of space, but nothing, a void so utter it was empty

even of space. The line where sky met snow, a thin bead of molten silver trembling under the pressure of the light, was so vivid it seemed the edge of creation. It was as if by some accident of pure light and geography you could see an aspect of the divine—a single, stunning face, a sidelong glance, an instant.

I could have turned away from it with indefinite feelings of gratitude and reassurance, were it not for the disillusionment of a contradiction: Nothing biological stirs here. It is not apparent from that loom of light and matter, deep and incandescent on the horizon, that creation has anything to do with biological life.

We had unconsciously assumed, with the good weather, that the land around us was tolerant. But the land, nightless, disinterested, was a caution. The Tree of Life did not grow here.

ANTARCTICA HAS SURFACED IN RECENT months like *glasnost*—the tip of a reorganizing principle with international implications. Scientists are coming here to gauge the impact of human activity on the fate of the Earth—the depleting of the ozone layer, for example, or the warming of the atmosphere known as the greenhouse effect—and, at the same time, to probe deep into galactic space looking for errant light from the Big Bang. It is the continent from which the Whole Earth vision implied in the famous Apollo 17 photograph is taking shape, though the work still consists at present of relatively small-scale experiments and research programs.

Our fieldwork on the polar plateau was simple—scientific, straightforward, physical. Several hundred feet upwind of our camp we dug a snow pit, about twenty feet deep, seven feet long, and four feet wide, with a series of landings coming up staircase fashion on one of the long sides. Opposite those landings (up which we had boosted snow from the hole as our work progressed) was a twenty-by-seven-foot wall from which we were taking, with meticulous care, a vertical series of more than thirteen hundred snow samples for chemical analysis.

Snow and ice chemistry, a very recent branching of earth and atmospheric science, has an unprecedented potential to clarify complex environmental issues. Falling snow preserves, in a relatively undisturbed state and apparently with great fidelity, a record of the chemical composition of the atmosphere through which it descends. From snow pits, and from ice cores pulled from deep within glaciers and ice caps, scientists can piece together a chemical history of the Earth's atmosphere—a record of climatic and environmental change.

Ice cores—the American effort to retrieve and analyze them is being led by the Glacier Research Group at the University of New Hampshire, with which I'd journeyed to the polar plateau—preserve a diverse and esoteric historical record. The ice itself retains particles of windblown pollen and fallout from thermonuclear tests. And chemical analysis of the ice produces information about changes in global temperature, precipitation, and atmospheric turbidity; changes in the chemistry of the atmosphere (increases and decreases, for example, in carbon dioxide, methane, nitrous oxide, sulfuric and nitric acid, lead, chloride, beryllium, and sodium); global volcanic events; and the varying extent of sea and land ice. The record goes back thus for 160,000 years (a Soviet ice core, from Vostok Station, on the polar plateau) and is precise in some instances down to the level of pin-pointing seasons in a particular year.

As techniques of analysis are refined and become more sophisticated, ice-core data become increasingly more reli-able and useful. (As with any analytic science, there is debate about the validity of certain techniques and over the inter-pretation of findings.) Among those most keenly interested in the development of this information are people appre-hensive about the accumulation of greenhouse gases in the Earth's atmosphere and puzzled by the cause and con-sequence of ozone depletion. (Although there is argument about precisely what is happening, and which data are accu-rate, the scientific consensus is that human activity has had a profound and perhaps deleterious effect on the chemical structure of the atmosphere.)

The specific hope behind our work on the plateau was that it would improve an understanding of ozone deple-tion. Paul Mayewski, forty-two, the field party leader and director of the Glacier Research Group—he also directs the most ambitious U.S. ice-core program, a 3,000-meter drill-ing project in central Greenland—had noticed something peculiar in an ice core taken from Antarctica's Dominion Range in 1984. The upper layers contained relatively high levels of nitrate and chloride ions. Something about the pat-tern of their fluctuation was familiar . . . it seemed to match, at least superficially, the fluctuation pattern of ozone over Antarctica. Could it be, he wondered, that a proxy record for stratospheric ozone depletion was preserved in the snow?

If the correlation proved to be more than a coincidence, if the match was perfect, scientists would suddenly have an ozone record going back centuries. They could determine when the recent episode of ozone fluctuation began and, equally important, whether similar episodes have occurred in the past. If they have, the current cause of stratospheric ozone depletion cannot be considered the result of human activity alone. (The prevailing scientific opinion is that it is—that holes in the ozone layer are caused primarily by chemical changes triggered by chlorofluorocarbons [CFCs], a manufactured product widely used as refrigerants, aerosol propellants, and cleaning agents. The Montreal Protocol, signed in 1987 and ratified by fifty-six nations, calls for a 50 percent reduction in CFCs by 1999. Privately, Mayewski fears that his work could undermine the scientific basis for this resolve.)

The answer to the question of a reliable proxy record, or the beginning of an answer, lay with the collection of snow samples at our pit. The Dominion-core data matched well with the ozone record at the South Pole, but the Dominion Range itself lies 250 miles north of the pole, on the 170° E meridian. Since the longest continuous ozone record for the Antarctic interior is of measurements taken at the pole itself, the obvious solution was to extract a chemical record from a nearby pit and match it to that ozone record.

Mayewski chose a site about twenty miles upwind of South Pole Station for the pit, to guard against any trace of contamination—carbon monoxide from the diesel generators at South Pole Station or exhaust gases from aircraft. We rode out in a tracked personnel carrier, flagging the route as we went so we could be found, or in case we had to walk back. Once we made contact with South Pole Station on our VHF radio, we bid adieu to the two men who had driven us out. A Canadian named Cameron Wake, a young graduate student of Mayewski's at the University of New Hampshire, and a biogeochemist named Mike Morrison, also from New Hampshire, occupied one tent, designated for cooking. I shared the other yellow, pyramid-type Scott tent with Mayewski and our radio. By the time we dug a latrine, secured our gear against high winds, and ate dinner, it was time to turn in.

Work the next day was arduous. We had to contend with cold temperatures and winds gusting to twenty knots. The altitude also affected us. (Because of the thinness of the atmosphere at the poles, the effective pressure altitude where we were working was about eleven thousand feet.) But it was also enjoyable. The four of us worked easily together, a rhythmic pattern of sawing snow blocks, of digging and heaving snow with spades and grain shovels in the morning; and a regimen of scientific sampling in the afternoon, wearing sterile masks and gloves and white, particle-free jumpsuits and hoods over our clothing. (Our thirteen hundred samples, packed carefully in heavy plastic cases, would eventually be moved by plane to the Antarctic coast, by ship to Port Hueneme, California, then by refrigerated truck to the University of New Hampshire, where, sometime in the spring of 1990, the results would be known.) Our conversation was laconic and droll. We marveled during the day at nacreous solar coronas in the clouds overhead and at brilliant sun dogs, the radiant physics of light.

I could not remember a camp as congenial or as comfortable as this. We were near the limits of exposure for a field party, but we were well-outfitted, experienced people. We took pleasure in each other's company and were happy with the efficiency and progress of the work. But our sense of felicity was sharpened by something else, by the degree of our isolation. To have satisfying work to carry out, clear tasks that, however humble, seemed useful in the world, and to also be free of any sort of interruption on that vast white stage had a salubrious effect on us all. This contentment countered the constant, vaguely deracinated feeling we had in being there, as out of place as polar bears in Jamaica.

BEFORE HEADING OUT TO MAKE camp on the polar plateau, we had spent two days adjusting to the altitude at South Pole Station, and I had a chance to tour the station and to inquire about some of the experiments being conducted there. Amundsen-Scott South Pole Station is a 165-foot-wide, 55-foot-tall, silver-colored geodesic dome with assorted outbuildings. The aluminum dome shelters a walk-in refrigerator and three two-story prefabricated buildings in which the station's permanent staff live and work. Heat comes from hot glycol circulating in pipes; there are flush toilets, showers, and a small sauna. Built in 1975 and half-buried now in drifting snow, the dome is connected by a 90-foot steel archway to a snow ramp leading directly to a taxiway and the base's 14,000-foot airstrip. At right angles to the dome's entry arch, and running roughly parallel to the runway, are two 400-foot steel archways. The one to the left as you enter

houses a biomedical facility and, beyond that, rubber blad-
ders that hold 225,000 gallons of diesel fuel. In the archway
to the right are the station's power-generating plant, a small
gymnasium, a carpentry shop, and a garage complex. A
four-story "skylab," cramped as a submarine but withal the
quietest and sunniest rooms on the base, is attached to one
side of the dome by an arched steel passageway. On the
opposite side of the dome is a tall, gantry-like structure where
weather balloons are launched.

Upwind of the dome, in an area called the science quad-
rant, the National Oceanic and Atmospheric Administration
runs a Clean Air Facility—a building the size of a two-car
garage on pilings, one of four it maintains in the Western
Hemisphere to monitor atmospheric chemistry. Wooden
shafts nearby descend to seismic pits that house the station's
seismometers. Among various other scientific apparatus here
is a splayed arrangement of elevated wooden boxes, receiv-
ers for a gamma-ray telescope that look like rabbit hutches.

Off another quarter of the dome, several hundred yards
out, is a bunker for snow for fresh water. Downwind is a
construction yard and storage area and a series of semi-
permanent, wood-and-canvas Quonset huts called Jamesways, which provide housing and work space for up to sixty
people during the summer.

The geographic South Pole, marked by a metal rod with
a copper cap a few inches above the snow, is situated about
200 yards from the dome entrance, in an infield that the taxiway loop forms with the runway. The polar ice cap is advancing about 33 feet annually (the station sits "upstream," on
about 9,300 feet of ice), so each year, in January, the U.S.

Geological Survey relocates the stake. A ceremonial monument, a short barber pole capped with a polished chrome sphere, stands about 150 feet closer to the station, in front of a semicircle of twelve flags, those of the original signatories to the Antarctic Treaty. During the austral summer, National Science Foundation LC-130 cargo planes land regularly at the pole, weather permitting. The young U.S. Navy flight crews rush out to take each other's pictures at the ceremonial pole, then bolt for the tiny commissary in the dome where they buy souvenir T-shirts and arm patches. The planes—which deliver the T-shirts, among other things—never shut off their engines; as soon as they're unloaded they depart. The commissary does about $60,000 a year in souvenir business.

Adjacent to the ceremonial pole is a confused array of hand-painted wooden signposts, commemorating the field seasons of scientists from Idaho to New Jersey. A picket ladder of neat wooden arrows on a high post lists the distance to seventeen New Zealand cities. Another post holds a county bus-stop sign. A solar-heated box with glass walls, up on stilts, contains a thermometer that registers 120°F. Among other oddities are a street sign from West Throop Street in Calumet Park, Illinois, and two pink flamingos.

About a mile downwind of South Pole Station is a cluster of three Jamesways designed to accommodate several cosmic microwave background-radiation projects, one of which flies the orange-and-black flag of Princeton University. Five miles away, out on the 90° E meridian and clearly visible on the flattened polar terrain, is a small solar research facility, built on skids.

During the austral summer, which begins in late November, as many as eighty people may be working at the pole at any one time. In mid-February, with the onset of winter, the temperature plummets and the population drops to eighteen or twenty. For eight months the station is cut off from the outside world except for daily radio communications and one airdrop of symbolic summer picnic food (for example, watermelons), high-priority cargo, and mail in mid-June.

In these prosaic and unpretentious circumstances, a small scientific program in upper atmospheric physics, meteorology, astrophysics, geophysics, and atmospheric chemistry operates year-round. Few locations in the world are so well suited to such work. Cosmic-ray activity is focused on the Earth's poles, and sun–Earth interactions—the auroral display, for example—are focused here as well. South Pole Station itself is situated in an ideal place for stellar and solar observation, on the highest, driest, coldest desert plateau in the world (snowfall at the pole is scant). There is less "sky noise" and water vapor in the air above the South Pole than anywhere else, and, because South Pole Station is located at the end of the Earth's rotational axis, it is possible to study the sun and various parts of the sky continuously, for months on end. Finally, Antarctica is seismically the quietest of the continents. One scientist put it this way: "We can, in effect, turn up the volume here and listen to seismic events that other stations, in Asia and North America, can't separate from background noise."

The instruments and programs at the pole probe the remotest parts of the universe, looking for relic light from the creation; monitor seismic activity in the interior of the sun;

listen to the deepest, most nearly inaudible murmurs of the
planet; and track satellites in polar orbit. If the pole weren't
so hard to reach for so much of the year, its scientific program would be much larger.

WALKING AROUND SOUTH POLE STATION, a visitor is struck by
the cosmic reach, the planetary perspective, of the inquiries
here. The focus, in fact, of much of the research now conducted in Antarctica is global or planetary, rather than local.
In an era of large, coordinated global geoscience projects
and space probes, and concern over global climate, the continent has come into its own. (We tend, I think, to imagine
Antarctica as an island the size of perhaps Texas, sheathed in
snow and ice and surrounded by a frozen ocean. It is nearly
twice the size of Australia—the East Antarctic ice sheet
alone is about the size of the United States. Antarctica is the
planet's heat sink; because of its size and its position at the
end of the Earth's axis—there is no comparable landmass
in the Arctic—Antarctica drives both the circulation of the
world's oceans and the circulation of the atmosphere.)

Greenhouse gases and ozone depletion have brought
Antarctic research into high public profile and created,
rather suddenly, a transnational perspective on human fate.
(Greenhouse gases such as methane and carbon dioxide, by
trapping heat in the Earth's atmosphere, can trigger a dramatic shift in the pattern of global climate. The ozone layer
protects biological organisms against ultraviolet radiation,
which causes cancer in humans and can be lethal in its effect on certain plants and smaller creatures, especially in the

upper layers of ocean water.) Interest in Antarctic research in these areas is apt to grow rapidly for one reason: Adverse effects on global climate are likely to appear in Antarctica first, because of the central role the continent plays in the Earth's weather and because of the pristine nature of its physical environment. Antarctica serves, then, as an early-warning station and, with the information in its ice cores, as a sort of archive for the atmosphere.

The accumulation of environmental and climatic records, and the rather recent realization of the pivotal role Antarctica plays in global research programs, are direct results of its having been dedicated to scientific research in 1956, in preparation for the International Geophysical Year. This arrangement was formalized in 1959 with the drafting of the Antarctic Treaty. (When the treaty was signed it set a precedent in disarmament negotiations; for mutual, on-site inspections; and for devising a legal framework for international management of the seafloor and space. Today no one need show a passport to visit the continent. Military maneuvers, weapons siting, and the disposal of nuclear waste are all prohibited. And the scientific work of any signatory nation is open to the inspection of any other signatory.)

Antarctica draws several hundred scientists each year from about twenty-five nations to pose questions about cosmology and climate, about the lives of penguins and seals and the behavior of ice, questions oddly eminent in this modernist landscape without a national politics.

To get a sense of direction at the pole, a visitor faces a Gordian knot. From the pole itself there is only one direction—north. East and west are unfetchable. A north

wind, passing the pole, becomes a south wind. To someone
from the Northern Hemisphere the sun's movement is a dis-
concerting right to left, not left to right. Local time, as in "the
sun sets in the west at night," is an utter mystery. People
revert to stating their position relative to the prevailing wind
or the flow of polar ice. (When people at South Pole Station
asked us where we were going to work, we took to offering
them white paper napkins from the galley—a map, we said.)
To counter the lack of specificity in the landscape, the vast
sameness, people plant flags to mark their courses and camps.
An eleven-by-seventeen-inch colored nylon flag, flapping
sharply in the breeze on the end of a six-foot bamboo pole,
is a ubiquitous sign of scientific research in Antarctica.

IT WAS NOT SCIENCE AS we practice it today but a desire for
acclaim and adventure and a wish to settle the geography of
the unknown, to tame space, that initially anchored the eva-
nescent idea of the pole. Roald Amundsen, four companions, and sixteen Greenland dogs were the first to arrive at
this undistinguished spot, on the afternoon of December 14,
1911. They remained in the area for almost four days, boxing the pole with three sets of readings so there would be no
dispute about where they had been. (A black bunting flag
fixed to a spare sledge runner and standing about fourteen
nautical miles from the pole was Robert Falcon Scott's first
indication, on January 16, 1912, that he had lost the race to
Amundsen. A later review of readings taken by both parties
led a navigational expert to conclude that, given the relative
crudeness of their instruments, the sextant and theodolite,

and the difficulty of employing them in the anomalous region of the pole, both parties had done remarkably well. Two men from Amundsen's group, Helmer Hanssen and Olav Bjaaland, probably came within at least two hundred yards of the pole; Scott's group, making a small but critical error at the end, technically missed the pole by about half a mile.)

Amundsen and Scott were driven men, their personalities made more complex by their notoriety. Amundsen, "proud, aloof, and quarrelsome," in the words of one biographer, never got the respect he deserved for his unexcelled technical skill and his extraordinary achievement. Scott, "insecure," "vacillatory," and "obtuse," in the words of the same biographer, was probably praised too highly in the face of a tragic failure (his party perished), a failure that could be traced in part to his own incompetence. On leaving the pole, Amundsen wrote in his journal, "And so, farewell, dear Pole. I don't think we'll meet again." Scott wrote, "Great God! This is an awful place." Neither man, it would seem, cared a whit for where he had been, only for the mathematics, the accomplishment of it.

IN A 1982 SHORT STORY by Ursula K. Le Guin called "Sur," three women are the first to arrive at the pole, two Peruvians and a Chilean, on December 22, 1909. Their journey, as arduous as Scott's or Amundsen's, is less grandiose, not so self-consciously heroic, and in pursuit of no fame. The nine women on the expedition, each of whom had had to employ a subterfuge to escape from a patriarchal family, decide to keep their journey a secret. Men are so keen on making these discoveries, they agree, it would be unkind to deprive them of the pleasure. Besides, says one character, if the secret did get out now, years later, Amundsen "would be terribly embarrassed and disappointed."

There is a barb in the last statement. Amundsen never appreciated the company of women, and Antarctica, until very recently, was an exclusively male domain. (The male naval tradition, of which Richard Byrd as well as Scott were a part, became deeply entrenched in Antarctica after World War II. American women were kept off the continent, largely at the insistence of the U.S. Navy, until 1969.)

After Scott departed on January 18, 1912, no one, save the members of Byrd's party on an overflight on November 29, 1929, visited the pole again until October 31, 1956, when a rear admiral landed in a DC-3 to officially open the U.S. research program. On January 21, 1988, the first tourists arrived by commercial aircraft, at $34,900 per ticket. On January 17, 1989, the first tourists to travel overland on skis arrived, having paid $80,000 each to do so.

When I first arrived at South Pole Station, I felt, as I think many do, somewhat sheepish. My three-hour flight in a heated cargo plane from McMurdo Station, the U.S. base on the coast, could in no way compare to the struggles of Amundsen and Scott; yet here I was, privileged to stand at this remote and terrifyingly beautiful place. I had been so disturbed by the insult to the English inherent in Amundsen's black flag, by all that it signified about the coarseness and brutality of nationalism, of the colonial imagination, so especially incongruous here, that I had brought a kite to fly. I flew it for an hour in a six-knot wind, at −36°F, over the national flags, over the American flag that stands, oddly, alone at the geographic South Pole, and out over the polar plain. It began as a symbolic gesture. As it quivered in my hand, however, I began to appreciate something else. I could feel, as the kite dipped and soared, as it ran out on the edge of the flow of air and luffed, the writhing, the curvetting of the wind. The wind is the only animal that lives here.

FROM OUR SMALL AND TIDY camp, South Pole Station seemed like a mother ship on a white ocean, or a space station. This environment, more than any other I know, its cold and silence, the abiotic stillness, the infrangible hollowness of the sky, the supreme indifference and intractability of the snow plain, with its wild raisin-scatter of meteorites within, rests at the threshold of space.

IN THE EVENINGS, WHEN I stood those moments before the sun, I thought of Scott, so disparaged now. Of Amundsen, his profound unhappiness. I thought of the curious emptiness of their achievements, of how Byrd had written almost despondently of his arrival at the pole, "One gets there and that is about all there is for the telling." The work here now is different, perhaps less consciously vain. I thought of the scientists I'd met at South Pole Station, whom I'd followed to ask questions about seismometers, gamma rays, and radio telescopes.

The work of these scientists, though it may be driven to some extent by pride or ambition or be compensation for insecurity or some grievous wound suffered in life, seemed to me humble in a fundamental sense. From a certain perspective they seem only to be trying to determine the coordinates of intelligence, to address again the persistent questions of time and space. These questions are larger by far than the imagination, the vision, of any one person. Where are we, literally, in the universe? they are asking. What is the nature of the Earth's magnetosphere, an enormous opera cape of energy trailing in the solar wind? Is there periodicity in the heartbeat of the sun, enough to tell a farmer not to plant, a fisherman not to sail? Does the Gondwanan bedrock of East Antarctica still track in some seismic murmur the departure of peninsular India from its shores? Can one tell from bits of snow and ice whether the planet is healthy, or infer that we are, or were, only a turbulent and passing episode in its journey through space?

Reminded of my own displacement on the white plain where we worked, I habitually sought on those evenings to bind myself into it, into the flow of events. I recalled historical narratives; and the land. The surface here is infinitely complex, its patterns of sunlight, minute shadows, and glare endlessly attractive. The trend of hard, dense runners of snow, called sastrugi, reveals the prevailing direction of the wind. The plain itself is not really flat; it rolls and is deceptively canted. In the distance lies a ridge, a white palisade that could be two miles or five miles away, thirty or a hundred feet high. The eye struggles constantly with dimension. The snow periodically collapses beneath one's feet, with a sound like a wave dropping concussively on a hard beach—I want, by these notations, to remember that I have been here.

On the way to my tent I would glance upwind at our snow pit. Our desire was so simple. It overlapped in some sense the professed aim of art, to make what is significant—here, the chemistry—apparent; to make what we know intelligible. Like Scott and Amundsen we were trying to locate ourselves, representatives of a human community, in the relative terror of space; and in time, within the complexities of history. Whatever our individual failings might be, many of us in the end, I think, wish only this, to make some simple contribution, a good one or an original one if that be our gift, to be recalled as having done something worthy and dignified with our time.

In remote Antarctica a reflective mind can easily develop a great fondness for the human race, a wistful sense of its fate, and not dwell on its capacity for violence, for evil, for duplicity and self-aggrandizement. The most poignant words I know in Antarctic literature are the last words Robert Falcon Scott wrote in his journal: "For God's sake look after our people." In that moment, knowing he was finished, Bowers and Wilson perhaps already dead in the tent with him, Evans and Oates dead on the trail behind, I don't know whom he meant by "our." Perhaps he meant only the immediate families. Perhaps he also glimpsed the outline of a larger responsibility that haunts many.

I usually went to bed about ten, of that time we were keeping, hoping the wind would hold calm so we could finish the work easily. I would scan the sky, one foot in the tent, as though it might hold somewhere in its vastness a flock of birds.

On Location

ONE SPRING AFTERNOON IN 1981 I MET A MARINE MAMMALOGIST
named Bud Fay for lunch, in Fairbanks, Alaska. He was the
country's foremost expert back then on the biology and ecology of the Pacific walrus (*Odobenus rosmarus divergens*), and
he'd traveled extensively in arctic and subarctic coastal
Alaska as a field biologist, mostly for the Alaska Department
of Fish and Game. A chance for me to observe walruses in
the wild in the Bering Sea was coming up, and I wanted to
have a conversation with him. One thing I wanted to ask him
about—my opening prompt, I guess—was the current size
of the walrus population in the greater Bering Strait region.
It was 250,000 and growing rapidly. Was this something that
he was concerned about?

Looking back that evening on our conversation, what
stood out most for me wasn't all I'd been able to absorb from
Fay about walruses—little-known behavioral details and his
informed speculation about the nature of the animal, which
he generously shared—but how my exchange with him had

reaffirmed the decision I'd recently made to travel out to St.
Lawrence Island the following week. I now felt there was
going to be more for me out there than I had originally imagined. I believed, in fact, that the experience on St. Lawrence
might easily open up onto something larger. For example,
Fay had described a type of walrus living around there that
I'd never heard of—a mammalian carnivore, like a killer
whale. It spent its life in the Bering Strait region alone, living
apart from all other walruses. For sustenance, it hunted down
other marine mammals smaller than itself, mostly ringed
seals and spotted seals. Except for polar bears, and a few species of toothed whale, I couldn't think of another mammal
that hunted seals—with the exception of humans, of course.
The Indigenous people of that part of the North Pacific, the
Yupik, called this animal *angeyeghaq*, said Fay. And he mentioned that when the walrus population around the Bering
Strait begins to approach 300,000 animals, *angeyeghaq*, usually rare, begin to turn up more frequently.

I THINK FAY AGREED TO have lunch with me partly because
he'd heard that Bob Stephenson, a colleague of his, was
planning to fly to St. Lawrence Island in a few days to visit
friends. He'd also heard that I was going along on that trip,
and that the two of us were hoping to accompany Yupik
hunters as they searched for walrus.

Before lunch was served, even before our conversation
really began, Fay asked whether Bob and I would do him a
favor out there. He'd been told that Yupik in Savoonga and
Gambell, the only two villages on the island, had recently

killed three *angeyeghaq*. He wanted to know if they'd examined the carcasses closely, and what their thoughts were about these animals. Also, could we try to secure a skull or a pair of tusks for him?

I said we'd be glad to gather whatever information and material we could.

LOOKING ACROSS THE TABLE AT Fay that afternoon, I felt acutely the paucity of my own knowledge about walruses, how little I really knew about their behavior and ecology, despite all the reading I'd been doing. Also, how little I really knew about the place Bob and I were headed—not to mention the Yupik living there, who imagined the world in a way quite different from the way I'd been taught to see it.

I'd brought a couple of topographic maps with me to the restaurant, hoping to get better acquainted with the physical geography Fay would be referring to during our interview. I'd also brought along some scientific reports about walrus behavior. Based on my readings of that material, I'd composed a list of questions for Fay. I anticipated feeling my way through this conversation. I didn't want to force it in any particular direction. I was looking for a dependable through-line as much as anything, some sort of structure for the story I anticipated writing about walruses' lives and our visit with Yupik hunters, a few of whom were Bob's old friends.

As Fay and I spoke about walruses and the marine environment of the Bering Strait generally, I hoped to be able to probe his feelings about a complicated, politicized, multi-layered topic I'd been thinking about for several years. It's a situation some whites living in larger towns in Alaska refer to pejoratively as "life in rural Alaska," a reference to human lives they perceived as mostly brutish. A year earlier, researching another story, I'd volunteered to work as a dive tender for a group of benthic ecologists operating out of Nome, a Bering Sea coastal village. They were documenting the way walruses actually feed on the bottom (that is, on the *benthos*), believing that they did not—as most guidebooks back then claimed they did—use their tusks to grub the bottom. So I'd already had some exposure to the idea of subsistence life in rural Alaska, both in Nome and in other places around the state. Now I wanted to listen to Fay's appraisal of subsistence hunting in rural Alaska.

A THOUGHT OFTEN ON MY mind when I travel through Alaska is the difference between one place and the next. Where, in this sprawling country, will I actually be standing when I arrive somewhere I've never been before? I always feel the need to go deep with this particular question, and I'd been pushing into it for some months before I met Fay, focusing mostly on the far northwestern corner of North America. I'd made a number of friends in Alaska over the previous few years, wildlife biologists for the most part, and a few birders, and I thought I'd learned my way around the state pretty well. I often speculated, though, that my grasp of its highly varied topography, hard as I'd worked to gain an overall picture of it, was really little more than a tourist's understanding of the place. Alaska is not merely vast—it's larger than Germany, Spain, and France combined—it's ecologically complex. Where, among all the physical landscapes of western Alaska I'd visited, would I imagine I was, relative to all other Alaskan landscapes, when Bob and I arrived on St. Lawrence Island, a location I'd never seen before? And, importantly, which of Alaska's many biological, cultural, and political ecosystems I'd already immersed myself in could I honestly claim I really comprehended? Enormous numbers of wild animals live in rural Alaska, in regions like the Yukon Flats, the Brooks Range, and the intracoastal waters of the state's southeastern panhandle. In most of these places, wild animals completely surround relatively small, widely scattered enclaves of the human population.

While people have lived in Alaska for more than fifteen thousand years, most of the state looks and feels not just pre-colonial but pre-anthropogenic. Landscapes without humanity.

IN THE EARLY RESEARCH PHASE of much of my work as a writer, I'm usually trying to develop an appreciation for particular places, mostly remote or far-flung. Once I determine where I'll be situating myself—within a certain settlement, say, or camped in a particular watershed, or on the road from Cape Town to the Namib Desert—the wealth of information I begin to accumulate about that area—local history, wild animals and their ecology, the archaeology and anthropology of the region, even its local politics—can quickly become unwieldy.

With regard to my current plan—to closely observe walruses in the Bering Strait with Bob and his Yupik friends (should they agree to this)—I wanted as well to inquire about the sea-based life of the people living in Savoonga and Gambell. And watch them try to manage a 2,500-pound walrus carcass while they were at sea in a small boat. And learn the basics of predicting weather in that place. And, if possible, organize a round-table discussion with the Yupik about the poorly understood (by non-native people) biology and ecology of *angeyeghaq*. I was confident of being able to do this, and of being able to compose an accurate and well-reported story, because I was, for one thing, so diligently doing my homework. In the parlance of the film industry, I was going to be working "on location"—the gateway, I believed at the time, to greater authenticity.

I was eager to gain an understanding of the authority of the place while I was sojourning on St. Lawrence.

WITH MY TOPOGRAPHIC MAPS OF the island, the Bering Strait, and the nearby Russian coast spread out on a table, cleared now of our lunch dishes, I felt as though I were laying down the first layer of context for the deeper meaning of what I was about to encounter in the Bering Sea. As had been the case with other stories I'd written about Alaska, while this kind of geographic orienteering usually gave me an initial measure of confidence about being able to sort out the complexities of a given place, it would inevitably diminish as I pushed ahead into the next phase of work, like having this conversation with Fay. New and sometimes unfathomable dimensions would emerge in the evolving structure of the story I was thinking about writing. The racist politics that surrounded the propriety of subsistence hunting by Native people, for example, or the degree of social change Yupik people, in this particular case, were forced to accept as they struggled to merge with the dominant, cash-based economy, induced in me a feeling of fading comprehension. The notion of proceeding like this as a writer, on the verge of confusion as I try to organize and integrate the material, is risible, but that anxiety has always been a sign for me that the work is going well. If I simply accept my limitations and push on with the research, I frequently find that the disparate pieces self-sort and come together on their own, merging like iron filings drawn to a magnet. I regain confidence from this, move on with more interviews and fieldwork, and try to ignore the obvious fact, that, once again, I feel like I am in over my head.

I gravitate toward environments of uncertainty like this—the intersection of cultural and physical geography, say—as I try to discern and manage the idiosyncrasies of a place. One day, I'm sure, I'll find myself entirely inadequate to the task while walking through a landscape I've never seen before. I'll have no option then but to give up. To put off this day—for a while at least—I always try to travel in the company of people steeped in several sorts of local knowledge. They can tell me at any moment exactly where we are—with respect to the geography we're moving through, with regard to any local custom we'd be wise to defer to, or, say, considering how much food and water we're carrying, whether our supplies are sufficient to get us to our destination.

BOB AND I FLEW WEST from Fairbanks to Nome, on the coast
of Norton Sound, then caught a twice-a-week flight from
there on a prop plane across the Bering Sea to Savoonga.
Over the next three or four days we interviewed five or six
hunters about their encounters with *angeyeghaq*, purchased a
single pair of that animal's tusks for Fay, and carefully photographed a single *angeyeghaq* skull, one with its tusks still in
place. (The tusks of *angeyeghaq* are distinctive. They bear the
claw marks of seals the walrus has caught, gripped tightly,
and eaten alive.) We moved in with a Yupik man in his thirties, George Noongwook, and his family. (George had gotten
to know Bob several years earlier, while doing fieldwork on
St. Lawrence Island with arctic foxes; Savoonga had been
their base of operations.)

As we began taking meals with George's family, I grew
more comfortable with our accommodations, and my relationships with George, his wife, and their three children
began to deepen. After supper, I sometimes got down on the
linoleum floor and played with the youngest child, while
George and Bob continued talking. I listened in as they discussed walrus behavior during different seasons of the year;
how other people in the village, whom Bob had met earlier,
were getting on; the effectiveness of certain types of ammunition in different hunting situations; and so on.

One night when I rejoined the conversation, after the
youngest child had been carried off to bed, I asked George
how he and the other hunters managed, psychologically, the
deaths of the animals they killed. (Instead of "killed," George
used the phrase "were given to me." He and the other men
in Savoonga were subsistence hunters, killing to feed them-

selves and their families, not "sport hunters" or "trophy hunters," whose approaches to taking an animal's life they held in unspoken contempt.) At one point, George was describing the way a young Yupik man typically matured as a hunter, the way he came to understand the nature of a fatal encounter with a wild animal, and the ethical responsibility that hunting entailed. To make this clearer for me, George asked if I was familiar with the writing of the American psychologist Abraham Maslow. I said I wasn't, hoping he would then explain what he thought of Maslow's theory of self-actualization. (After graduating from the University of Alaska Anchorage, George had returned to Savoonga, where he was now one of the village leaders.) I marked the seeming incongruity of this particular situation: a widely read, bilingual, subsistence hunter, living in a remote, subarctic village, using a well-known academic from my own culture to explain to me how a young Yupik man developed his ability to hunt and gained an awareness that he was ethically implicated in a fatal encounter with a creature that he himself had initiated.

You couldn't locate the multicultural content of our exchange that night on any topographic map, but it helped me to better understand where I was.

A FEW DAYS AFTER WE arrived in Savoonga, Bob and I flew on to the larger village of Gambell. One of the people who met our plane recommended that we stay with Vernon Slwooko and his family. During walrus-hunting time, in May, Yupik people actively discourage—even physically block, if they must—the arrival of white people on the island. (Bob and I had been able to travel there and stay solely because people in both villages had good memories of Bob, and Bob was vouching for me.) In the past, white people have traveled to St. Lawrence, via Nome, from as far away as Miami in order to upbraid the Yupik for killing and eating wild animals. They've told them that they were uncivilized, and that God despised them.

One of the experiences I enjoyed most on our visit to St. Lawrence was the opportunity it offered to overhear, every day, an ongoing conversation about the lives of wild animals: about the different species of seabirds nesting in colonies along the coastal cliffs (the Yupik collected and ate their eggs); about ice fishing for sculpin and tomcod in winter; about the lives of bowhead, minke, and gray whales, ceta-ceans they actively studied and hunted; about arctic foxes, which they sometimes trapped for their fur; and about the social lives of every other species of animal they regularly encountered, including all 141 species of birds to be found on the island at different points during the solar year. Their knowledge was encyclopedic, their descriptions nuanced and detailed, and their recollections of meetings with wild ani-mals distinguished by the fact that, for them, the life of every single animal was fundamentally unplumbable, in a way that a highly analytic or adamantly rational mind might resist, or simply reject. Every day I spent with them reminded me of my own shortcomings as an observer; on the other hand, they consistently responded to my questions with respect and enthusiasm, no matter how uninformed those questions were.

THE DAY AFTER WE ARRIVED in Gambell, our host told us that the time had come for a meeting with the head man in the village, Merlin Kanooka. On the way over to his home, Bob emphasized that this would be an important visit, that Mr. Kanooka was going to ask us for our opinions on subsistence hunting. Depending on how we answered, Bob said, we could expect to be told either to leave the island on the next plane or that we were free to stay—which was not the same thing as being told that our presence was welcome.

Our conversation with Mr. Kanooka took place around a kitchen table. Its Formica surface was crowded with condiment bottles, rounds of live ammunition, empty soda cans, small tools, and children's toys. The talk was casual but halting. Tense. Mr. Kanooka's demeanor was more circumspect than confrontational, but he soon asked us directly what we thought about killing walrus for food (in a place where the ground never thaws any deeper than an inch, and the climate is too harsh, anyway, to maintain a vegetable garden). When it was my turn to speak about why I had come to the island, I related what I'd learned over the years in Native villages in Alaska about subsistence hunting. I said that, although I had come to respect and support subsistence hunting, I was not myself a hunter. When I volunteered that I was a writer, Mr. Kanooka's eyes flared in his otherwise expressionless face and I could feel the story I wanted to write collapsing right in front of me. Mr. Kanooka held my eyes for a long moment, but he heard me out. I tried to explain, as a white man and an outsider, that I was not in a

position to offer any worthwhile opinion on subsistence hunting. I told him I was on St. Lawrence Island to learn. To listen to the hunters and other people. After another long
moment he made a small, dismissive gesture with his left
hand, as if brushing something trivial away.

He thanked us for coming by and we said good night.

I can still recall vividly the scene afterward, Bob and
I walking back to Vernon's house in the dark, crunching
through the snow with our arms slung across each other's
shoulders, affirming our friendship and belief in each other—
one man long-acquainted with Indigenous life in the bush,
the other serving the early years of an apprenticeship, trying
to understand the ways human lives differ. Two white men
who'd been able to present themselves successfully that evening as neither racist nor colonial in their thinking. We'd not
asked Mr. Kanooka about going out to sea with the hunters
in the coming days, but if we were truly trusted and welcome, said Bob, we would be invited. Or the possibility might
arise and then fade away, unremarked upon. We would then
return to Fairbanks with our notes and photographs and
angeyeghaq tusks, to be debriefed by Fay. Until someone told us
otherwise, we felt free to go ahead with our interviews and
socializing, and to accept an invitation from anyone who
asked us to share a meal.

THE YUPIK DESCRIBED *ANGEYEGHAQ* AS almost always being
young males. When they haul out on a floe in the moving
pack ice to rest, they told us, they lie there conspicuously
alone. They don't slide off quickly into the water when they

see you. They raise their heads and remain alert. If you pass by too close in a boat, they said, *angeyeghaq* will glare at you; and if you slow down to observe them, or linger nearby, they will charge off the ice and swim straight for you. They'll dive under the boat, roll over, and drive their tusks through the bottom. Or they'll rise up in the water, hook their tusks over the gunwale of the boat, and try to flip it.

In Savoonga, I had asked an older man whether he ever feared being attacked by a killer whale, if he happened to fall out of his boat. No, he said. Orcas never attack people. (Killer whales, also called orcas, however, will mob a lone walrus on occasion, pummel it to death, and then depart without feeding on the carcass.) The only marine animal the man said he feared—other than *angeyeghaq*—was the polar bear. Whenever the Yupik hunters killed *angeyeghaq*, the man continued, they opened its stomach to see what it had been eating. Usually they found narrow strips of seal skin with the blubber still attached. *Angeyeghaq*, he explained, will grab a seal and, holding it tightly against its tusks with its front flippers, rotate it like a corn cob, suctioning off strips of the animal's flesh.

Bob and I spoke to a half dozen hunters while we were in Gambell, a village of about 450 people. We collected a few more tusks and photographed others. The world, I remember speculating at the time, was likely full of things as little known, as unanticipated and unsettling, as *angeyeghaq*. My increasing knowledge of this kind of walrus slowly became a warning. It's always a challenge to understand deeply where you are in your travels. The more you're convinced, however, that you know precisely where you are, the more likely it is that you'll be in danger, because of what you don't know.

A FEW DAYS BEFORE WE planned to return to Fairbanks, Bob and I were having breakfast at Vernon's kitchen table, staring out a triple-paned window at the loose pack ice drifting past, out beyond the edge of the shore-fast ice. Closer to us, on the island's dark beach of basalt cobbles, we could see more than a dozen sixteen-foot aluminum skiffs, sitting empty, with fifty-five-horsepower engines tilted up on their transoms. Vernon padded through the kitchen wearing unlaced skin boots with bearded-seal soles. He had a high-caliber rifle slung over his shoulder and was cradling some loose gear in the crook of his right arm.

"Want to go for a boat ride?" he asked, meaning, "Want to hunt walrus with us?"

We quickly got our things together.

The Yupik searched for walrus far into the afternoon, heading generally north and west. We saw hundreds of them, and killed some, before we reached a high wall of bluffs that looms above Markov Bay on the Russian coast. The nearness of Russia—the Soviet Union back then—while mildly alarming to me, wasn't alarming at all for my companions, many of whose relatives lived here along the coast, a physical extension in their minds of their own "country." As we motored back and forth over the international date line, crossing into tomorrow as we headed west and, heading east from there, crossing back into Russia's yesterday, the Yupik showed no interest in time zones. In their minds, where we actually were was apparently not where I imagined we were. My companions were hunting in waters they had hunted in for dozens of generations. For them, it was the same day of the week, no matter where we were.

A FEW YEARS BEFORE THAT spring afternoon I spent hunting and observing walruses with the Yupik, I was flying in and out of Nome every day in a large amphibious plane, accompanying a group of marine scientists from the U.S. Navy's Naval Ocean Systems Center, in San Diego. They were tracking the spring migration of bowhead whales moving north through the pack ice and on into the Beaufort Sea. One morning two Soviet MiG fighter jets pulled up alongside us, one on either side of the plane. The pilots throttled their engines back, lowered their landing gear, and fully extended their flaps in order to match our slower air speed. The pilot on our starboard side gave us all the finger, then pulled ahead, banked slightly, and leveled off, taking up a position barely a hundred yards ahead of us and creating a violent stream of turbulence. The plane bucked and yawed in it. We would drop forty or fifty feet and then as quickly surge upward, while our pilot struggled to hold his course. Eventually, losing interest, the Soviet pilots roared off and everything was quiet again.

In those days, the late 1970s, Soviet merchant ships anchored regularly off Nome. Crew members would come ashore with bottles of vodka to share, and loaves of black bread. They drank in the waterfront bars, shot pool with local residents, and joked with everyone who came in. When

Ronald Reagan was voted into the White House in 1980, these occasional forays suddenly ended; four thousand miles away, the new president had forbidden any more such visits. The Yupik were confounded. No explanation for the Russian sailors' abrupt disappearance seemed to satisfy them. We were no longer in the place we thought we were. We were somewhere else now.

BEFORE BOB AND I LEFT Gambell, I questioned one of the hunters there about the unusual conformation of a few of the village dogs. Russia, he said. They come across from Russia. In the winter, he explained, they walk out on the sea ice and head straight for St. Lawrence Island. From their shores, he told me, the dogs can see the six-hundred-foot heights of Sevuokuk Mountain, at the base of which stands Gambell. Sometimes, my acquaintance told me, when Yupik hunters find dogs traveling out on the sea ice, they pick them up and carry them onward to Gambell. Presumably, some of the Gambell dogs make this same journey across the ice to the Russian villages. Other dogs, swept southward into the Bering Sea and the Gulf of Anadyr, never see land again.

One day I went for a long walk on the shore-fast ice at Savoonga. I discovered about thirty dead dogs there, some with short hanks of yellow polypropylene tow rope still tied around their necks. They'd been killed on that year's "dog day," a time set aside each spring to shoot any dog not secured on a tether. When the ice melted, the dead dogs would drop to the bottom of the sea, along with hundreds of black plastic bags filled with village garbage.

TEN YEARS AFTER THAT WEEK on St. Lawrence Island, and after thousands of miles of sojourning in places all over the planet, most of them unknown to me until I arrived, I was working on a story in the eastern Mojave Desert, in Southern California. Hiking across a narrow valley in that basin-and-range country, I spotted a man in the distance. He was carrying a bright green satchel over his shoulder. Its wide strap cut diagonally across his chest; through my binoculars I could see that he was gripping some loose pages in his left hand.

The air was clear that particular winter morning. Warm and dry. No wind stirred. The man was the sole bit of color and animation in an otherwise desolate valley. Suddenly he stopped walking and bent over to study something on the ground near him. I recognized a shoulder patch on his tan shirt—Bureau of Land Management (BLM), an agency in the U.S. Department of the Interior.

I was hundreds of yards from him, standing partly hidden behind a slight rise in the desert floor. I couldn't see his vehicle but assumed it was parked, like mine, somewhere in the folds of the terrain. He was squatting down on his haunches, scrutinizing something, picking away at it with light blows from a rock hammer.

I stepped up onto the crest of the rise where I would be clearly visible to him and raised my hand. He spotted me right away. Slowly he rose up. I waved again and started walking toward him. As I approached, he took several considered steps in my direction, his way, it seemed, of politely agreeing to my intrusion. We were still some yards apart when we began conversing. I could see plainly that the pages he was holding were satellite images. I expressed surprise at our meeting—we were likely the only two people for miles around—and identified myself as a writer, researching a story for *National Geographic* about the eastern Mojave. In answer to a question of mine he described what he was doing as "ground-truthing," and offered me one of the satellite images. It depicted a section of the extensive sagebrush basin that surrounded the two of us. He said a few of the images he was gripping showed "terrestrial anomalies"—puzzling geographic features—or were otherwise unclear. Some of the lack of clarity in them, he announced, was due to obscuring shadows that had been present at the moment when the satellite was making its pass overhead.

It wasn't until the man told me he was a geologist that I saw that I'd initially made a mistake in imagining the scale of his work. It wasn't square *feet* he was ground-truthing but square *miles*. I'd pictured him making refinements to the satellite images at a microscopic level, but this was only part of what he was doing. His larger purpose, he told me, was to survey more closely the surface geology of this particular stretch of land. He was mostly searching for any significant indication of mineral deposits.

Although I'd never heard of ground-truthing, I was immediately attracted to the idea of contrasting the *rendering* of an object with the object itself. The hurtling satellite above, indiscriminately recording whatever presented itself to the lens, did not make apparent all that it observed. On scales large and small, dozens of issues were left open to

interpretation. The surveyor told me that his primary responsibility in this desert basin was to "amplify" the satellite
images by comparing them with what he was actually seeing
in front of him; he was then to append any notes he thought
relevant to the images.

I asked if I could follow along while he continued his
work.

The image on each piece of paper he showed me was an
overview, a large-scale impression of a particular section of
terrain; what I was seeing at my feet, by comparison, was a
limited view, a small-scale impression. Where was the most
dependable truth about exactly where I was in this place?
Most of us believe a satellite camera offers a true image of a
specific location, in this instance a small, elongated basin in
the eastern Mojave Desert. We also understand, however,
that any such image is actually missing certain crucial information. It is two-, not three-, dimensional. It presents no
infrared, ultraviolet, sonic, or olfactory data, and it registers
scant information about biological activity. It captures a single, arbitrary moment during Earth's daylit hours. To produce a richer, more complete, more reliable picture, given
the limitations of the technology involved, would require far
more ground-truthing than this surveyor seemed prepared
for. Where was the record of Spanish exploration here, in
the sixteenth century, or of Amerind immigration fifteen
thousand or more years before that? How can one really say
where one is, given such a dearth of information?

The man and I parted company that morning in the
Mojave with an unusually firm handshake, looking directly
into each other's eyes. It was my guess that he and I did not

share the same political views. Also, I believed his training might incline him to be more comfortable with the logic of empirical science, while I was steeped in the metaphors and allusions of the arts and humanities. His employers, I knew, hoped his work would identify areas of interest to mining companies, to which the BLM might lease some of the lands over which it had jurisdiction. As for me, I was thinking more about the rapidly changing desert climate here, from one year to the next; about mountain lions hunting feral donkeys in this basin, which I had seen evidence of; about ephemeral creeks that occasionally flooded the playa with rainwater; about centuries-old potsherds I'd picked up to inspect, and then put back; and about other components of this still-undeveloped area that might be of more interest to readers of *National Geographic* than any prospects for profiting financially from the leasing of mineral rights to this basin.

THE MAN I MET THAT day was no more a resident of this place than I had been a resident of St. Lawrence Island. You can never say precisely where you are, of course, state your position definitively, even if you've been resident in the same place all your life and have, moreover, been paying attention, stabilizing as that information might be to any person's sense of identity. In the decades to come I think it will be less important, however, to know exactly where you are than it will be to know, wherever you are, that you are safe.

　　I was young the morning I sailed off with a band of Yupik hunters to look for walrus in the northern Bering Sea. In the coming years, I would understand better how dangerous it could be to rely on my own way of knowing the world, especially when far from home. And whenever I found myself in those situations, I came to understand that it was always good to hold in suspension my own ideas about what the practical, wise, or ethical decision might be in any given set of circumstances. The reservoir of knowledge some, but not all, Indigenous residents possess reminds me of the phenomenon of the king post on a nineteenth-century whaling boat. It ensures structural integrity during times of heavy seas or when the boat is being strained to its utmost by a harpooned whale desperate to escape.

It provides safety in a world of looming threats.

AS A FORMER WORLD TRAVELER, situated comfortably now within a so-called developed-world culture, I think often on those who've been driven out of their homes, or otherwise marginalized or destroyed, by poverty, famine, thirst, sectarian war, the twentieth-century wave of corporate colonization, marauding bandits, and the indifference of the ruling classes; or they've been driven out because too many others simply hated the way they spoke, or looked, or worshipped. Tens of millions of people alive today are refugees or otherwise displaced, according to Amnesty International. For some, memory still provides a strong sense of home. Others feel more profoundly lost with each week that passes. In every direction you see families holed up in temporary quarters, eager to descry any avenue of escape.

The overriding goal in a gathering storm, many are convinced, is to commit to being firmly anchored in a known geography, within a familiar cultural space. Such an approach, they believe, will provide each person with a protective network of friendships and a deeper sense of personal identity, and it will strengthen in each individual the sense that they are living lives of significant purpose. In times of upheaval and social chaos, knowing exactly where one is standing seems imperative.

Change is coming fast, though, on multiple fronts. Most of us begin the day now uncertain of exactly where we are. Once, we banked on knowing how to respond to all the important questions. Once, we assumed we'd be able to pass on to the next generation the skill of staying poised in worrying times. To survive what's headed our way—global climate disruption, a new pandemic, additional authoritarian governments—and to endure, we will have to stretch our imaginations. We will need to trust each other, because today, it's as if every safe place has melted into the sameness of water. We are searching for the boats we forgot to build.

¡Nunca Más!

The plane to Kraków is held forty minutes at the gate in Paris, but the delay does not distress me. No one is waiting for me in Kraków. My plan is to work alone and anonymously there, having spent the last five days in Paris with colleagues.

I have not discussed what I've planned in Poland with anyone, because I do not know what I am doing. For the hundredth time I am going somewhere with the simplest of ideas, trusting to an intuition driven by desires that have compelled my life as a writer, and which, sooner or later, I act on. This time it is just to look at Auschwitz.

I have been visiting slaughter grounds in my own country over the past year, places where Native Americans were killed without warning by racists and the many and various acolytes of Progress, acts of genocide in which my government was either directly involved or complicitous. Auschwitz, it is my hope, will clarify something for me, even if it is only the barest glimmer of comprehension about how such murderous enforcements of policy can occur. What happened at Auschwitz, of course, is widely known and publicly condemned; the genocidal history of the United States remains, regrettably, a region of political oblivion.

The first place I visit in Kraków is the Princes Czartoryski Museum, but it is not to see, as I have been urged by Peter Matthiessen, the famous da Vinci, *Lady with an Ermine*. It is to see a Rembrandt, *Landscape with the Good Samaritan*. I have recently reread the story in Luke 10:30–36, the parable Christ offered in response to the question Who is my neighbor? In Rembrandt's painting, it is not just the priest and the Levite who have ignored a man stripped, beaten, and left for dead on the roadside by robbers, but a gentleman fowler and his servant, standing nearby. Two children look on in fright as the Samaritan tends to the man. Everyone else, the artist seems to be saying, has more pressing business in the beautiful, sunlit landscape beyond, which dominates the painting.

I go to sleep reading the last few pages of Imre Kertész's *Fatelessness*, a novel in which the narrator struggles to understand why he has been condemned to Auschwitz, the infamous *Konzentrationslager* on the Soła River south of Oświęcim, Poland.

SUNDAY

At several stops on the standard three-and-a-half-hour tour of Auschwitz, I must leave the group. I have come here deliberately to try to open myself up. Despite a conscious effort to be otherwise, I am afraid I have become inured to contemporary human plight—in Somalia, Haiti, Syria. The depravity memorialized on the grounds of Auschwitz is beyond human comprehension, beyond Primo Levi, Elie Wiesel, Imre Kertész, or Tadeusz Borowski. Walking past some of the exhibits within the barracks buildings, I feel the onset of panic, as if I were suddenly trying to swim in gasoline. The State Museum here recommends that no children younger than fourteen enter the compound, but there are young children everywhere. The museum also requests you make the guided tour in silence, that no cell phones be used, no flash photographs, no fast-food consumption, no immodest dress. All of it is ignored. I reflect, though, that if it were not for this indifference to those who were murdered, the exhibit might be emotionally unmanageable for many. The denial of history is a form of self-protection.

I tell the guide I need the remainder of the day to myself and drop out of the tour. I'll get other transportation back to Kraków. I spend the hours studying the Topf ovens in Crematorium No. 1 while tours glide past; trying, again, to look directly at the exhibits in the cellar of Barrack 11, the "Death Block," and walking the shaded grid of dirt lanes that separate the prisoners' barracks. In these precincts, Pol Pot, Pinochet, Mobutu, and the architects of apartheid insist on being remembered. Images of the impositions of bloodshed come back to me, and with them their seductive theme: solution. *We will give you a solution to your frustrations*, the politicians tell us. *Just allow us to act.* In America, my twice-elected president seems to believe that, if what you feel compelled to do you

know to be right, legal restraint is misguided, and that tor-
ture has its place. He sneers at Amnesty International for
daring to question "the leader of the free world" about
Guantánamo Bay, Abu Ghraib, or any other developing
monument to this ongoing horror.

I eat by myself in the evening in Kraków, at Restauracja
Farina on Marka Street, making notes. What I saw today—
the starvation cells, fingernail marks in the plaster walls of a
gas chamber—cannot be understood. You endure it and
leave bewildered, believing yourself not a part of it. Not now,
not ever.

Monday

I've been awake for only a few moments when I realize I
must go back to Auschwitz today. I did not break down in
my heart, only in my mind. My obsessions yesterday were
with historical contexts, with the literature of witness and
resistance, with the current Polish government's incomprehensible nod of approval toward anti-Semitism, and with
the insidious ways in which my own country has so often
looked the other way while tyrants elsewhere did away with
civil liberties—whenever it looked right for American commerce. I had been walking in a landscape of murder and
abject sorrow, but it was all taking place in my head. In the
margins of the novels I'd been reading—Philip Caputo's
Acts of Faith and José Saramago's *Blindness*—I'd been making
note of self-deception, of injustice and innocence. I'd been
telling myself about the obdurate stance of my incurious and
willfully uneducated president, his harmful and adolescent

conviction that he has been called upon to teach others how to behave.

But this is the intellect at work.

On the sixty-kilometer ride from Kraków to Oświęcim today, I am more absorbed than distracted by the bucolic countryside, the color and texture of its small-scale mixed farming, the behavior of men with horses, older couples laboring side by side. Evidence of the dignity of this ordinary task, growing food carefully and successfully in the same place, century after century, is an anodyne for my ennui, the existential indulgence of my despair.

I confront the few exhibits I could not manage yesterday, try to plumb them. It is in Barrack 13 that I finally break down and cry before a memorial, eloquent in the simplicity of its blue light and granite, to Romany-speaking people gassed and burned here by the Schutzstaffel. This barrack is one of the least visited of the museum buildings. For twenty minutes I am the only person there.

TUESDAY

I leave Kraków at dawn for Munich, change to another plane for Chicago, take a third plane to San Francisco, and climb aboard a fourth flight for my home in Oregon. A phrase Primo Levi uses has been reverberating in my mind, words to expose the morbid wretchedness of the Auschwitz camps (they included Birkenau and Monowitz—where Levi was— along with the main Auschwitz camp and about forty other incarceration centers nearby): "the mystique of barrenness." The attractant within oblivion. The main Auschwitz camp was planted afterward with birches, oaks, poplars, and cottonwoods, which have grown full-crowned and robust. While I was there yesterday, the air was full of bird calls and song—gray wagtails, swallows, sparrows, hooded crows, cuckoos. Bees swarmed audibly over the neat, foursquare lawns, thick with flowering clover. Light winds had come to fill the vacuum left by a violent Carpathian thunderstorm that had passed through the day before. The relict camp seemed benign, its aspect nearly salubrious. The destruction of personality, the boredom behind the compulsion to inflict pain, the lascivious urgings of the guards around degradation and perversion, the tedium of industrialized murder— they were not so much in evidence yesterday. But I know these flames flicker among the people I pass in the airports, and with whom I fly, and that if we, everywhere, continue to live in political denial and naïveté, our children will curse us. When officials in government tell us they have a plan for the triumph of good, but deny us a knowledge of the particulars of these plans, we are on the verge of arrangements that lead to murder if we say yes.

WEDNESDAY

I spend the day unpacking and reading mail. In the afternoon I go for a long walk in the woods around my rural home, troubled by the many human scenes of grief, embarrassment, and disbelief I witnessed at the main Auschwitz camp and at Birkenau. I wonder why there are no billboards on those grounds, telling us, say, of Stalin and the Gulags in Siberia that were to come later. Of the rise of Marcos, Stroessner, Charles Taylor, Milošević. I recall the Mothers of the Disappeared in Buenos Aires in the 1980s, shouting "¡*Nunca más!*" And then later those same words in Chile. And after that, in Nicaragua.

THURSDAY

While I was in Paris I visited the Memorial to the Martyrs of the Deportation at the western point of the Île de France. Today, organizing my thoughts, I have come across notes I made in that hour about the necessity—"the imperative" is what I had written—to resist. The scope of what must be resisted today—imagine, by itself, the juggernaut of ever-present advertising, its promises of wealth, beauty, ease, youth, power, its Orwellian and beguiling dead ends—is breathtaking. It is so vast that the very idea of resistance seems ludicrous and unsophisticated. Did the residents of Berlin, in August 1944, when on a single day the SS murdered twenty-four thousand Jews, homosexuals, Roma, and resistance fighters at Birkenau, find the assertion that death camps existed a generally extraneous, impertinent, and un-patriotic idea?

FRIDAY

This morning I called a man, an American reporter, who travels regularly in that world that some Palestinians and some Israelis are trying to share. He is as insightful about the Gordian knot of achieving justice in the Middle East as any-one I know. I need to hear his erudition, his expressions of morality. Visiting Auschwitz, I tell him, can leave you fearful about your own numbness and lack of resolve. I ask him whether he thinks it possible for American government to take up the question of genocide and slavery, upon which the Republic has been built, take it up in the way of South Africa's Truth and Reconciliation hearings. Or would it now have to be the citizens, acting on their own, resisting the interference of the government in controlling the definition of these matters.

State of Mind: Threshold

WHEN I BEGAN TRAINING SERIOUSLY AS A SCUBA DIVER, I STARTED reading a series of reports on the deaths of American divers. The publication, *Report on Diving Accidents, Injuries, and Fatalities*, is published annually by the Divers Alert Network, a group of medical doctors associated with the recompression (hyperbaric) chamber facilities at Duke University, in Durham, North Carolina. The case histories in these reports, describing virtually every fatal dive accident involving a U.S. diver that year, offer medical and technical information in the hope that future, potentially fatal, dive accidents might be avoided. In many cases, it was a small mistake in a stressful situation that led to death.

It's entirely possible that some of these incidents were running through my mind as I prepared for my first dives in Antarctica. I was working with a group of benthic ecologists, six people I knew well and with whom I'd dived before in different locales. Our plan was to make a series of scientific dives under the sea ice in McMurdo Sound. Divers characterize working underneath solid ice as operating in an "overhead environment," meaning if you get in trouble you must first swim a certain distance laterally before you're able to ascend vertically. (The term refers more frequently to cave diving or to exploring the interiors of sunken ships.) In addition to working under a thick, hard roof we'd be working in very cold water—28.6°F, or 3.4° below the freezing point of fresh water—which creates certain technical problems. For example, the moisture in human breath is fresh water. This exhaled vapor will crystallize in very cold seawater environments, where it can begin to wedge open "demand" valves in a diver's air delivery system.

I possessed advantages that should logically have put me at ease in these circumstances. I eventually became a certified Master Scuba Diver. I was using excellent equipment, and I had studied the dive logs of people—including a few on my own team—who had dived in McMurdo Sound before. I prepared carefully and I knew the personalities and habits of my companions. Still, there was the problem of dropping through a narrow, six-foot-deep hole in the sea ice and entering a frigid world where equipment must endure maximum stress and where there is only one exit.

I cannot explain how I managed to do this. The draw for me was knowing that the world down there was brilliantly lit, rich with life, and beautiful. (I'd viewed it obliquely three years before as a dive tender. I knew the waters of Antarctica, before the plankton bloom in November, were the clearest waters on the planet, by nearly an order of magnitude. And that the team would be encountering between 100,000 and 150,000 organisms in every square meter of bottom we inspected.) I knew, too, that in order to write about this kind of scientific work, I had to be an active participant.

This wasn't the first time I'd had to face my own fears on a scientific expedition. One of my oldest apprehensions about doing this kind of work involves the necessity of having to sail offshore in big seas. Whenever I board a small plane to help with a wildlife survey, I know the tight maneuvering required and constant changes of direction and elevation will likely make me sick. In northern Kenya once, searching for the fossil evidence of early human ancestors, I knew the heat of the day would buckle me at some point—slightly dizzy, hands on knees, dripping sweat—but, still, I went out each day. It is not bravery that comes into play in situations like these. Possibly it's commitment to the work, work I feel I must do if I am to write credibly. The question for me really isn't whether I'm afraid, it's whether I wish to commit. Once I've committed I've crossed the starting line, and my thoughts turn swiftly to how incredibly beautiful, confounding, mysterious, and elevating the natural world is—the raging seas, the Antarctic benthos, the remote and dark wood.

The commitment in these circumstances, I believe, is actually to something larger than the self. You get in the right frame of mind to drop through that narrow hole in the ice by recalling the love you bear your friends, and that they bear you; by stimulating the professional need to make thorough, accurate notes; and by appreciating an opportunity to give curiosity its full rein. You can't do this every day but you can once in a while. You can enter that place inside yourself where you privately meet your fears and say, "Yes. I know.

But please, come with me. What we're about to see is greater than the thing you're running from."

Successfully locating the proper frame of mind and then acting is not, I think, about refusing to accommodate fear. It's about the cultivation of love.

SKY

Missing California

THIRTY-FIVE YEARS AGO I JOINED A FRIEND ON A FLOAT TRIP down the Green River in Utah. One of the passengers was a commercial nurseryman from central California. He had a habit at the end of the day of walking off by himself along the riverbank and, it appeared, dictating into a small recording device. One day I asked him if he was recording his daily impressions. He said he was making a record for his two-year-old daughter, so that she would one day know how much he missed her and that he was thinking about her every day.

One of the boatmen, my friend, was also originally from California. The three of us became fast friends on that eight-day trip. I was living in Oregon at the time but had spent my youth in the San Fernando Valley, in Southern California. This further affirmed our growing sense of camaraderie.

Dave, the one who was recording the trip for his daughter, ran a large commercial nursery specializing in native California plants in Arroyo Grande, on the central coast. Cort, the boatman, who'd grown up in the East Bay and finished a law degree at Berkeley, was living in Boise. Dave's nursery, Native Sons, was named after himself and another California native who'd founded the business with him. One evening I told Dave that since childhood I'd harbored a dream of becoming a nurseryman. This aspiration, I told him, grew out of my friendship with a man who was courting my mother at the time, several years after her second divorce.

It was his gentleness, the way he spoke softly and in wonder about plants, and how he handled them when I was with him in the potting shed where he worked. His respect for the plants and the grace of his movements attracted me to him.

Dave asked me where he worked. I told him the Santa Barbara Botanical Garden.

"Was his name Dara Emery?"

When I said yes, Dave told me it was Dara who had mentored him years earlier when he was planning to open Native Sons. And it was Dara who had helped sharpen and focus his desire to grow plants.

On that same trip Cort invited me one evening to climb back into the boat he was rowing. He opened a war-surplus ammo can and removed something that was carefully wrapped in cloth. A clay *kylix*, a two-handled drinking cup from an archaeological site in Greece. About 2,500 years old. He poured a little red wine in the vessel and we alternated sips. We recognized a budding friendship with Dave. We had the Green River rolling by in weak moonlight, hearing it plashing and burbling against the boat, and we had the promise of the days ahead, moving through this spectacular desert canyon country together.

Both these men, when they got to know her, became fond of my first wife. The four of us later floated rivers together every summer after the Green River trip. We shared Thanksgivings and got together whenever we could. When I divorced ten years after our Green River trip, it strained my relationships with both men to the breaking point. It was another fifteen years before the three of us were able to put things back together.

During those years I went on living in the same house in rural western Oregon, on the banks of a whitewater river, that I'd lived in since 1970. Cort moved to a couple of new addresses in Boise. Dave remained in Arroyo Grande. My former wife moved to western Ireland and bought a home there.

My mother's divorce in 1956 had disrupted our lives in Southern California—hers, my younger brother's, and mine. Our father moved away abruptly to Florida, where he rejoined a wife he had never divorced, and their son. Looking back on it, I can see that my mother forged a new life for the three of us that felt undisturbed and dependable. With my father's departure, the physical violence in the house disappeared. My mother worked three jobs. As I recall, we didn't want for anything. Into this peaceful existence came a pedophile and for four and a half years, until we left California, my life was very difficult.

Five years after my mother's divorce, she married again and the family moved to New York. I missed California—the clement weather, going barefoot every day, weeks on the loose in the Mojave Desert, the groves of trees with fresh fruit waiting to be swiped, afternoons on the beach, hot-rod culture—terribly. As bad as the days there were, in some ways I also remembered what was good. I went back for the first time eight years later, in 1964. My brother and I drove there from New York following a zigzag course in the summer of that year and I felt, when we arrived, the kind of nostalgic waves of fulfilled desire that penetrate your skin and tug at you when you depart—for Oregon, in our case.

I've tried to sort this out for years. After four and a half years with the pedophile, after my father's violence toward the three of us, how could I long for California in such a way? I always believed as my life took its turns and I ended up in pain that if I could just get back to California, I would be all right. I took to visiting a monastery in Santa Barbara, high in the hills above the city, for several weeks at a time, following the same rule of silence the monks did. As a young writer I visited every couple of years to report on wildfires, on rodeo cowboys, on a new national park. When I met Cort and Dave on the Green River that time, I felt such relief. I was not *from* California the way they were, but when we met and conversed I felt drawn to them as if they were magnetized. They recalled vividly my childhood pals and the adventures and pranks and fall-to-the-ground laughter we shared.

The summer my brother and I returned to California we had two encounters driving in from Nevada to the northern Mojave that have stayed with me for half a century, as strong as my desire to see birds in flight.

The first was not much more than a glance as I pulled into a rest area. A father and son were climbing out of an old 1950s Jeep with a canvas top. They were towing a short steel trailer with a tarp lashed over it. Their camping gear, I assumed. A boy and his father making their way through the mountains and alkali flats together on their open road.

The other encounter was at a roadside stop on the highway from Death Valley to Trona, where we'd pulled in to get gas and a couple of cold drinks. Another person was getting gas alongside us. He had a large cab-over camper mounted on a four-wheel-drive Dodge Power Wagon with oversized tires, which gave him greater ground clearance. A dedicated cross-country vehicle. After we'd both gassed up, we pulled away from the pumps and parked to continue a conversation about the country we were in and about his life as a prospector.

He was self-sufficient to the point of being nearly invisible. He prospected for minerals on government land. He had no social security account and paid no taxes. He found enough gold and silver to cover his expenses, and a metals appraiser in San Diego handled his business needs and provided a phone number for him to use, as well as a mailbox.

I was entirely taken with the apparent freedom of his life. It never occurred to me to ask the questions I should have. Any family? How do you manage the loneliness? Where do you belong? Do you feel any sense of belonging anywhere? Some place you can return to in the face of failure or illness?

There was something in his life I wanted. Anonymity. Detachment. Freedom from responsibility. When he drove off, I wanted to be him. Almost.

After my divorce I lost contact with Cort. Dave kept in touch, but it was hard for both of us. It was like walking on

glass. My wife planned a large party for my seventieth birthday and on the phone one night I asked Dave if he'd ever
think about joining us. He said yes. He saw me at that birthday party, for the first time, in the context of my family. He'd
met my second wife but not my four stepdaughters and my
two grandchildren. Two years later he drove up my driveway
with Cort. He'd called ahead to ask if this would be all right.
And it was.

The three of us are as close now as we were in the late
eighties after the Green River trip, hugging each other goodbye at the end of another river trip or after Thanksgiving at
Dave's place or mine. Age has something to do with this reconciliation. We're all in our mid-seventies and no longer
capable of the great physical exertion that we once took for
granted as a way of life. We've shared the same politics from
the beginning. We share affection for each other's families:
our seven daughters and six grandchildren.

In my early days in California I understood that people
came to California to start their lives over. Some succeeded;
others, like my parents, who moved there from Westchester
County in New York when I was three, couldn't manage it.

The theme of darkness and light has formed the spine of
hundreds of short stories, books, and movies about moving
to or growing up in California. The drama goes to the heart
of something universal among humans. You're wounded by
something awful—traumatic sexual abuse, violent divorce,
the unresolved longing for the lost father—and it takes you
decades to work through it. But the linchpin of my existence
as a California boy was the ever-forgiving, ever-soothing
light, the way it so beautifully bathed everything around it,

the slender leaves of gum trees, the pale surfaces of adobe buildings, the surfaces of moving water. That, and for me the flocks of birds that pulled me into the sky, pulled me up and out of myself—and gave me what in my life I would call hope.

I am a peripatetic person, but as I write this I can say I have occupied the same house in rural Oregon for fifty years. I never moved back to Southern California, though in some way I longed to be situated there again. It was not the place itself that I missed; it was the 1950s ambience of my childhood I pined for. The barefoot days at the edge of suburbia.

You can never have the childhood again, though the desire for the innocence of those days overwhelms you from time to time. And then you learn to love what you have more than what you had. Or thought you had.

Of course, it was the pedophile who gave me eight tumbler pigeons on my birthday, the pigeons that deliberately lose aerodynamic life and plummet to earth as though shot by a gun, only to pull out of it a few feet from the ground and soar stiff-winged toward the open sky.

Madre de Dios

I ENTERED A JESUIT PREP SCHOOL IN NEW YORK CITY AT THE AGE of eleven and later finished two degrees at the University of Notre Dame. During those years in the city, I served regularly as an altar boy at Low Mass and also at Catholicism's most complex public ceremonies, including the solemn High Mass at Easter, when the paschal candle is ritually prepared and light begins to fill the cavernous dark of a cathedral, ending the purple-shrouded silence of Good Friday and Holy Saturday. At the Masses at which I served, I felt no doubt or cynicism about what I was doing. Whatever my moods might have been, I believed and understood that I was in the presence of a great mystery.

As a freshman and sophomore at Notre Dame, I attended Mass three or four times a week. No matter what pangs of adolescence I might have been feeling then, and they were in my case severe, or whatever family troubles I might have been embroiled in, I felt the support and consolation of this Catholic ritual and the theology beneath it. Catholicism,

though, was not a religion I was formally born to. I was baptized in the Church at the age of five, the son of a Roman
Catholic father and a Southern Baptist mother. Soon afterward my father, a bigamist, abandoned my younger brother,
me, and his spouse to return to his other wife and son. My
mother—inexplicably, it would seem later—insisted on raising my brother and me as Catholics, though she herself
would never convert. She supported us while working as a
teacher and, years later, told me that the Catholic schools in
the San Fernando Valley back then were better than the public schools. Maybe for her that was all there was to it.

In college, I came to see that the Jesuits had encouraged
in me a more metaphorical than literal understanding of
Catholic liturgy, and that they had also encouraged me to
develop an informed, skeptical attitude toward organized
religion in general. The Jesuit approach to spiritual life,
famously, was cerebral, but, importantly for me, theirs was
a tradition also at ease with mysticism as a path to God. By
the time I was thirteen—my mother had gotten remarried
by then, to a twice-divorced Roman Catholic who moved
us from California to New York—I had found a spiritual
home in Catholicism. I reveled in Catholic iconography
and ritual. I was fascinated by the difference between the
regal Jesus of religious institutions and the historical Jesus.
And I was a diligent student of the overarching Catholic
history of medieval Europe (though not very well informed
about the foul underbelly of the Crusades or the behavior
of the Borgia popes).

AT THE END OF MY senior year in high school, I accompanied my classmates to a Jesuit retreat house at Cornwall-on-Hudson, New York. I was fixated at the time on leading a life like that of Teilhard de Chardin, the Jesuit paleoanthropologist, a life of inquiry into secular and sacred mystery, and a life of service to God and man. We spent three days in prayer, silence, and contemplation (as the Jesuits characterized it) in order to become more certain each of us was taking the right next step as we prepared for college. I hoped to return to the city convinced that my future lay with the Jesuit order, but that was not what happened. I felt no calling. I entered, instead, the University of Notre Dame, declaring aeronautical engineering as my major.

It turned out that aeronautical engineering was not my calling either. By the middle of my freshman year, with some pointed advice from my physics professor, I came to see that I was enthralled not with the mechanics of engineering but with the metaphors of flight, with Icarus's daring and the aerial acrobatics of tumbler pigeons, which I had raised in California after my father left. I moved over to the College of Arts and Letters, and there took up writing, photography, and theater. At the time—the mid-sixties—every Arts and Letters undergraduate was required to take four years of philosophy and four years of theology. As the reading and classroom discussion in these particular courses went successively deeper, my understanding of the lives of mystics like Teresa of Ávila and John of the Cross expanded, along with my curiosity about what ordinary daily life was like for people like Francis of Assisi and Martín de Porres.

During my graduate and undergraduate years at Notre

Dame, if I prayed in public at all, it was usually at a shallow shelter of fieldstone built into a slope between the campus's two lakes. A statue of the Mother of God stood there on a pedestal above a barrier of wrought-iron pickets. It was flanked and fronted by dark wrought-iron stands, on which racks of votive candles burned in deep-red and dark-blue glass vessels. The Grotto, as it was called, was lit day and night by these hundreds of flames. The flickering yellow light, swept regularly but rarely extinguished by gusts of wind and so arranged as to not often be extinguished by rain or snow, represented for me the elusiveness of what had attracted me and others to organized religion, to that sphere of incomprehensible holiness which, in the Western imagination, stands beyond the reach of the rational mind. On some frigid nights when I knelt there, alone in the effervescent swelling of candlelight holding the darkness at bay, I felt a streaming convergence of inert stone, gleaming light, weather, and shadowed trees, all of it presided over by an unperturbed and benevolent Queen of Intercession, a woman hearing my prayers.

I drifted away from Catholicism in my junior and senior years, though without anger or denouncement. Most of the friends I made at Notre Dame broke with the Church during their time there, but I did not experience the fury they felt, the sense of betrayal they described. (We were a decided minority at the school, listening to Bob Dylan in our dorms and protesting against the Vietnam War in our Carnaby Street bell-bottoms.) My friends imagined themselves trapped in a risible and suffocating superstructure of religious doctrine, cut off from the very empirical experiences that could make for a full life. The Church, in their view, was asking them to embark on lives that had already been led.

I drifted away because the religion I sought was, finally, not to be found at Notre Dame. The environment in which we learned was not just exclusively male; hardly a single Protestant attended class with me, let alone an agnostic or Jew. No philosophy but that which had produced the culture of the West was examined. We were middle-class white youths, being taught to perpetuate our religious and economic values throughout the world. We were largely innocent of the world, however, so innocent it should have scared us.

When I graduated, I took a job with a publishing house in New York, but the question of both my vocation and my religion remained unsettled. A few months into my employment, I asked for a week off and traveled to Kentucky, to make a retreat at Gethsemani, the Trappist monastery near New Hope where Thomas Merton lived. I wanted to address one more time the possibility of a religious life. This monastery, with its daily routine of liturgy and manual labor—it was a working farm—seemed a right place for me, a Cistercian community in the tradition of the French Carthusians and Benedictines. As attractive as I found the lives monks led there, however, the answer for me still seemed to be no.

In the decades following that decision to look elsewhere, I was fortunate to be able to travel often and widely, from Greenland to Tierra del Fuego, from Tajikistan to Namibia, from Poland to Tahiti. Much of what I would see, to employ a noun popular in some Catholic circles when I was young, was the culture of heathens, though these foreign epistemologies and metaphysics always appeared to me, on reflection, to be recondite and profound. In traveling with Indigenous people in Alaska, with Kamba tribesmen in Kenya, and with Warlpiri people in the Northern Territory in Australia, I found a spirituality and a capacity to engage with mysticism that I have come to think of as universal among people. The utility and strength of these ways, of course, is often obscured by the ordinary failure of every human society to live up to its own expectations. How a particular society reconciles its history of seemingly intractable failures, its strains of injustice and irreverence, with its spiritual longing for perfection is, to me, a succinct expression of its religion.

In those many years of travel, long after I had lost touch with my Catholic practice, I continued to rely, anyway, on the centrality of a life of prayer, which I broadly took to be a continuous, respectful attendance to the presence of the Divine. Prayer was one's daily effort to be incorporated within that essence. I continued to believe, too, in the immanence of the Blessed Mother, for me a figure of compassion and charity, a female bodhisattva (not meaning here to slight either strict Catholics or Buddhists). She was simultaneously a figure rooted in my religious tradition (including the tradition of the Black Madonna, of which the Church of my youth never spoke) and a figure who transcended religion. Like her Son, the battered Jesu nailed to a gibbet at Golgotha, she did not need a religion to inspire belief in her existence. Further, if one had any imagination, she did not need the papal bulls of Pius IX and Pius XII to gain credibility in the eyes of either a devout Catholic or an apostate.

I HAVE FELT THE PRESENCE of the Blessed Mother only twice. I was in the northern part of the Galápagos archipelago once, in 1989, passing just to the north of Isla San Salvador late on a May afternoon, when I saw a slight disturbance on the shoreward water, about a mile away. Just inside Buccaneer Cove, the low rays of the setting sun were catching what seemed to be the vertical strikes of blue-footed boobies diving for fish. The repeated splashes, however, were occurring only at one spot. With a pair of ten-power binoculars I finally made out a herd of sea lions trapped in a net.

We were on a course for distant Isla Genovesa, and I knew the captain might not want to detour. I located our guide, Orlando Falco. I gave him the glasses and he quickly confirmed what I thought—sea lions drowning in a net set illegally by local fishermen who intended to use the carcasses as bait to catch sharks. The sharks would have their fins cut away and then be turned loose to drown. (Over the past few days, we had seen four or five de-finned sharks washed up on Galapagean beaches.) The fishermen were selling the shark fins—another illegal act—to buyers aboard Asian factory ships who, as it happened, were supplying the fishermen surreptitiously with the expensive nets and other gear.

Orlando was conflicted. He said the captain, who was his employer, would be very reluctant to get involved in what would appear to be a judgment about the livelihood of other men on the islands, illegal or not, and he would not want to get caught up in Galápagos National Park politics. Nevertheless, we went to the bridge and he argued our case. The captain glared briefly at Orlando, then changed course.

Once the *Beagle III* was anchored in the cove, Orlando and

a crewman lowered a motor-powered, fourteen-foot panga into the water and, with four other tourists traveling aboard the *Beagle III*, we approached the sea lions. Some of them were trussed so tightly in the net's green twine that their eyeballs bulged from their heads. To get a short breath one animal, closely bound to three or four others in a knot, might have to force the others underwater, only then to be driven underwater itself by another animal struggling to breathe. The high-pitched whistles and explosive bellows of animals gasping for air rent the atmosphere in the cove again and again. Their desperation and sheer size made an approach in the small panga dangerous, but we had no choice now. Orlando and I braced ourselves to work on the port side. Two people leaned out on the starboard side, to balance the boat. The crewman kept the lunging jaws of the sea lions away from us with an oar blade, and Orlando and I went after the net with our knives.

I ran a hand under the constricting mesh, pulled it toward me, and began cutting. In their efforts to climb into the panga—they were biting frantically at the port gunwale to gain purchase—the animals threatened to pitch both of us overboard. How they had survived, I couldn't begin to understand. Braced hip to hip, Orlando and I cut away at the twine, trying not to nick the sea lions' flesh. It was full dark now on the equator, where dusk is brief. A second panga arrived with flashlights from the *Beagle III* and stood away after handing them over. The light beams swept wildly through the night, catching the mesh pattern of the net, pink mouths, white canines, and the glistening conjunctivas of the sea lions' eyes. Orlando and I nicked our forearms and hands, and our shins cracked repeatedly against the boat's gunwale.

In the heaving chaos something yanked at the hilt of my knife—a sea lion flipper, the net—and it was instantly gone. Snatched into the night. Without it I could not continue to help. I was briefly paralyzed, then swung around to help Orlando. Someone was bailing the panga around my feet. Like a tightrope walker I reached out to maintain my balance. When I closed my empty hand in the dark air above the water, it closed around the haft of the knife. Orlando, adjusting his stance to accommodate me, saw the knife appear in my hand. He looked at me without expression and then fell back to work. Orlando and I became aware then that whenever our hands touched an animal, the moment it felt a knife sliding between the twine and its skin, it went limp, while the sea lions next to it continued to bawl and thrash. With this help from them we were able to work more quickly.

In the weak beams of the flashlights we could not be certain, but it seemed we finally freed about fifteen animals, all but one of which swam slowly away. Before we left, Orlando and I pulled ourselves hand over hand along the entire length of the float line all the way to the anchor buoy, cutting the net's mesh to shreds.

Back aboard the *Beagle III*, everyone save Orlando and me stepped into the main cabin for a late dinner. The two of us sat on the open deck in silence, barefoot, our T-shirts and shorts soaked. Orlando, a young Argentinian, was not a man particularly reverent about anything, certainly not mystical. In the deck lights we could see that our shins were turning black-and-blue, that the small cuts on our hands and arms were swelling shut from the salt water.

I said, "Did you see what happened with the knife?"

"La Madre de Dios," he said, staring into the night.

Later that evening, unrolling my sleeping pad on the deck, I recalled a single one of her many appellations: Mediatrix of Graces.

THE OTHER TIME I FELT the Blessed Mother near, it was not another man's observation that I accepted without hesitation, a moment when something made perfect sense. It was thirty-six years earlier. I was eight years old, trapped in a pedophile's bedroom. This man, who first sodomized me when I was six, went on doing this until I was eleven. He enjoyed the complete confidence of other adults in our community. He commanded their respect as a medical doctor. I was a rag doll in his bed, an object he jerked around to suit himself. He had carefully arranged the many fears of my childhood life—insecurity, lack of physical strength, a desire to do the right thing—to create a cage. I could not see any way out.

That afternoon, gazing into the shabby bedroom in catatonic submission, I saw the Blessed Mother, a presence resolved in the stagnant air. She was floating barefoot a few inches above the floor, clothed in a white robe. Over her head she wore a pale blue veil. Her hands were extended toward me. She said, "You will not die here." I took her to mean that something else lay beyond this. As bad as it could still get, she seemed to be saying, she would be there.

The Queen of Heaven, I might have thought then. And would say now.

A Scary Abundance of Water

A FEW HOURS AFTER THE JAPANESE BLITZKRIEG AT PEARL Harbor, a Czech national, a combat pilot who'd been shot down over the French Alps in 1918 by a German flying ace, rapped briskly at the door of an apartment in Birmingham, Alabama. A handsome young woman answered. The man, dapper in a linen suit, ushered himself in, courteously acknowledging another woman in the room, and came straight to his point. He was afraid they hadn't heard what had just happened, far out in the Pacific. More precisely, he wasn't sure either of them understood how dramatically different everything was now going to be.

The anxious messenger with his intuition of upheaval was an artist, a muralist and portrait painter, as well as an aeronautical engineer, working then on the wing design of the B-24 bomber for Bechtel-McCone. A fused neck from the World War I air crash, his French schooling, and cosmopolitan clothes gave him a slightly aristocratic air, dubious in the Deep South of 1941. The person who opened the door was currently one of his fine-art students. The other woman, an attractive writer for *The Birmingham Post*, a stylish dresser with raven-black hair, fourteen years his junior, was his former wife. The women, both divorced native rural Alabamians, were as controversial—then—as he was.

In a matter of weeks the writer, with a yearning for the broader world, would marry a businessman not yet divorced and move with him to Mamaroneck, a suburb of New York City. In the winter of 1945, before the holocausts occurred at Hiroshima and Nagasaki, I would be born to her and three years later there would be another son. Her Birmingham roommate and best friend, Esther Kelton, would also choose a second husband and move with him to Southern California, where he planned to join the navy and fight in the Pacific. The artist, Sidney Van Sheck, with a slew of patents and work on the B-29 and the first satellites still ahead of him, would remain in Birmingham. In a year or two he would marry another one of his art students.

While Esther adapted to single life as a war bride in Van Nuys, my mother settled into a Westchester County apartment with her husband and two sons. What Sidney envisioned for each of them that morning in 1941, however, had little to do with these new arrangements. The change he imagined occurring was more akin to the opening of the Jazz Age or the economic shift that brought with it the Goulds and Carnegies and Ford's assembly line.

Esther's letters during the war, describing the good life in Southern California, and later the opportunities for employment with the advent of peace, had a personal impact on my mother and on Sidney. In the late 1940s, within a year of each other, they both arrived in Los Angeles. As enticing as Esther's letters had been, promising a renewal of their close camaraderie, Mother and Sidney were driven as well by a siren song. It emanated from an imperfectly understood but catalytic and evocative image Southern California projected then to war-weary Americans—a fresh start in a balmy and promising land. Along with your overcoat, you could check your personal history at the door. You could pick oranges from your own trees for breakfast. No region of the country had ever, or would ever again, burgeon as Los Angeles did in those postwar years.

In 1947, Sidney and his wife, Grace, bought a house in Pacific Palisades, and he began a long and wide-ranging career as a design specialist with Hughes Aircraft, tackling everything from high-speed cameras to Hughes's *Spruce Goose*. Esther and her husband, Bobby—"the love of my life" she would later call him—had already been working together for a couple of years on the back lot of Republic Pictures in Studio City when the Van Shecks arrived. With families surging into the San Fernando Valley, however, and industry expanding, Esther decided to move into real estate. When my family arrived, my father opened a business in Reseda in advertising and consulting. The narrow but robust economic order that defined the region—aircraft design, the motion-picture industry, real estate development, and corporate advertising—also defined the financial well-being behind these three families.

During the Depression, a new style of American leisure living had evolved in Southern California among people largely able to ignore the effects of the Depression. After the war, that elitist, upper-class life—barbecuing for friends on a backyard patio, driving the Pacific Coast Highway in a

two-seater, casual clothes for golf and tennis weekends, a
Spanish Revival bungalow with a swimming pool—would
become, with bewildering swiftness, part of people's expectations for middle-class living.

My parents, Mary and Jack Brennan, aspired to these
amenities—"the cult of Valley living," as it came to be
called—but something festering in their marriage soon went
terribly wrong. Jack recast his dreams and walked out, rejoin-
ing the wife he had never divorced and a young son from that
marriage living in Florida. (Unbeknownst to us, he would
soon return to Los Angeles with them, pick up his outdoor-
advertising business again and also do very well with real
estate development.)

With Esther's and Sidney's help, Mother anxiously began
to cobble together a financial life. Her most immediately
marketable skills lay with dressmaking and cooking, with
what in the 1950s was called homemaking. The first junior
high school in the Valley had just opened in San Fernando.
Like other Valley schools confronted with a rapidly expanding population, this one was desperate for instructors. Mother
got a job teaching home economics there with no credential
beyond her considerable skill and gracious personality.

Mary had a knack for getting along with people different
from herself. It was more than an ability to smooth over rifts
with the light touch of Southern manners; it was a tenet of her
constitution. Young Mexican girls, the daughters of braceros
working in the northeast Valley, along with the daughters of
other, similarly marginalized workers, flocked to her classes.
They liked her verve and egalitarian approach. Her success
with them, I believe, was at least partly attributable to the stu-

dents' sense that she understood class distinction went nearly as deep as race did in characterizing the nation's prejudices.

Mary also taught two nights a week at Pierce Junior College, and further supplemented our income by working as a dressmaker at home. On the odd Saturday morning, she'd whisk my brother and me off to L.A. to tour the fashionable department stores on Wilshire—I. Magnin, Bullock's, May Co. She'd disappear into a dressing room with three or four couture outfits, then tell the waiting clerk that nothing quite fit her. Later at home, using the penciled notes from her purse, she'd pattern and sew identical outfits for herself and her clients in the Valley.

Her friends from those days have told me that, unable to call on child support, Mary simply pitched herself into the harrowing economic reality she faced. Hers was more than what many other women might have been looking at in her circumstances, because she insisted on buying her own home. After her divorce, she purchased a small two-bedroom house on a quarter-acre of land in Reseda, a lot that gave her room enough to plant two dozen fruit trees. She dated various men (including a successful poultry rancher from Canoga Park and a nurseryman who landscaped the Reseda place), set a beautiful table, and, as she repeatedly reminded us to do, held her head high.

It was, I can believe, just such an enterprising woman as this that James M. Cain had in mind when he wrote *Mildred Pierce*, dramatizing the difficulties of a divorced woman with two children, making a way for herself in the San Fernando Valley and periodically weighing the advantages of taking another husband.

WATER, ITS TRICKLE, POOL, AND flow, is the dream image I
recall most often from those years. And with it the fecundity
of vegetable fields and flower gardens in the Valley; big
marine winds boiling through the eucalyptus trees; and the
ineffable breadth of farmland opening to the west of Reseda
and to the north of Northridge. To this day, I locate in these
bucolic images the impelling power of that mythic injunc-
tion to American children: Hit the road. Straddling the
crossbar of my bike at the foot of a windbreak row of poplars on some dirt road between Reseda and Calabasas in
1953, looking out across the truck farms, walnut groves, and
orchards, the dark-green reaches of irrigated alfalfa to dry
chaparral on the fan slopes of the Santa Susanas, I would
wonder where fortune lay for me.

The intimate water of my childhood—easy to surmise—
was the Los Angeles River. From my house on Calvert Street
it was only a short walk to Caballero Creek, a dry wash
mostly, but the best-defined stream course on the north side
of the Santa Monica Mountains. Caballero Creek empties
into the L.A. River just past Victory Boulevard, near Lindley
Avenue. Though the river was channeled to the west of
Reseda in the late 1940s, it wasn't paved, and we hiked it
regularly. The soft river bottom formed a sonic tunnel,
alive with red-winged blackbirds and house finches, black
phoebes and yellowthroats, egrets, barn swallows, and teal.
To us, the L.A. was a different river here than the one running in a concrete shunt to the east, beyond Sepulveda Dam.

This way of imagining the Valley—urban and domesticated to the east, wild and agrarian to the west—fixed my way of seeing many things in life as extensions from a borderland. In grade school in Encino (at that time the most refined of Valley towns), boys like me from north of the Southern Pacific tracks were called dirtballers, kids who fought each other with dirt clods from the fields. We were from the outlands. We didn't build our play forts in backyard trees but out in the open, in decks of baled hay.

The rural character of the west Valley was changing so fast back then that only a child riding the crest of this wave of suburban development might remember it as gradual or isolated. In that pivotal decade of 1950 to 1960, the population of Granada Hills, for example, increased by 1,001 percent. Canoga Park grew by 576 percent, Chatsworth by 361 percent. In that same ten years the Valley as a whole, growing at two and a half times the rate of the rest of Los Angeles, doubled its population from 402,538 to 840,531. This change in population density had an almost sharply delineated edge. It was surging west and north from the southeast corner of the Valley, moving toward Calabasas, Chatsworth, and Granada Hills from Encino, Van Nuys, and Pacoima.

In 1953, Reseda stood on the narrow, anomalous boundary between town-lot subdivision and small-scale irrigation agriculture.

The northwest and northeast corners of the Valley were marked for me by formidable icons in 1953: the Simi Hills above Chatsworth to the west and the Cascades of the Los Angeles Aqueduct near Sylmar to the east. The former incorporated several movie ranches seen often in B Westerns, of the sort Esther and Bobby Davis were helping

Republic Pictures to make in those years (and which I and
my pals watched as avidly as did any other group of American boys). The Cascades, lit up at night like the fabulous
debouchment of a liquid silver mine, was the tumbling riot
of water pumped over and through the mountains from the
Owens Valley.

I can imagine no other but a Southern California childhood of this particular era that might have been tensioned in
such a peculiar way. A boy could easily anchor himself, his
innocent psyche, midway between the hay field and the public swimming pool in the San Fernando Valley, finding the
two but a few minutes apart on a bicycle. He could position
himself, as well, midway between a preeminent American
symbol of mythic (though misleading) bounty in the east
and, to the west, a rugged landscape of earnest but spurious
histories, around which the country was reinventing itself in
the Eisenhower years.

To visit the Cascades as a boy, to stand in silence in a
wash of water-chilled air before Mulholland's altar, was to
experience something like spiritual exhilaration. It was sol-
ace and Edenic magic. To drive through Santa Susana Pass
on the other hand and see a distant posse chasing cattle rus-
tlers, to hear the pop and crackle of gunfire, did not seem in
the least otherworldly. Recording these dramas was what
your parents—or other parents you knew—did every day.
They made up what you would later see at the movies or on
television. Such scenes viewed from the car, however, were
not entirely prosaic. The cowboy dramas embodied a serious
code of behavior. The heroes rooted out and destroyed evil,
and they were brave and eminently trustworthy in a world

threatened by such as Hitler, by such treachery as Pearl Harbor represented.

We were not so removed from World War II in Southern California in those days as other American boys might have been. Fighter jets from Edwards, Miramar, and other air bases all streaked across the west Valley regularly, sometimes breaking the sound barrier and shattering a living-room window. Perfecting aerial combat, making cowboy dramas—that's what we imagined adult work to be. That and, for boys living in Reseda, field and orchard work, or maybe a blue-collar job at the General Motors assembly plant in Van Nuys.

The backbone industries—moviemaking and aircraft development—were brought home to me symbolically and tangibly by Esther and Sidney. Esther presented my brother and me with Roy Rogers sweaters and signed photos of cowboy stars like Hopalong Cassidy. When Sidney visited, he would often bring a new model plane to assemble, like the B-36 bomber he had worked on. The planes I most liked to put together were flying boats: a military aircraft called the PBY Catalina, built in San Diego during the war; the Martin M-130 (one of which was the *China Clipper*); and the Boeing B-314 (among which was the *California Clipper*).

My vision of life's goals, imagined at various times beneath poplars and eucalyptuses on dirt roads somewhere west of Reseda, was infused, of course, with romantic notions of justice and rescuing the unfortunate, which I took from cowboy pictures. I had, as well, a yearning to run away, to wing far out across the Pacific in the *China Clipper* and there take up another life. More deeply, though, a sense of how my life might work hinged on my perception of that peculiar

borderland that Reseda defined for me in 1953. One's hopes
for a good life might depend entirely on the direction in
which one looked.

During my years on Calvert Street, a huge alfalfa field,
bounded on the east and west, respectively, by Etiwanda
Avenue and Reseda Boulevard, on the north by Victory Boulevard and on the south by Southern Pacific's right of way,
was plowed up for tract housing. This was the breaking wave
of urban development, but you couldn't say the landscape
was thereby irrevocably changed. Something of the original
land, something deep and elusive, remained. I can see it still
today, like the memory of a thunderstorm awakened by sunlight glinting off a car bumper.

When the L.A. River channel west of Reseda was
cemented in, we adapted to it almost without thinking.
Instead of slogging through the cattails, trying to avoid sting-
ing nettle and seeing which of us was quick enough to grab
a water snake, we arbitrated our friendships in new games.
Who could roll an automobile tire down the freshly grouted
cobblestone bank of the river the farthest? You had to get
just the right pattern of bounces to make it sail over the low
water channel and roll partway up the other side. When tract
houses came in where the alfalfa field had been, and we
could no longer squirm around on our tummies in games
of hide-and-seek, we learned to attach roller-skate trucks to
two-by-fours and go hurtling down the new sidewalks. Where
curbed gutters gathered the runoff from lawn sprinklers, we
constructed elaborate check dams of mud and leaves and
fashioned Popsicle-stick rafts to bob on the flow.

When we lost a squash field at the corner of Lindley and

Oxnard to subdivision, we lost our last good source not only of dirt clods but of squash, a vegetable for which we found many uses. (One day we found a pile of empty cardboard boxes dumped by the trestle that took the Southern Pacific tracks across Caballero Creek. We filled them with squash and stacked them in a barricade on the tracks. The engineer bringing the afternoon train east from Canoga Park plowed straight through, sending shattered rind and stringy fistulas of seed flying out over the dry wash and streaming back along the flanks of the locomotive. The man's laconic wave to us, hiding in the brush, made us giddy with pleasure. Beyond rotting melons, nothing could replace the splatter appeal of squash. We believed that they were growing elsewhere now, not that they were gone.)

I saw large orange groves torn up in Granada Hills in the early 1950s but did not feel anxiety or regret. It was change. If change didn't go well, it seemed it might be our fault, for failing to adapt. I remember watching a sculptor friend of Mother's in those years, a Pole named Stosh. He worked in a ramshackle studio in an old poultry shed off Reseda on Sylvan. The way he took marble away with his mallet and chisel to make a torso seemed no less magical because I had to walk through a housing tract instead of an alfalfa field to see it. Such change in the landscape itself did not at all mean our aspirations were diminished, nor our capacity for wonder. For us, the world waiting to be known was still vast, more so than it could be for boys growing up in the Belgian Congo or Tierra del Fuego.

Looking back, I might say that in those days we didn't take in with sufficient awe, with enough incredulity, that sparkling chute of water tumbling out of the mountain at

Sylmar. If the adults understood a deeper message in it, in
the magisterial change wrought in the Valley by water from
the Aqueduct, they didn't let on.

They weren't afraid of it.

TWO BOYHOOD EXPERIENCES ENCAPSULATE FOR me the Reseda
I knew as a borderland in the early 1950s. One was my
involvement with a flock of homing pigeons; the other was
with what occurred at John Ford's Field Photo Memorial
Farm, a neighborhood property that was sold and subdivided shortly after I left California.

Domestic pigeons and rock doves (their feral relatives)
derive from cliff-dwelling stock in the Mediterranean. They're
most at home amid bridges and buildings. Historically, they
would not have been the type of pigeon to take up residence
on the San Fernando Valley's broad, treeless plain. It was
only with the advance of a built environment across the Valley that they found that landscape suitable—and they followed it.

I was given eight pigeons on my birthday. They were a
source of indescribable joy, especially the tumblers. I could
not convey adequately to anyone what their soaring and
homing meant to me. They seemed to exult in life, and no
other kind of reassurance could match the emotion I felt
when they returned each afternoon to the small coop I'd
built. I spent hours with them, trying sometimes even to keep
up with their far-Valley wanderings on my bike. It seemed in
my child's mind that, together, the birds and I were exploring
a shifting country between the city—that conurbation of

towns in the east Valley, with its ruler-straight yards and immaculate cars—and the countryside, with its traipsing coyotes, dirt roads, and cactus fences.

The birds took in the Valley from above; I had the ground-level view. We were watching something emphatic move across the land, implacable, unfolding like the flaps of a cardboard box.

The John Ford place I remember as huge, but it was only eight acres, on Calvert Street off Lindley. Ford had it built in 1946, a retirement home and recreation center to honor thirteen men from his Field Photographic Unit killed while filming frontline combat in World War II. (The unit's films won Oscars for Best Documentary in 1943 and Best Documentary Short Subject in 1944.) A horse paddock and big swimming pool at Field Photo lured us to these private grounds. We'd sneak in for night swims, and during the day try to steal bareback rides on the horses, mounting with a fistful of mane and a boost from two friends. The men who worked around the big barn, with its racks of elaborate Western tack and its fresh hay and grain smells, hardly paid us any mind.

We were also greatly impressed by a sign at the gate: No Women Allowed.

Every Memorial Day weekend (when women were welcome), a celebration began with services at the farm's small war-memorial chapel. It continued on a parade ground with an equestrian show and finished with a torchlight dinner at picnic tables around the pool. An aluminum canoe filled with iced cases of beer (no charge) and a band in Western regalia kept revelers going into the night. My friends and I, some having slipped away from home in pajamas, studied the final blowout from the cover of oleander bushes, fully expecting someone to fall into the pool.

The weekend festivities included stagecoach rides, a bonfire, and flamenco, rancho events resembling those that might have unfolded in the Valley a hundred years earlier, during the waning days of the Spanish dons. Much of the festive life of Valley residents in the 1950s, in fact, which played itself out at places like Ford's movie-set hacienda and at horse farms in Northridge, recalled the privileged life of the dons, with its sharp class, race, and gender distinctions, its emphasis on horsemanship, its whole-beef barbecues, and its disinclination toward labor.

IN ELEMENTARY SCHOOL—I ATTENDED Our Lady of Grace in Encino, at the corner of White Oak and Ventura—we were taught to carve bars of Ivory soap to resemble the different façades of the churches in Junípero Serra's "rosary" of twenty-one California missions, but we learned nothing of the Gabrielino, the original inhabitants of the Valley. We did not suspect their language lingered in the names Simi, Pacoima, and Cahuenga. Characterized as grubbing or "digger" Indians, the Gabrielino were in fact a culturally advanced people when Gaspar de Portolá's party first encountered them on August 5, 1769, in a village on the L.A. River the Spanish named Rancho Los Encinos, for the coast live oaks in the bottomland. Arguably the most populous and powerful ethnic group in Southern California at that time, they had by 1900 ceased to exist as a culturally identifiable group.

A few years after Portolá's party passed through, El Valle

de Santa Catalina de Bononia de los Encinos was loosely apportioned between two Spanish lessees. In 1797 the leases were terminated, and virtually all of the Valley's 155,000 acres came under the control of the new Misión del Señor Fernando, Rey de España. Mexican republicanism replaced Spanish feudalism in 1811, and following secularization in 1834 the mission system of land tenure gave way to a more formalized rancho system of pastoral and agricultural leases. These operations were largely replaced by dry-land wheat farms in the 1870s after a series of catastrophic droughts killed great numbers of sheep and cattle.

Platted towns first appeared in the east Valley around 1875; breakneck land development began about 1905, amid rumors of abundant water soon to be delivered from the eastern Sierra. (Under the so-called pueblo right, the city of Los Angeles laid claims to *all* Los Angeles River water, including the San Fernando Valley's immense subterranean aquifer from which the river itself arose.)

In 1911, a huge public auction of farm machinery and implements marked the end of the forty-year reign of King Wheat in the Valley. Four years later, William Mulholland's water surged through a network of steel and cast-iron pipes, and the Valley changed swiftly and radically. Immense reaches of dry-land farm suddenly became a bocage landscape: small-scale, mixed truck and garden crops, alfalfa fields, walnut and avocado groves, and citrus, apricot, and peach orchards. (To avail themselves of Los Angeles's Owens Valley water, Valley residents had to agree to annexation, most of which took place on May 4, 1915.)

By 1917, with its irrigation system completely in place,

the Valley had become a nearly contiguous expanse of small two- to three-acre rural lots centered on farm towns— Marian (soon to be renamed Reseda), Owensmouth (Canoga Park), Zelzah (Northridge), Girard (Woodland Hills)—and somewhat larger, outlying farmsteads, these demarcated by windbreaks of Lombardy poplar or Italian cypress and by "eucalyptus alleys," one-track farm maintenance roads bounded by rows of blue gums.

The lands that would one day be called Reseda began their modern history as part of the first Rancho Los Encinos (1787). They were then included in Eulogio de Celis's post-secularization purchase of 121,542 acres from the Mexican government in 1846, his Rancho Ex-Mission de San Fernando. In 1869, Celis and his partners, the Pico brothers Pío and Andrés, sold most of the Valley south of present-day Roscoe Boulevard to a group of San Francisco area investors, among them Isaac Lankershim and his son-in-law Isaac Newton Van Nuys. The syndicate managed its 59,000-acre property under a variety of plans (and titles), the last of which was a series of six ranches operating as the Los Angeles Farm and Milling Company (one, Patton Ranch, approximated the future site of Reseda). Anticipating the bounty of water soon to come, LAF&M sold its holdings in 1910 to the Los Angeles Suburban Homes Company, which immediately began to subdivide. With similar subdivision going on in the north Valley, nearly 100,000 acres—two-thirds of the Valley—was in real estate development that year.

By the time the first pipeload of Sierra water arrived, Reseda had been a town site for three decades. Along with Van Nuys, it had established itself as a poultry-raising center.

Its outer lands were mostly in sugar beets and other field crops—lima beans, lettuce, spinach, melons, squash, carrots—and alfalfa, grown to fodder dairy cattle and for chicken feed.

When my family arrived, Reseda was still about this kind of farming, though by 1948 it was rapidly coming to a close. The population of Reseda in 1930 was 1,805. By 1940, 4,147. By 1950, it had topped 16,000—but the Ventura Freeway lay ten years in the future, and like many other Reseda residents, my family still bought most of its fresh eggs, milk, honey, and vegetables at stands along Ventura Boulevard. The name "Reseda" was given first to a siding on a branch of the Southern Pacific in the south Valley. In 1919, after Edgar Rice Burroughs bought 550 acres near the intersection of Reseda and Ventura Boulevards and named it Tarzana (after his famous fictional character), Reseda came to refer more directly to an area farther north. In about 1920, Reseda—after a fragrant North African yellow-dye plant, *Reseda odorata*—replaced Marian as a designation for a stop on the Pacific Electric interurban railway running along Sherman Way. (Marian was the daughter of the *Los Angeles Times* publisher Harrison Gray Otis, a director of the Los Angeles Suburban Homes Company syndicate.)

I recall an evening in 1952 when Mother drove my brother and me over to Pacific Palisades to have dinner with Sidney and Grace. I spent some of that time in Sidney's workshop, watching him fashion aluminum struts for a model-railroad bridge. (It would turn up later under our Christmas tree, part of a large train layout he built and painted for me.) Crossing back over the mountains that night in our 1932 Ford coupe, Mother had me aim a flashlight beam at the shoulder of the road to guide her, there being no money in the budget for new headlamps. With the car beams out and little traffic coming up the hill toward us, we could see the grid of the Valley's lights clearly, and dark patches to the north where farm-style houses still occupied small holdings—the last remnant of working land, of old Valley life.

Los Angeles County was the most productive agricultural county in the United States in 1950. By 1955, its agriculture had become largely vestigial. Faced with one of the most astonishing phases of urban development in modern history, commercial agriculture in the San Fernando Valley came and went in a span of forty-five years, between 1915 and 1960. In 1915, about 3,000 of the Valley's 155,000 acres were irrigated; by 1920, according to one estimate, it was 50,000 acres. The number of irrigated farms peaked in 1937 and then began to decline, decreasing not through consolidation but by elimination. Between 1940 and 1958, an average of 2,500 acres per year went out of agricultural production.

An abundance of water brought an abundance of people. Along with irrigation, agriculture, and annexation, the Valley got, in virtually the same instant, urban subdivision and industrial development. In 1911, by one estimate, only about 2,000 people lived in the unirrigated Valley, the land out beyond Van Nuys, North Hollywood, Burbank, Pacoima, and San Fernando. By 1950, 402,538 people were living on the same land, an almost incomprehensible increase of 20,000 percent. Urban subdivision, bringing with it freeways, supermarkets, and apartment buildings, overwhelmed a young agricultural landscape. Water that had once grown food now filled swimming pools (a per capita amenity in which the Valley led the nation) and kept golf courses green. It served tens of thousands of plumbed dwellings and supported a suburban horticultural architecture of Babylonian proportions.

It is hard to grasp completely the change wrought in the Valley by water. A hundred years after Portolá crossed Sepulveda Pass in 1769, only a handful of immigrants, few of whom spoke English, were occupying the Valley floor. It remained a place of casual property bounds, a dry steppe landscape without fences, a flatness relieved only by a few hills. At one point, around 1876, some forty-eight square miles of the Valley was standing in wheat, "league upon league of grain," wrote a traveler, "waving ready for harvest" in a "landscape flickering under an ardent sun." A hundred years on, irrigation agriculture having passed like a migrating bird, the Valley's population stood at more than one million. Its sprawling and vigorous economy was fueled almost entirely by newly developed technologies—television and movie production, automobile assembly, and the aerospace and electronics industries.

It is tempting to say that what was once grand and beautiful about the Valley, a place of Steinbeckian dignity, undercurrent, and innocence, had all but vanished by the time we came over the mountains that night, guided by the beam of a flashlight, but the truth is the river still flowed down there in the dark, however restricted and burdened its channel; in scattered single fields, food crops still matured in the indigenous light and wind and rain; and my pigeons, the aerial component of my fertile imagination, still circled the last of

the Valley's rural districts—Platt Ranch, Porter Ranch,
Shadow Ranch—before coming home.

In July 1952, I ran out of the house during an earthquake, which made the trembling ground seem willful and
aware. One winter night in 1953, Caballero Creek backed
up Calvert Street to lap at the stone tiles of our porch, and
that primal communion I felt with water, the visceral disturbance that completely silenced me whenever I went to the
Cascades, told me that something essential was around and
before me, something older than the Gabrielino, more essential to human life than economic solvency: The white coin of
an August sun in Santa Ana skies, the fault-riven ground, this
El Niño climate could not be paved over. It could never be
lost, never destroyed.

Insofar as I was able as a child, I put my faith in that.

I LIVE IN A DIFFERENT sort of landscape now, a temperate rain
forest on the west slope of the Cascade Range in Oregon. It
is lightly settled country, a place with no streetlamps, no
curbs or sidewalks. I'm twenty-nine miles from a stoplight,
and there's only one road to town. In some ways I still live in
the borderland of my Reseda youth. Driving into Eugene, I
will stop for fresh vegetables, for honey, berries, and eggs at
roadside stands. In the few broad bottomlands where hazelnut orchards grow, I can picture the walnut groves I once
knew around Van Nuys, and on a hot day I can smell the
sweet air rising off a sugar-beet field.

Like everyone else, I've no simple way to measure where
I've been between these episodes of childhood and middle

age. I've traveled through thirty-five countries, ended a thirty-year marriage, and written fourteen books. I believe that I could as easily have become an orchardist as a writer. I simply found a different shape to the passion I felt as a child, watching things grow and wanting to participate in the cultivation and harvest.

Like my neighbors, then and now, I've broken down alone or with others in tears of adult despair, and known a joy so transporting, so serene, I've believed I was within the realm of the Divine. I've come to assume that these emotional extremes are a part of every human life, that they were known to the braceros whose daughters my mother taught and also to the movie-star fathers of some of my classmates at Our Lady of Grace.

I have also come to assume that one of a writer's obligations to society is to make this equality clear. As I see it, in a democracy such as ours the writer is called on especially to expose the notion of entitlement, which posits that some of us should receive more, solely on the basis of skin color, education, gender, ethnicity, supposed gifts, or accumulated wealth. Such a writer, growing up like me, white in a white man's valley, must look back at the social and economic customs, the real estate covenants, the prejudicial legislation and ethical oblivion that made it so.

The peculiar task of many American writers today—though, again, only as I see it—is to address what lies beyond racism, class structure, and violence in American life by first recognizing these failings as real, and then by helping with the invention of what will work in such circumstances to ensure that each life endures less cruelty, each life is less painful.

I cannot recall the agricultural richness of the San Fernando Valley in my youth without remembering that the Valley I grew up in was brought to life through schemes of
injustice, at several crucial junctures. The early settlers used up
the Gabrielino as a kind of grout and mortar, first to build the
mission at San Fernando and make it economically viable, and
then to work the ranchos designed to augment the wealth of a
dozen or so men. Chinese laborers were brought in to build
the railroad through San Fernando Pass, and then handed the
Chinese Exclusion Act of 1882 to read. After the turn of the
century, those who could most easily direct the fate of the Valley imposed on it, for profit, a regime of imported water. They
created an Eden of fruit and vegetables, of jasmine and bou-
gainvillea, and put it up for sale in a seller's market. They
seemed, to some observers, intoxicated with their own gran-
deur. Mulholland stood there like a god at the Cascades on
November 5, 1913. "There it is," he said. "Take it."

IT IS A LONG WAY, of course, from the policies of abuse that
extinguished the cultural life of the Gabrielino to the assumptions Mulholland made about what might be bought and
sold with impunity. But the policies and assumptions are
rooted in a similar indifference to the sanctity of complex
life. As much as the Gabrielino selected the Valley as a comfortable abode, the Valley itself exerted a selective pressure
on the Gabrielino and their culture. And Mulholland con-
strued water not as life but as a commodity, a market lever.

To effectively address the ordinary difficulties of human
existence, each generation must relocate and protect the

ground that will not give way, the ground that will sustain the dreams of its ancestors in the face of waywardness. An American writer today can hardly miss, anywhere in the country, the emergence of a culture increasingly mestizo in its ways, and yet he or she knows that many Americans still cling silently to the hope of a rule by one race, and continue to believe in a land that will produce no end of water, timber, coal, gasoline, and the other fuels of culture. When the lessons come—infernos in the chaparral, the Watts riots, rolling blackouts—they are met with new technologies and new infrastructures that often prove only weirdly cosmetic.

Some fundamental shift in cultural awareness now seems called for. The economic assessment of a stretch of land, it might be argued, can be made more accurate now by taking into account what comes out of the Earth that cannot be bought.

When I read the journals of eighteenth-century travelers to the San Fernando Valley, I can grasp that they were mesmerized by the same things I was as a boy. These essences, it seems to me, no kind of development can truly erase: The heartbreaking light clear as grain alcohol, then "weathered like aluminum," in the phrase of contemporary California poet Robert Vasquez. Spring winds bursting along the river through bosques of native walnut and oak, those complexly graceful limbs riding the buffet. And the all-or-nothing of the streams—Tujunga Wash running one day like the upper Missouri, another day standing as sleepy as a bajada at noon.

I am inclined toward these natural elements, toward them as a foundation for culture, because they saved my life as a child. It is not nostalgia I feel for them but respect.

ON DECEMBER 23, 1955, MY mother married her third husband, a businessman from New York who offered us financial security, elevated social status, and private schools. At
the least, this marriage represented for her the realization
of what she had been seeking in the Valley for years—
dependably stable, even generous economic circumstances,
a more graciously appointed home, and a measure of
privilege—but this life would now unfold for us in Manhattan, not in working-class Reseda.

The relief I felt at the news that we would be leaving
California was the kind of relief an animal might feel if that
animal had been electrocuted to unconsciousness every few
days by an indifferent owner, and then had awakened one
morning to find the owner dead, the cage door standing
open. Along with three other boys at the time (whom I've
never met, and only learned about years later from two
detectives in the Los Angeles Police Department), I had been
sodomized repeatedly in the mid-1950s by an older man
who ran a drying-out clinic for alcoholics on Riverside Drive
in North Hollywood. He preyed, I would now speculate,
largely on the sons of single mothers who brought a friend or
relative in for treatment. He posed as a compassionate MD
but was neither. In the way of a true sociopath, a pathologi-
cal narcissist, he insinuated himself into a family with timely
gifts on birthdays, extra cash for groceries and school clothes,
and the offer to give a parent an evening off.

According to the detectives, Harry Shier fled L.A. in
1959, one step ahead of a grand jury indictment, and not

his first. He had fled earlier indictments in Canada and Colorado.

Like tens of thousands of sexually brutalized children, I lived in silent compliance. My patient hope was somehow to walk away, to no longer have to endure his compulsions in the small, nasty apartment he kept on the roof of his sanitarium. But when my dreamed-of escape became reality, when I was rid of him, I missed California to the point of grief. The sound of mourning doves at first light; the unpopulated middle stretches of Topanga and Laurel Canyons, with their bolting jackrabbits; the long beaches at Zuma and Leo Carrillo, where it seemed to me the biggest waves in the world came to their crashing ends—these sounds and places were my refuge from the threat of ruin in that room. Without them, without the surgical sharpness and (on another day) the smoky nature of the sun's light as it spilled into the Valley, without the astringent smells of fresh eucalyptus buttons and pepper-tree leaves clinging to the skin of my fingers—without these things I believe I would have perished. Left like a wet rag doll in the bed of a beast, I might have gone through some other door.

In a dry, fault-block basin in the transverse ranges of Southern California, where the Gabrielino once lived well on sixty different kinds of plants and a hundred types of seed, another group of people built a world of well-watered fields. However they may have reasoned the water was theirs, they made an arid land bloom. And so I understood as a boy I could do the same. I could address the thing in me that threatened to become a vast and spreading desert. I had only to discover the water to make it happen.

The water, it turned out, was ordinary life. The water was the braceros, working every day in the fields, making a curiously knowing nod to a young white boy passing on his bike. The water was the ordinary determination of everyday people to contain something deep in their lives. It was a detachment from distraction, which led many of them to eschew both nostalgia and the pages of *Sunset* in a search for what they hoped for from life in the Valley.

My pigeons, in all the rise and fall of their aerial scripture, were the water. (In one of the ironic twists that give life its signal, curious spine, these were the gift of Harry Shier.) As I understood them, lining the ridge of their coop in the morning, waiting for the air to warm, they were happy for the light. It did not seem that they would later return home disappointed because the ground they found beneath their wings had changed in the night. Whatever they might encounter, it would take neither energy nor beauty from their flight.

WHEN, EVERY FEW YEARS, I return to the Valley I make the same rounds to pay my respects. I drive out to the first home we lived in, a ranch-style house still standing on Wilbur Avenue in Reseda. In 1948 it was isolated, surrounded by alfalfa and barley fields as far as a small boy could imagine walking. Today it sits hemmed in by other houses and sheltered from the street by a row of sawleaf zelkova trees planted where another twenty feet of the front yard once was. Out back, Aliso Creek, the first seasonal water of my life, lies strait-jacketed in concrete. In the late 1940s, Wilbur was a narrow, paved trough, a steep-sided street designed to carry heavy winter rain south to the river. When the river was in flood, we parked out on Sherman Way and walked in to our place. And sometimes on summer days we had to ease the car through a tide of sheep being driven to pasture along the same corridor.

Today, Wilbur is as tame a road as Aliso is a creek.

We lived for a while in a second house on Wilbur, this one in Tarzana. It, too, lost most of its front yard to the widening of the avenue before being razed in 1988. I happened to drive by that year on the last day the bulldozer and the loader worked. The lot had been scraped clean and subdivided with flagged lath stakes. House, garage, chicken coop, horse barn—all of it had been hauled away, along with the walnut, apricot, and grapefruit trees. I pocketed the single apricot pit I found.

The house I lived in the longest, the one on Calvert Street, I could easily move back into today if it were mine. The current owners have been obliging enough to let me come by to visit. The lot is smaller by half, and the house has an addition and has been remodeled inside and out, but the family has preserved a measure of its old Valley stature.

I brought a friend with me on a recent visit to the Calvert Street house, a man who grew up in Lakewood in the 1950s and who now runs a commercial nursery in Arroyo Grande. All I could recognize in the front yard from the past were two camellia bushes my mother planted in 1954, from which I now take an occasional blossom. At a glance, Dave identified seventeen different flowering plants and trees around the house, a landscape he compared to that at the Getty Museum—"something from the Mojave, something from the Alps, something from India, something from riparian Botswana."

"It breaks the horticultural rules, having so many different plants growing right next to each other, but it works," he said. "It's like L.A."

On that same visit, I asked Dave to drift us out across the Valley to Chatsworth. I wanted to take advantage of his knowledge to identify some of the jungle of what now grows there, most all of which didn't when I was a boy. We recalled to each other the sensations of our boyhood days on the suburban perimeter of L.A., how the blooming of jacaranda trees signaled the end of the school year, and how we fought the crabgrass in our lawns and tried to sell our parents on dichondra turf as a replacement. We remembered hauling trash to backyard incinerators and pulling foxtails out of our socks, the tenacious seed cases of ripgut bromegrass.

When we crossed Santa Susana Pass and drove over into Santa Clara Valley, we both had the same thought: It looked like the Valley in 1953. We came back through San Fernando Pass, and then followed the river all the way to Long Beach. We walked the boardwalk at Venice Beach and watched a purple evening emerge from light dismantled in the sky above the ocean.

The night before, we'd had dinner with the writer and historian D. J. Waldie and a friend of his at La Serenata de Garibaldi in East L.A. The four of us discovered, without attempting to, that the L.A. River had played an important psychic role in each of our lives when we were boys. Our affection for the river, though, and our hopes that it might one day be stripped of some of its revetment, were not a

yearning for restored scenery, or even for wild nature renewed in an urban corridor. What we felt was a desire like
wanting a tourniquet removed. The river, in the very way of
its trickle-and-flood personality, its El Niño essence, had
shaped something vital in us, and we missed it now, as if it
were a finger lost in an accident.

I intuited again the next day, on that long zigzag drive to
Chatsworth with Dave, that the Valley of my childhood was
not gone, only dormant. Like the Gabrielino, it has ceased to
exist as an obvious force, but it's still present, vibrating in the
shadow lines. A cursory glance might incline you to think the
Valley has been thoroughly ruined—subdivided, automobi-
lized, scorched by venal dreams of wealth. But its spirit remains
intact. The oblivion is an illusion. When I drive the back streets
of Winnetka and Reseda today, I see people of ordinary means
with routine struggles standing in their front yards, watching
the wind blouse sentinel eucalyptus and watering their array
of exotic plants. In the trimness and intense fragrance of their
mestizo yards, they have erected a barrier against much that
insults and hounds them. When I stop to talk, I sometimes
find these people have preserved a centerpiece of my era—
backyard agriculture. A few chickens, some fruit trees and
berry vines, a clutch of beehives, a kitchen garden. These individuals' sense of where they are, and how to manage, tran-
scends what has been imposed on the Valley. The Gabrielino
could have explained a life to them they would understand.

MY OCCASIONAL TRAVELS THROUGH THE Valley are only incidentally meant to find whether a restaurant I ate at as a boy

is still in business on Ventura, or if two of my three childhood homes still stand, or if the field where I played Little
League ball is still in use. Deeper emotions of gratitude, tenderness, and wonder come over me when I study the eyes of
rock doves on rooflines along Calvert Street. (Were birds I
raised ancestors to these?) They come when I cross the Santa
Monicas to find—so suddenly—the Pacific and recall Charles
Wright's description of that sight: "the ocean like a sleeping
dog, its side rising and falling and twitching occasionally in
the aftermath of some dream or other." The deeper emotions come when I bend over to sip again from a drinking
fountain at Our Lady of Grace, turning the same spigot handle I did as a boy, when I thought water the most delicious of
all foods.

At its core, the Valley is a particular modulation of light
and water, an imbalance of aridity and flood, of stagnant air
and wind. As civilization has done in every landscape where it
has made its pitch, settlers here thought they would get closer
to paradise if they could simply adjust these amplitudes—
have water coming on a more predictable schedule, completely eliminate aridity, create a consoling and beautiful
horticulture, pave over the dust, and brighten things up by
getting rid of as much of the night as possible.

I watched as a ten-year-old boy for clear, moonlit nights
in the Valley. I would ride my bike for miles through the
great dark expanses of cultivated land between Chatsworth
and Reseda on those evenings. I'd look up to the high, pale
lit walls of the basin, the lower one to the south named for
Saint Monica, the mother of Saint Augustine, the other
range for a third-century virgin martyr, Saint Susanna. I

saw in the fields through veils cast by night sprinklers the heads of deer come down to graze from the dry mountains in a luxuriant and wet paradise. I cannot imagine them wondering why paradise was there that night, only thinking it was fabulous.

The slow *chuck, chuck, chuck* of the big sprinklers and the moon-shot fields felt mythic and comforting. They held no threats for me. They carried no mean notices, like the sign I once saw in a restaurant window downtown: SE SIRVE SOLA- MENTE A RAZA BLANCO. It was simply the dampened soil doing its work under the magic wand of the sprinkler. I knew the water came from somewhere far away, that it had not always been like this. But the vistas of worked and well-watered land, seen in the intense heat haze of a stifling July afternoon or on a cool starlit night such as this, seemed stronger, more enduring, than any violation I knew, the residue of which I sometimes felt clinging to me like a smear.

I returned to the Valley again and again to encounter, again, the physical ground of this understanding.

ON THE FINAL DAY OF a recent trip, I slipped away from the home of friends before dawn, came across Topanga Canyon into Canoga Park, and turned right onto Sherman Way. The sun was still below the San Gabriels, but it had filled the sky with a milky blue color, backlighting the crowns of Mexican fan palms lining the avenue. It seemed I could see all the way to Van Nuys Airport down this promenade, modeled, I had always understood, after the Paseo de la Reforma in Mexico City.

I saw people getting their coffee at the twenty-four-hour stores. It's no longer outdoor work for most of these early risers in the west Valley, and it is no longer the simple racial mix of my boyhood—white and Mexican, perhaps a few Japanese. Today I see Vietnamese, Chinese, West Africans. I see faces I would call Nordic, East Indian, Aboriginal. Here was one dramatic change from my time, reiterated in the remarkable array of ethnic restaurants now in the Valley.

I had two thoughts I wanted to follow out that morning. One was about trees, the other about the river, that great, constricted shadow-life moving through the Valley.

As a boy, I imagined trees the most enduring and grace-ful of all creatures. Historically, the river watered an inter-mittent gallery forest of Frémont's cottonwood, California black walnut, hackberry, California sycamore (the *aliso* of Aliso Creek), coast live oak, and varieties of willow. By the 1950s, the idea that trees were associated only with the river and its big washes—Tujunga and Pacoima—was long gone. Trees grew northward from the river all the way to the allu-vial fans of the Santa Susanas and westward to the Simi Hills. Among the dominant ones were species of eucalyptus from Australia, Lombardy poplar from Italy, pepper tree from the Peruvian Andes (but often mistakenly called Cali-fornia pepper tree), and types of pine, many of them from the Mediterranean.

Settlers frequently assumed early on that although the San Fernando Valley was blessed with a favorable climate and good soils (both true), it could never become farming country because it lacked water. (All it lacked, of course, was surface water.) When Owens Valley water came in, trees

could be planted and sustained far across the formerly treeless plain. These trees, especially blue gums growing to a
hundred feet or more, gave the west Valley its first vertical
relief. And where they were planted as windbreaks, they
demarcated its first volumes of space.

I oriented myself toward trees as a boy. I slept under
them. I sought them out as I might otherwise have gone to
grandparents. Now, I clip a few sprigs to take home.

The L.A. River, like the Gabrielino people, could not be
accorded a place in the Valley unless its fundamental nature
was altered. Coffined, bound in such a way as to suggest
imprisonment, civilized in the most vehement ways, it still
manages to raise its fist to the ruling party. In an open gallery
of graffiti, it proclaims the city's ethnic and class divisions
and registers the degree of people's alienation and marginal-
ization. In these scrawled and sometimes stunningly executed
outbursts of pride, of self-actualization, one can imagine the
voice of the river itself, whose behavior for so long has also
been proscribed. The difference lies in the great maturity of
the river. It came before. It will outlast. Its wish is not for
vengeance, a young man's goal, but for release.

For many Angelenos today, the city is a bizarre, exagger-
ated, and superficial environment, but it never was to me.
And I knew, making the turn onto Sherman Way that morning, it was not to those I grew up with. Once unearthed, the
transcendent essence of the Valley, the sense of what is eternal about its expression of life, deeper than race, deeper than
money, deeper than a creed, cannot be misplaced. Once discovered, it can defend an otherwise terrified person against
the intrusion of ordinary evil, against the banal horror of the

truly deviant, which we persist in declaring is shockingly
unfamiliar to us.

MY MOTHER, MARY BRENNAN, DIED of cancer in New York City
in 1976, less than thirty years after she heeded her friend's
call and came west to try to make a life for herself in the Valley. She is buried in the community graveyard of the small
Alabama farm town from which she came. Sidney Van Sheck
died in 1991, having become something of an icon at Hughes
Aircraft. Esther, following his wishes, scattered his ashes in
the Pacific. She is now ninety-one. She lost her second husband, Bobby, to a heart attack in 1951. Remarried, she was
widowed again and now lives in Sun City. Whenever I'm in
town, we go to dinner. I do not know, really, what any of the
three of them hoped to find in L.A., and I wouldn't presume
to ask Esther now. We spend our lives trying to say what it is
we want, sometimes in denial of all we have. L.A. is perhaps
more symbolic of this syndrome than other cities, and it
likely accentuates more the leisure circumstances that can
make such contemplation an obsession.

I ENDED THAT FINAL DAY of my recent visit at Reseda Park, at
the corner of Reseda and Victory Boulevards. I sat at a concrete picnic table, reading Blake Gumprecht's exceptional
history, *The Los Angeles River: Its Life, Death, and Possible Rebirth*,
now and then shielding my eyes against the setting sun to
take in some event. Like Waldie's *Holy Land* and Robert
Adams's *Los Angeles Spring*, Gumprecht's book made palpable

a landscape I have never wanted to be too long absent from. I'd walked through the park for an hour before I sat down with the book, brushing the flanks of trees with my hand to see if I remembered the textures—stone pine, holly oak, and cork oak from the Mediterranean; redwood; tree of heaven from China; Canary Island pine from the eastern Atlantic—the familiar heterogeneous mix.

I had passed a camarilla of older men playing serious cards, mothers anxiously eyeing children feeding animals (many of the latter missing digits and tails) at the edge of a murky pond. I'd bought a cold drink from a vendor on a bicycle, discreetly watched a young man and woman in physically passionate conversation, taken in the enthusiasms of Spanish-language talk radio, the *thwack* and return *thwack* of a tennis match, the gleeful screams of girls at jump rope, and the apparently detached but actually quite scandalized looks of a conservatively dressed Middle Eastern family strolling through.

The most exotic component of this late-afternoon tableau may have been a gorgeous male Mandarin duck swimming the pond. (Small numbers of these brightly feathered Asian birds are now feral in California.) I thought the most striking element in the park, though, the hour I watched, was the unadorned love of these people, the pleasure they were taking in each other's company. Here were fathers giving the children of other fathers (presumably) hour upon hour of gentle encouragement in pursuits no more exalted than the fundamentals of base running. Here were mothers, pleased merely to see their children at play, showing no signs of distraction from the task, no need for a book or CD player. Here were old men who, but for the presence of another old man on the other side of the backgammon board, might be in the relentless, dark grip of some other emotion. Here were young men in close, emphatic discussion, perhaps of the political affairs of the day.

I am sufficiently aware, I hope, of the possibility for seduction in such a scene, the danger of imputing to it more than is there. Still, I recognized something here that I had first seen in the demeanor of the braceros I had encountered as a boy. You could build anything on the backs of such people. They, more than any couture boy on a cell phone passing the park in a spotless, air-conditioned Hummer, were the ones to be reckoned with if you wanted a society capable of perpetuating itself.

The river, with its battered chain-link barrier fence, is very close here. The shallow stream running in the low-water channel, swirling bright-green algal fronds, is runoff from storm drains, not treated sewage. The arroyo chubs, three-spined sticklebacks, and crayfish of my youth I suppose are entirely gone, but what I see in the water is not nostalgia or despair. I see the infinite patience we associate with the still ocean. And I see behind me here on the river's banks the ebb and flow of diverse humanity, engaged, adapting to whatever mean threat or wild beauty may lie in its path.

As always when I return, I have found again the ground that propels me past the great temptation of our time: to put one's faith in despair.

Sliver of Sky

ONE DAY IN THE FALL OF 1938, HARRY SHIER ENTERED THE operating room of a Toronto hospital and began an appendectomy procedure on a prepubescent boy. He was not a trained surgeon; he nearly botched the operation, and the boy's parents reacted angrily. Suspicions about Shier's medical credentials had already surfaced among operating-room nurses, and the hospital, aware of other complaints related to Shier's groin-area operations on young boys, opened a formal investigation. By the time the hospital board determined that both his medical degree, from a European university, and his European letters of reference were fraudulent, Harry Shier had departed for the United States.

A few years later, a police officer in Denver caught Shier raping a boy in the front seat of his automobile. Shier spent a year in prison and then slipped out of Colorado. In the late 1940s, he surfaced in North Hollywood, California, as the director of a sanitarium where he supervised the treatment of people with addictions, primarily alcoholics. In the summer of

1952, at the age of seven, I was introduced to him when I visited the sanitarium with my mother.

At the time, I lived with her and my younger brother in
Reseda. My parents had recently divorced, and my father had
moved across the country. To support the three of us, my
mother had taken a day job teaching home economics at a
junior high in the city of San Fernando and also a job teaching
dressmaking two evenings a week at Pierce Junior College in
Woodland Hills, on the far western edge of the Valley.

Early that summer, my mother had somewhat reluctantly agreed to take in a houseguest, her first cousin Evelyn Carrothers. Evelyn, who was my mother's age, lived an
hour away in Long Beach and was struggling with a drinking
problem. Her marriage was also in trouble. Mother couldn't
accommodate Evelyn for long in our one-bedroom house, so
she began inquiring among her friends about other arrangements. People advised her to call Alcoholics Anonymous.
Someone in the organization's Los Angeles office suggested
that she contact the North Hollywood Lodge and Sanitarium.

One morning, Mother drove us all to the facility at 12003
Riverside Drive, known then around the Valley, I would later
learn, as "Shier's dryer." In those years, Shier was renowned
as someone who could "cure" alcoholism. He was also able
to relate sympathetically to the families of alcoholics. When
we arrived at the clinic, Mother introduced my four-year-old
brother and me to "Dr." Shier. We shook hands with him,
and he escorted the two of us to the sanitarium's kitchen,
where we each selected a fresh doughnut from an array laid
out on trays for the patients—frosted, sugared, glazed, covered with sprinkles. A nice man. I remember the building's

corridors reeked that morning of something other than dis-
infectant. Paraldehyde, I was later informed, which Shier
used liberally to sedate his patients.

Shortly after Evelyn had, in Shier's estimation, recovered
enough to return to Long Beach—she would begin drinking
again and, a year later, would return to his facility—he
started dropping by our home in Reseda. He had gotten to
know something of Mother's marital and financial situation
from Evelyn, and during one of his early visits he told Mother
that he was concerned: Her income was not, in his view,
commensurate with her capabilities. He said he might be
able to do something about that. (Mother's divorce settlement required my father to send her ten dollars a month in
child support—an obligation he rarely met, according to
correspondence I would later find.) Shier said that one of his
former patients was in a position to speak with the school
board about Mother's value to the school system. This appeal
was apparently made, and a short while later she received a
small increase in salary.

She was grateful. Harry was pleased to help. He conducted himself around Mother like someone considering
serious courtship. She was a handsome woman of thirty-
nine, he a short, abrasively self-confident, balding man of
fifty-six. He complimented her on the way she was single-
handedly raising her two polite, neatly dressed sons. He complimented her on her figure. Occasionally he'd take her hand
or caress her lightly on the shoulder. After a while, Shier
began dropping by the house in the evening, just as my
brother and I were getting into our pajamas. He'd bring a
tub of ice cream along, and the four of us would have dessert

together. One evening he arrived without the ice cream. He'd forgotten. He suggested I accompany him to the grocery store, where I could pick out a different dessert for each of us.

A few minutes after we left the house, he pulled his car up alongside a tall hedge on an unlit residential street off Lindley Avenue. He turned me to the side, put me facedown on the seat, pulled down my pajama bottoms, and pushed his erect penis into my anus. As he built toward his climax he told me, calmly but emphatically, that he was a doctor, that I needed treatment, and that we were not going to be adding to Mother's worries by telling her about my problem.

SHIER FOLLOWED THIS PATTERN OF sexual assault with me for four years. He came by the house several times a month and continued to successfully direct Mother's attention away from what he was doing. It is hard to imagine, now, that no one suspected what was going on. It is equally difficult, even for therapists, to explain how this type of sexual violence can be perpetuated between two human beings for years without the victim successfully objecting. Why, people wonder, does the evidence for a child's resistance in these circumstances usually seem so meager? I believe it's because the child is too innocent to plan effectively, and because, from the very start, the child faces a labyrinth of confused allegiances. I asked myself questions I couldn't answer: Do I actually need protection in this situation? From what, precisely? I was bewildered by what was happening. How could I explain to my mother what I was doing? Physical resistance, of course, is virtually impossible for most children. The child's alternatives, as I understand them, never get much beyond endurance and avoidance—and speculation about how to encourage intervention.

An additional source of confusion for me was the belief that I had been chosen as a special patient by Harry Shier, an esteemed doctor and the director of a prestigious institution. A weird sense of privilege was attached to his interest in me, and to the existence of an unspecified medical condition too serious or exotic to share with Mother. Also, being the elder son in a lower-middle-class and fatherless family, I came to feel—or he encouraged me to feel—that I was shouldering an important responsibility for my family.

I understood that I was helping my family, and he complimented me on my maturity.

WHEN SHIER CAME TO OUR house he would inform Mother that we were just going out to get some ice cream together, or, on a Saturday afternoon, that he was going to take me to an early movie, and then maybe out to dinner at the Sportsmen's Lodge on Ventura Boulevard in Studio City. We would say goodbye and he would walk me to his car and we would drive off. If it was dark, he'd pull over soon in a secluded spot and rape me in the front seat; or we'd go to the movie and he'd force my head into his lap for a while, pushing at me through his trousers; or it would be dinner at the restaurant, where we'd hook our trout in a small pool for the chef to cook, and then he'd drive on to the sanitarium, where he'd park behind the single-story building. He'd direct me up an outside staircase to a series of rotting duckboards that led across the clinic's flat roof to a locked door, the outside entrance to a rooftop apartment, where I was to wait. He'd enter the front of the building, check on his patients, say good night to the nurses, and ascend an inside staircase to reach the interior door of his studio-size quarters. I'd see the lights go on inside. A moment later he'd open the door to the roof and pull me in.

One night in these chambers, after he was through with me, he took a medical text from a bookshelf. He sat me down beside him on the edge of the bed and showed me black-and-white photographs of men's genitals ravaged by syphilis. This, he said, was what came from physical intimacy with women.

In bed with him, I would try to maneuver myself so I could focus on the horizontal sliver of sky visible between the lower edge of the drawn blinds and the white sill of the partially open window. Passing clouds, a bird, the stars.

From time to time, often on the drive back to my home, Shier would remind me that if I were ever to tell anyone, if the treatments were to stop, he would have no choice but to have me committed to an institution. And then, if I were no longer around for my family . . . I'd seen how he occasionally slipped Mother a few folded bills in my presence. It would be best, I thought, if I just continued to be the brave boy he said I was.

I know the questions I initially asked myself afterward about these events were not very sophisticated. For example: Why hadn't Shier also molested my younger brother? My brother, I conjectured, had been too young in 1952, only four years old; later, with one brother firmly in hand, Shier had probably considered pursuing the other too much of a risk. (When we were older, my brother told me that Shier had molested him, several times, in the mid-1950s. I went numb with grief. After the four years of sexual violence with Shier were over, what sense of self-worth I still retained rested mainly with a conviction that, however I might have debased myself with Shier, I had at least protected my brother—and also probably saved my family from significant financial hardship. Further shame would come after I discovered that our family had never been in serious financial danger, that Mother's earnings had covered our every necessity and more.)

MY MOTHER REMARRIED IN 1956. We moved to New York City, where my stepfather lived, and I never again saw the malachite-green-and-cream-colored Pontiac Chieftain pulling up in front of our house on Calvert Street. After we moved into my stepfather's apartment, I felt a great sense of freedom. I was so very far away now from Harry Shier. A new school, a new neighborhood, new friends. I had surfaced in another ocean. This discovery of fresh opportunity, however, which sometimes gave way to palpable euphoria, I nevertheless experienced as unreliable. I couldn't keep a hold on it. And then, two years after we moved East, when I was thirteen, Harry Shier flew into New York and my sense of safety collapsed. He arrived with my stepfather at our vacation home on the Jersey Shore one summer evening in 1958. He was my parents' guest for the weekend. A surprise for the boys.

Weren't we pleased?

The next morning, a Saturday, while my parents were preparing breakfast in the kitchen, Shier eased open the door of my attic bedroom and closed it quietly behind him. He walked wordlessly to the edge of my bed, his lips twitching in a characteristic pucker, his eyes fixed on mine. When he reached under the sheet I kicked at him and sprang from the bed, grabbing a baseball bat that was leaning against the headboard. Naked, cursing, swinging at him with the bat, I drove him from the room and slammed the door.

While I dressed, he began a conversation downstairs with my parents.

Eavesdropping on them from the hallway next to the kitchen door, I heard Shier explain that I needed to be committed. He described—in grave tones, which gave his voice a kind of Delphic weight—how I was prone to delusions, a dangerous, potentially violent boy. Trouble ahead. Through the hinge gap in the doorway, I studied my mother and stepfather seated with him at the breakfast table. Their hands were folded squarely on the oilcloth. They took in Shier's measured, professional characterization with consternation and grief. In that moment, I couldn't bring myself to describe for them what he had done. The thought of the change it would bring to our lives was overwhelming, and, regardless, my own situation felt far too precarious. Having abruptly gained the security of a family with a devoted father, I could now abruptly lose it.

I left the house without delay, to play pickup baseball with my friends. In the afternoon I rode off alone on my bicycle to the next town inland. When I returned that evening, I learned that Shier had asked my stepfather to drive him straight back to New York that morning so that he could catch a plane west from Idlewild. I had insulted the doctor, my mother told me, and embarrassed the family. She presented his analysis of my behavior. When I tried to object, her response was, "But he's a *doctor!*"

Shier, she said, would confer with her and my stepfather in a few days by telephone, about accommodations for me in Los Angeles.

I was not, finally, sent to California, though the reason for this was never discussed with me. If my parents harbored any misgivings about Shier, I didn't hear them. I studied hard, came home on time, did my chores: I continued to behave as a dutiful son, a boy neither parent would willingly give up.

THE TRAUMA STAYED WITH ME, however, and in the spring of 1962, when I was seventeen, I gave in to a state of depression. I had become confused about my sexual identity and was haunted by a sense of contamination, a feeling that I had been rendered worthless as a man because of what I had done.

When I was immobilized in the elaborate web of Shier's appetites and undone by his ploys to ensure his own safety, I had assumed I was the only boy he was involved with. It was the sudden realization that there might have been—probably were—others, and that he might still be raping boys in California, that compelled me to break my silence and risk, I believed, disastrous humiliation. I phoned my stepfather at his office. He agreed to meet me in the lobby of the New

York Athletic Club on Central Park South, where I thought
he would feel comfortable.

He strode impatiently into his club that afternoon and
took a seat opposite me in one of the lobby's large leather
chairs. He was a busy man, but he was prepared to listen. I
gave him a brief account of Shier's behavior and of my history with him, and I made two requests of him. First, that he
never tell anyone what had happened; if he ever came to
believe that Mother had to know, he was to let *me* tell her.
Second, that he help me stop Shier. He listened with rising
interest and increasing ire. He was especially angry, I later
realized, at the idea that he had been duped by Shier that
summer in New Jersey.

Early the next morning, he took a plane to Los Angeles,
and late that same afternoon he met with two LAPD detectives. When he returned to New York three days later, my
stepfather told me that the detectives he'd spoken with were
going to scrutinize everything—the North Hollywood Lodge
and Sanitarium, Shier's criminal record, his network of
acquaintances. They were going to gather all the evidence. I
only needed to be patient. The detectives would contact us.

That week gave way to another. My stepfather waved off
my anxious inquiries. He was in touch with the detectives, he
said. They were working on it. When I finally confronted
him, he admitted that, in consultation with the detectives, he
had decided it would be too great an undertaking for me
to go up against such a clever deviant, to endure cross-
examination in a trial. So he was choosing not to press
charges. Besides, he said, Shier had bolted as soon as he had
suspected an investigation was under way.

A week or so later, my stepfather told me that he had just heard from the LAPD detectives that Harry Shier had been killed—an automobile accident in Arizona. This was, I now believe, my stepfather's preemptive effort to force closure.

IN 2003, FORTY-ONE YEARS AFTER these conversations with my stepfather and some years into my own effort to comprehend the psychological effects of what had happened to me, I phoned the LAPD. An officer there, an intermediary, was able to locate one of the two long-retired detectives who had begun the investigation of Shier in 1962. The detective did not want to speak with me directly, but he authorized the intermediary to pass on his recollections. (Because this information is at best thirdhand, I cannot be certain about either the dates or the circumstances surrounding Shier's early criminal history. The police department's official records of the case, including the detectives' notes from their conversations with my stepfather, were destroyed, along with other inactive records from that time.) The officer informed me about the botched operations at the hospital in Toronto and the sodomy charge in Colorado, gave me the approximate dates, and confirmed that the investigation had ended soon after it began because Shier had fled the state. The detective also recalled that Shier might have been killed shortly after he left California, possibly in South America, but he could not remember precisely.

In 1989, years before this conversation with the LAPD officer took place, I interviewed Evelyn Carrothers at her home in Studio City about her experiences with Shier. She said that "behind a façade of solicitous concern," Shier was a "mean man." A bully. She had never liked him, she said, but he had been very successful treating alcoholics in the Los Angeles area in the 1950s, and she herself had referred many people to him over the years. At the time I spoke with her, Evelyn had not only been sober a long while but had become a prominent member of Alcoholics Anonymous in Southern California. She was upset, I thought, by my revelation that Shier was a pedophile, but she wouldn't give me the names of anyone who might have known him. She said she never knew what became of him, but she was sure he was dead. She even argued a case for Shier: Whatever wrong he might have done in his private life, he had been of great value to the larger community.

I've never been able to comprehend Evelyn's sense of the larger good, though her point of view is a position people commonly take when confronted with evidence of sexual crimes committed by people they respect. (A reputation for valued service and magnanimous gestures often forms part of the protective cover pedophiles create.)

A more obvious question I asked myself as I grew older was: How could my mother not have known? Perhaps she did, although she died, a few years after she was told, unwilling to discuss her feelings about what had gone on in California. I've made some measure of peace with her stance. When certain individuals feel severely threatened—emotionally, financially, physically—the lights on the horizon they use to orient themselves in the world might easily wink out. Life can then become a series of fear-driven decisions and compulsive acts of self-protection. People start to separate what is deeply troubling in their lives from what they see as good.

To use the usual metaphor, they isolate the events from one another by storing them in different rooms in a large hotel. While these rooms share a corridor, they do not communicate directly with one another.

I'm not able, today, to put the image I have of my mother as her children's attentive guardian together with the idea of her as an innocent, a person blinded by the blandishments of a persistent pedophile. But for whatever reason, she was not able, back then, to consider what might be happening in the hours after she saw Shier drive away, her son's head, from her point of view on the porch, not quite clearing the sill of the car window as the two of them departed.

In June 1970, my stepfather related to my mother, without my knowledge, a distorted and incomplete version of what her friend Harry Shier had done, breaking the promise he had made to me that day eight years earlier when I'd spoken to him. They were having lunch together in Midtown Manhattan; she became hysterical and was taken from the restaurant by ambulance to a hospital. When she called me that evening, all she could bring herself to say, in a voice resigned and defeated, was, "I know what happened. I know what happened to you."

And then she never spoke of it again.

Six years later, in July 1976, my mother was dying of lung cancer. I asked her whether she wanted to speak to me about California. She lay on her bed in a private room at Manhattan's Lenox Hill Hospital, rocking her head slowly back and forth like a metronome. Her face averted, she wept silently while I sat mute in a chair by the bed. She would not take my hand.

Some of the pathways of a debilitating sexual history are simply destined never to be mapped.

THE REASONS MONSTROUSLY ABUSIVE RELATIONSHIPS persist between people are as complex, I think, as the mathematics of turbulence. The explanation I gave myself for decades, partly to avoid having to address any question of my own complicity, was that I had done this in order to keep our family safe and intact. After my father abandoned us, my mother told me that I would now be the man of the house. I took her remark literally. I began to double-check the locks on the doors at night. I mowed and weeded the lawn and took the trash out to the incinerator in the backyard to burn. I got the day's mail from the box on the street. Whenever Shier showed up at the door, I would bear down on myself: Just see the business with Shier through, I said to myself. Maybe another man, one of the more likable men Mother dated, would come and stay with us. And this one wouldn't walk out. Standing in the shower in Shier's filthy apartment, washing the blood and semen off my legs, I hammered this thought into my mind: You cannot quit.

I bottled the anger. I hid the blood. I adamantly focused anywhere else.

WHAT MY STEPFATHER ACTUALLY DID when he went to California in 1962, and how he presented Shier's crimes to the detectives, I will never know. And though I know he saw Evelyn at that time, I don't know what he discussed with her. Over the years, right up to his death, whenever I asked him about what he'd done, he became evasive. In an effort to seem sincere, he would occasionally recall a forgotten detail from one of his conversations with the detectives. This additional fact would sometimes shift my basic understanding of the longer story he had already told, raising new questions. Or, alternatively, trying to demonstrate compassion, he might suddenly recall a fact meant to soothe me but that made no sense. He told me once, for example, that during his 1962 visit Evelyn had taken him to see Shier's grave at Forest Lawn Memorial-Park in Glendale—several weeks before Shier was supposedly killed in an out-of-state automobile accident.

My stepfather, a recovering alcoholic, became, like Evelyn, a regionally prominent figure in Alcoholics Anonymous in the late 1960s. Whenever I inquired, in those early weeks of the investigation, about what sort of progress the detectives were making, he would find a way to mention how many alcoholics Shier had helped. Alcoholism, he said, was a "terrible disease," a more pervasive and serious issue, he wanted me to understand, than pedophilia. He suggested I would benefit from a slightly different perspective on all this. Shier, he conceded, was an awful man—but he had done a lot of good. I should consider, instead, how well I was doing. At seventeen I was student-body president at my Jesuit prep school. I had the highest academic average in my class senior year; I was lettering in two sports; I was escorting debutantes to balls at the Plaza, the Sherry-Netherland, the Pierre. Whatever might have occurred in California, he said, things had actually worked out all right. I should let it go.

For thirty years this was exactly the path I chose. Silence.

I believed that in spite of Shier's brutalizations I could develop a stable, productive life, that I could simply walk away from everything that had happened.

THE CONCLUSION I EVENTUALLY REACHED about my stepfather's refusal to pursue charges against Shier was that he did not want the family to be embarrassed by a trial. He was unable to understand that the decision to face cross-examination in a courtroom was not his to make. He could not appreciate that the opportunity to stand up in a public forum and describe, with Shier present, what he had done, and what he had forced me to do, was as important to me as any form of legal justice. Not to be allowed to speak or, worse, to have someone else relate my story and write its ending was to extend the original, infuriating experience of helplessness, to underscore the humiliation of being power-less. My stepfather's ultimate dismissal of my request for help was an instance, chilling for me, of an observation that victims of child molestation often make: If you tell them, they won't believe you. Believing you entails too much disruption.

From what I have read over the years in newspapers and magazines about scandals involving serial pedophiles, I have gathered that people seem to think that what victims most desire in the way of retribution is money and justice, apparently in that order. My own guess would be that what they most want is something quite different: They want to be believed, to have a foundation on which they can rebuild a sense of dignity. Reclaiming self-respect is more important than winning money, more important than exacting vengeance.

Victims do not want someone else's public wrath, the umbrage of an attorney or an editorial writer or a politician, to stand in for the articulation of their own anger. When a pedophile is exposed by a grand jury indictment today, the tenor of public indignation often seems ephemeral to me, a response generated by "civic" emotion. Considering the number of children who continue to be abused in America—something like one in seven boys and one in three girls—these expressions of condemnation seem naïve. Without a deeper commitment to vigilance, society's outrage begins to take on the look of another broken promise.

UP UNTIL THE TIME I interviewed Evelyn in the late 1980s, I had grown to more or less accept my stepfather's views about what had happened in California—which was, of course, my own form of denial. Whatever had been done to me, I held to the belief that things had actually turned out fairly well. By the time I was forty I had experienced some national success as a writer. I was friends with a large, if geographically scattered, group of people. And I was living happily in a rural, forested area in western Oregon with my wife of twenty years. Significantly, since I had moved to this mountainous place in 1970, the emotional attachment I felt to my home had become essential to any ongoing sense of well-being I had. My almost daily contact here with wild animals, the physical separation of the house from the homes of my neighbors, the flow of a large whitewater river past the property, the undomesticated land unfolding for miles around, the rawness of the weather at the back door—all of it fed a feeling of security.

During the years of "traumatic sexual abuse," the term psychologists use for serial sexual abuse, the deepest and some-times only relief I had was when I was confronted with the local, elementary forces of nature: hot Santa Ana winds blow-ing west into the San Fernando Valley from the Mojave Des-ert; Pacific storm surf crashing at Zuma and the other beaches west of Malibu; winter floods inundating our neighborhood when Caballero Creek breached its banks on its way to the Los Angeles River. I took from each of these encounters a sense of what it might feel like to become fully alive. When I gazed up beneath a flock of homing birds or listened as big winds swirled the dry leaves of eucalyptus trees or sat alone somewhere in a rarely traversed part of the Santa Monica Mountains, waiting for a glimpse of a coyote or a brush rab-bit, I would feel exhilaration. Encouragement.

But deep inside, I knew things remained awry. (It is rela-tively easy today—it wasn't then—to find pertinent and explicit information about childhood sexual trauma. How one interprets that information or chooses to act on it remains a perilous second step.) I could not, for example, shake the old thought that by not having acted sooner I was somehow responsible for what happened to other boys after I left Cali-fornia. According to my stepfather, one of the investigating detectives said I had been lucky to walk away in 1956. Con-tinuing their investigation after Shier disappeared, my step-father told me, the detectives had located three other boys, "none of whom had fared well." The detectives' advice to my stepfather had been that neither he nor I should inquire further into what Harry Shier had been doing with young boys during his years in North Hollywood.

When I began a deliberate inquiry into my past, starting in 1989, I thought of myself as a man walking around with shrapnel sealed in his flesh, and I wanted to get the fragments out. The doubts and images I had put aside for years were now starting to fester. I felt more or less continually seasick, confronting every day a harrowing absence within myself. I imagined it as a mine shaft of bleak, empty space, which neither the love of a spouse nor the companionship of friends nor professional success could efface. The thought began to work on me that a single, bold step, however, some sort of confrontation with the past, might sufficiently jar this frame of mind and change it. I could, I thought, dramatically cure myself in this way.

I phoned Forest Lawn Memorial-Park. No, there was no Harry Shier buried in any of their cemeteries. I couldn't find an obituary for him in any of the Southern California papers either. I called Evelyn and asked whether I could come to California and interview her. I would begin my healing, my ablution, by speaking with someone who had known him well. And on that same trip, I decided, I'd drive the rental car to 12003 Riverside Drive in North Hollywood. If the sanitarium was still there, I'd walk through the front door.

SHIER'S ROOFTOP APARTMENT, NEARLY HIDDEN behind the branches of several Norfolk Island pines, remained just visible from the sidewalk. I parked in the shade of a pepper tree on Ben Street and walked through the main entrance of the white stucco building, which now housed a private secondary school, a yeshiva. No one took any notice of me standing in the foyer. If someone had come up to inquire about my business, I was prepared to say that I had been a patient in this place thirty years earlier, when it had been a hospital. But I seemed to be invisible.

I walked down the main corridor. In rooms to my right, where I'd once seen the bedridden lying in dim shadow, lights now blazed. Attentive students sat at desks, avidly scribbling while someone lectured. I arrived at an intersection and suddenly found myself staring at the foot of an interior staircase. The door to the stairs, slightly ajar, revealed steps winding upward to the left. My throat clenched like a fist in my neck.

I left the building as soon as I was able to turn around. I ran across Riverside Drive into an outdoor nursery with a fence around it. I went down a pea-gravel path, past potted camellias and oleanders, past blooming primroses and azaleas. After a few minutes, breathing easily once more, the rigidity gone out of my back muscles, I crossed back to where I'd parked the car and drove away.

Later that afternoon, at the Central Library on West Fifth Street in downtown Los Angeles, I gathered several San Fernando Valley phone books from the 1950s, trying to remember the names of my mother's friends, guessing at the spellings—Emery, Falotico, Ling, Murray—hoping to dislodge a memory, to find a thread to follow. When my right index finger came to Shier's name, it halted there below the stark typeface. My bowels burst into my trousers.

In the men's room, I threw my undershorts into a waste bin and washed my pants in the sink, trying to keep the wet spot small. I was in my stocking feet, putting my pants back on, when a guard entered abruptly and stood alert and suspicious in the doorway. He informed me that the library was closing. I'll be only another moment, I assured him.

A few minutes later, shielding the wet seat of my pants with my briefcase, I met a friend for dinner nearby. When the maître d' asked whether we preferred eating outdoors or in, I suggested we sit outside. I didn't tell my friend where I'd been that day.

Over the years, I'd spoken to very few people about Shier—my brother, serious girlfriends, my wife, a few close friends. I didn't feel any need to be heard, and the chance of being misunderstood, of being taken for no more than the innocent victim, long ago, of a criminal's heinous acts seemed great. Pity, I thought, would take things in the wrong direction for me. What I wanted to know now was: *What happened to me?*

IN THE MONTHS FOLLOWING MY visit to the building on Riverside, I placed an occasional call to state and county agencies in California, trying to track down some of the details that might have framed my story. Doing this, I came to suspect that I was missing the memory of certain events. I could recall many scenes from my childhood in the Valley, even remember some vividly; but I also became aware of gaps in that period of time from which nothing surfaced.

In the fall of 1996, I visited a therapist for the first time.

I'd briefly seen a psychiatrist when I was in college, but we were not able to get anywhere. Years later, I understood it was because I hadn't been capable at the time of doing the required work. My expectation was that she would somehow simply fix me, get me over the anxiety, over the humiliation.

I chose therapy because my own efforts to clarify my past seemed dramatically unproductive, and because I was now, once again, of a mind that something was wrong with me. I had begun to recognize patterns in my behavior. If I sensed, for example, that I was being manipulated by someone, or disrespected, I quickly became furious out of all proportion. And I'd freeze sometimes when faced with a serious threat instead of calmly moving toward some sort of resolution. I suspected that these habits—no great insight—were rooted in my childhood experience.

Also, a persistent, anxiety-induced muscular tension across my shoulders had by now become so severe that I'd ruptured a cervical disc. When a regimen of steroids brought only limited relief, my doctor recommended surgery. After a second doctor said I had no option but surgery, I reluctantly agreed—until the surgical procedure was drawn up for me on a piece of paper: I'd be placed facedown and unconscious on an operating table, and a one-inch vertical slit would be opened in the nape of my neck. I said no, absolutely not. I'd live with the pain.

From the beginning, the therapist encouraged me to move at my own pace through the memories I was able to retrieve, and to resist the urge to fit any of these events into a pattern. I remember him saying in one of our first sessions, with regard to my apparent inability to protect myself in complex emotional situations such as my stepfather's betrayal, that I did "not even understand the concept of self-protection." I resented the statement. It made me feel stupid—but it also seemed like a start.

We worked together for four years. I described for him the particulars of the abuse: the sandpaper burn of Shier's evening stubble on my skin; his antic Chihuahua, which defecated on the floor of the apartment and raced around on the bed when we were in it; Shier's tongue jammed into my mouth. I described the time he forced me to perform fellatio in my home while my mother and brother were away. Shier lay back on Mother's sleeping couch, self-absorbed, palming my head like a melon, supremely at ease. I told the therapist about my inability to break off the relationship with Shier, and about my mother's apparent intention to look the other way.

At the start of therapy, I speculated that the real horror of those years would prove to be the actual acts of abuse—my choking on his semen, the towel forced over my face to silence me, the rectal bleeding. After a while, I began to see that the horror was more elusive, that it included more than just betrayals and denials and being yanked around in Shier's bed like a rag doll. The enduring horror was that I had learned to accommodate brutalization. This part of the experience remained with me long after I walked out of Shier's apartment for the last time.

Caught up in someone else's psychosis, overmatched at every turn, I had concentrated on only one thing: survival. To survive I needed to placate. My response to emotional confrontation in the years following that time, I came to see, was almost always to acquiesce, or to overreact angrily, with no option in between. Therapy led me to comprehend that I had not, as I wanted to believe, been able to tough out the trauma. I had succumbed, and others besides me had experienced the consequences of my attempt to endure. I had ahead of me now a chance to do better, to be a person less given to anger.

I visited the therapist twice a week to start with, occasionally for double sessions; then it was once a week or less frequently until we decided we'd come to a resting place. In our final sessions, I fitted the pieces of my story together differently, creating "another narrative," as therapists are wont to say, of the early years in California, a broader context for the physical and emotional damage. After that, long-term sexual abuse no longer organized the meaning of my life as it had during the years I believed that I'd simply walked away from it.

One night in 1998, driving from the town where I had been seeing the therapist forty miles upriver to my home, I suddenly felt flooded with relief. The sensation was so strong I pulled over and got out of the truck. I walked to the edge of what I knew to be an unfenced, cultivated field. At first I thought I was experiencing physical relief, the breakdown of the last bit of tension in my upper back, which, after many weeks of physical therapy, no longer required surgery. But it was something else. A stony, overbearing presence I'd been fearful of nearly all my life wasn't there anymore. I stood in the dark by the side of the road for a long while, savoring the reprieve, the sudden disappearance of this tyranny. I recalled a dream I'd had midway through my therapy. I burst through

a heavy cellar door and surprised an ogre devouring the
entrails of a gutted infant, alive but impassive in the grip of
his hand. The ogre was enraged at being discovered. What
seemed significant was that I had broken down the door. It
didn't matter whether it was the door into something or the
door out.

Therapy's success for me was not so much my coming to
understand that I had learned as a child to tolerate acts of
abuse. It was discovering a greater capacity within myself to
empathize with another person's nightmare. Most of the
unresolved fear and anger I once held on to has now meta-
morphosed into compassion, an understanding of the pre-
dicaments nearly everyone encounters, at some level, at some
time, in their lives.

A COMMONPLACE ABOUT TRAUMA, ONE buried deep in the
psyches of American men, is that it is noble to heal alone.
What I've learned in recent years, however, is that this choice
sometimes becomes a path to further isolation and trouble,
especially for the family and friends of the one who has been
wounded. I took exactly this path, intending to bother no
one with my determined effort to recalibrate my life. It took
a long while for me to understand that a crucial component
of recovery from trauma is learning to comprehend and
accept the embrace of someone who has no specific knowledge of what happened to you, who is disinterested.

We need others to bring us back into the comity of
human life. This appears to have been the final lesson for
me—to appreciate someone's embrace not as forgiveness or

as an amicable judgment but as an acknowledgment that, from time to time, private life becomes brutally hard for every one of us, and that without one another, without some sort of community, the nightmare is prone to lurk, waiting for an opening.

I'm not interested any longer in tracking down the details of Harry Shier's death, or in wondering how, if it is still there, I might reenter his apartment above the building on Riverside Drive to gaze out at the sky through the corner window. I'm on the alert now, though, for an often innocuous moment, the one in which an adult man begins to show an unusual interest in the welfare of someone's young son— especially if it's my grandson. He still, at the age of nine, reaches out for my hand when we start to cross a dangerous street.

RIVER

The Near Woods

A BEAR CAME LAST NIGHT. IT CAME DOWN THROUGH THE TREES
into the clearing around the house, most certainly in the
bright moonlight. I did not see it. I did not hear it dismantling a shed where I keep supplies, snapping wall strakes off
like matchsticks. He was rooting after some odor, and he
scattered my things in his search and not for the first time.

At dawn when I saw the havoc I got my tools and began
to make repairs, and while I worked I wondered where the
bear had come from and why. Where I live is both rural and
wild, on the west slope of the Cascades in Oregon, country
with a shallow white history compared, say, to Maine's or
Florida's. It is lightly and recently settled compared to rural
Illinois or Mississippi. The grizzlies are gone as are the
wolves, but black bears and mountain lions pad by the house
on a track of deer and elk, and Chinook salmon the size of
my leg spawn on gravel bars I can see from the living room.

I have lived here for many years, and though I can still
find the deep woods within a few miles and go in, it's getting

harder. I don't believe the bear came from the deep woods. Like many of us who occupy these margins, he is from the near woods.

The deconstructionists write that the deep woods is only an idea. I wish I could take these people on a tour of the planet, into Antarctica's whale- and seal-packed Weddell Sea, into Australia's poorly mapped Tanami Desert, into the boreal forest north of the Yukon River. What is striking about these places is not wild animals or even spectacular or sublime scenery. It is not even space with no artifact, as far as a straining eye can resolve. It is the way the vastness is permeated by silence. The volume of space is tensioned by silence. The increments between sounds, a goose pounding through overhead, a human shout, only reify the silence.

The bear did not come from such a place. In his daybed he can hear the sound of trucks coming up the valley toward the pass. He can hear passenger jets en route to Denver. He can hear the whistles on the yarders where workers are logging. The integration, the joinery of the space he inhabits with the sounds that penetrate his silence, is awry. He naps in the near woods. If he had ambled two hundred feet down the hill from my house into the road last night, and stood there gazing at moonlight on the river and been oblivious, a truckload of flooring headed for Minneapolis could have killed him.

I sometimes think the singular privilege of my life has been that I have gone inside the deep woods. I could never live there. I have sat enthralled by too many books. The best I can do is to make a life in the near woods, and when some opportunity to go once more into the deep woods arises, to go. I think it must be the same for a bear, though with him it's not having read books. It's the taste of the apples in an orchard nearby, and the honey in another neighbor's hives. And my compost.

The bear and I are not enemies. I do not tire of his violent inquiries. I repair the shed and in the afternoon sit nearby in the filigree of sunshine coming through the 150-foot Douglas firs and read Philip Levine's *The Mercy*. I like the poems enough to read them out loud (perhaps the bear listens if he is near). I imagine from the compassion, the intelligence and grit in the poems, that Mr. Levine would understand the bear's dilemma. I would like to fix Mr. Levine lunch and sit here in the woods and talk with our plates balanced in our laps.

Sometimes when I stand in the woods at night I am afraid. I don't believe the bear will attack me, but things are not so plain in the near woods, where we're shoved up against each other. If he opens up the shed again, should I shoot him as a neighbor advises? If he is hungry and has had an eye torn out on a barbed-wire fence or a foot broken in a trap and I'm easier than a deer, would he just swat me down? Should I stay inside? Should I consider that I would be safer inside where the books are and the telephone and a Brahms concerto on the stereo? Inside, in the magazines I read, are essays that say the bear comes from a place that is only an idea, and that it is in Brahms, not the woods, that you can better discern the increment between tones, and in Mies van der Rohe that you can better understand space.

I am not so sure. The way to catch the bear, to preserve the shed, is to shoot him with a dart or trap him in a box in the near woods. The only way to hold him afterward is to cage him, take that deep woods space-time away from him. Get rid of that notion, then it's safe. I'm not confident about this kind of safety. It feels like the safety the Spanish thought they had when they moved Native people into encomiendas.

When I go to sleep tonight, the bear will be out there in the woods somewhere, lifting his head to the night breeze. What am I to do if he turns up in my dreams?

Lessons from the River

WITHIN TWENTY-FOUR HOURS OF NOON ON SEPTEMBER 17, IN any given year, spring Chinook salmon arrive on gravel bars in front of my home to spawn. The females dig their redds, the males fertilize the eggs, and then both breathe their last. I've watched this event for forty-eight consecutive years on the middle reach of the McKenzie River in western Oregon. Each year I wait for the reassurance they bring, that even though things abstract and concrete are looking bad everywhere in the world, these fish are carrying on. If the salmon don't arrive by the evening of the 17th, I walk down through the woods to stand in the dark and listen for them. I know most all the sounds this river makes, and there is no other sound like their caudal fins breaking the surface of the water as they mill. If I hear them, then I know things are good for this particular strain of salmon for at least another three years. If I don't hear them, I toss and turn through a sleepless night and go down to look first thing in the morning.

They always arrive. I've never had to wait more than a few hours.

Much of what I know about integrity, constancy, power, and nobility I've learned from this river, just as I've learned the opposite of these things—impotency, feckless-ness, imprisonment—by walking across the dam on Blue River, a tributary of the McKenzie, and by standing on Cougar Dam on the river's South Fork, another tributary. I stare at the reservoirs from the tops of these dams and see the still-ness of the impoundments. The absence of freedom there.

I COULDN'T SAY THAT I knew the McKenzie after my first year here. I had to nearly drown in it once, trying to swim across from bank to bank one day and dangerously misjudging the strength of the river's flow. I had to watch a black bear wade through a patch of redds, biting through the spines of adult salmon. I had to come into the habit of walking its stony bed upstream and downstream, in daylight and at midnight, bracing myself with a hiker's pole and calculating each slippery step, the water vibrating the pole in my hand like a bowstring and breaking hard over my thighs. I had to see how the surface of the river changed during a rainstorm, with the peening rain filling in the troughs and hammering down the crests. I had to become more than just acquainted with the phenomenon. I had to study beaver falling alders into its back eddies, great blue herons stab-fishing its shal-lows, and lunging otters snatching its cutthroat trout. I had to understand the violet-green swallow swooping through ris-ing hatches, and the ouzel flying blind through a waterfall.

I had to watch elk swimming in the river at dusk. But still, I can't say I know it.

As I showed continuing interest in the McKenzie over the years, the river opened up for me. I began to feel toward it as I would a person. I learned that it had emotions and moods as subtle as any animal's. I learned that, in some strange way, the river had become a part of me. When I was away traveling I missed it, the way you miss a close friend.

THE FIRST RIVER I DEVELOPED any strong feeling for was a stretch of the Snake that winds through Jackson Hole. In 1965 I was working a summer there in Wyoming, wrangling horses and packing people into the Teton Wilderness. Some afternoons when I was free I volunteered as a swamper on float trips, eager to get a feeling for the undulation of that water. Since then I've been able to float the Middle Fork of the Salmon in Idaho, the Colorado through the Grand Canyon, the upper Yukon in Alaska, and the Green in Utah, gaining from them experience with more formidable water. I've since seen rivers far from home, like the Urubamba in Peru, perhaps the wildest river, in terms of its miles of continuous commotion, that I've ever stood before. And I visited some way-far-off rivers like the Onyx, a name that brings a wrinkled brow to every river rat I've ever mentioned it to.

The Onyx, Antarctica's longest river, flows for only a few months in the austral summer, from the base of the Wright Lower Glacier in the Wright Valley to perennially frozen Lake Vanda. During a week I spent there, at New Zealand's Vanda Station on the shore of the lake, I decided to hike a few miles of the river's north bank, wishing keenly all the while that I had a kayak. The Onyx is about thirty feet across and a foot deep, and it runs flat. A little bit of experience with the Onyx, though, helps you grasp the breadth of meaning behind the term "wild river." The designation includes everything from the virtually unrunnable, like the Urubamba, to pristine but tame rivers, like the Onyx.

I've also spent time in the thrall of another, singular type of wild river—ones that are perfectly runnable but that have gone, in my lifetime, from being virtually unknown to being popular destinations. In the boreal summer of 1979, Bob Stephenson and I were camped on the Utukok River, on the north slope of the Brooks Range in western Alaska. During the week we spent there, we not only saw no person but the bush pilot who brought us in, but also no evidence of *anything* from the man-made world. A tundra grizzly had torn up a ground squirrel's burrow twenty yards from the tent just before we arrived. We watched wolves hunting every day. We saw gyrfalcons, snow buntings, horned larks, and jaegers on their nests. One night, thirty or so caribou crossed the river in front of us at a run, throwing up great sheets of water— diamonds backlit by a late-night sun.

When Bob died last year, we held a memorial service for him in Fairbanks, and I caught up with a retired biologist who told me that commercial float trips now take people regularly down the Utukok. It's certainly a wild river, provid- ing an unforgettable experience for adventurers, some of whom have become river activists as a result. To my way of thinking, however, the Utukok is not so wild now as it was when we were camped there forty years ago, when the country, for as far as you could see, belonged to the animals.

HOME FROM SOME TRIP AND here on the banks of the McKenzie, I always feel that I've come back together again as a person. In spring, when I notice the first few flowers blooming in the riparian zone—trillium, yellow violet, purple grouse flower, deer's head orchid—I'm aware of similar changes in myself. I've lived here long enough now—intimate with the McKenzie's low- and high-water stages, its winter colors, its harlequin ducks, its log jams and aerial plankton (tens of thousands of spiders "balloon drifting" in summer on breezes above the river)—to know that without this river I'm less. Listening to osprey strike the river, watching common mergansers shooting past me at sixty miles an hour, a foot off the water, hearing the surging wind roiling the leaves of black cottonwoods close around me, I become whole again.

Many people, I have to think, have wilder and more inspiring stories to tell than I do about illuminating and staggering moments spent with a wild river. I have to believe, though, that we all share equally a love for the great range of expression this particular kind of being offers us, whether we're with it in the moment or must call up remembered feelings from former encounters. And, of course, today we all share a fate with them, during these days of the Sixth Extinction, and we know how late it is in human history to finally be thinking about protecting rivers.

We're only just now getting started with it. Congress

passed the Wild and Scenic Rivers Act in 1968, fifty years
ago this year. The bill was designed to protect eight different
rivers from development—among them, the Middle Fork of
the Clearwater in Idaho, the Eleven Point in Missouri, and
the Middle Fork of the Feather in California. In 1988, after
another twenty-seven rivers had slowly been incorporated
into the system, Oregon passed an omnibus river bill that
added another forty rivers, including the McKenzie, each
one with designated stretches of "wild," "scenic," and "rec-
reational" water, and each one of these sections subject to
increasingly stricter levels of management. Today, there are
208 wild and scenic rivers across forty states—12,743 miles
of protected river water. It's a paltry sum, actually, less than
a quarter of one percent of the nation's river miles. But each
year our understanding of the nature of this kind of planetary lifeblood grows deeper. As more land trusts come into
being, like the McKenzie River Trust here, the number of
champions and custodians grows larger.

Over the years, I've learned much about the McKenzie
that is obvious and much that is subtle. On this waterway
that supplies the city of Eugene with virtually all of its drinking water, for example, state and federal agencies have coop-
erated to protect bull trout and to restore the spring Chinook
salmon run on the upper South Fork of the river. And for
subtlety, I would offer you obsidian tools buried in the river's
riparian zone, evidence I've found of the very early presence
of people here, some of it from before the days of the historic occupants, the Kalapuya and Molalla, tribes who traveled to the upper McKenzie in the summer to gather a great
profusion of berries—blackberries, salmonberries, huckle-

berries, elderberries, osoberries, and thimbleberries (all of which remain a priority today for local residents and others to gather).

The goal for most of us on the McKenzie today is not simply to protect the physical river from miscreants by implementing various layers of necessary regulation from ridgeline to ridgeline, but to revitalize and protect the entire community associated with the river. To help all who are interested understand that this river began its life long before human beings arrived, and that the wildness it offers us all can still be accessed, engaged, and offered to our children. We're living today, of course, in a time of true political, social, and environmental upheaval and growing threat. You can select living creatures like rivers, if you choose, and take your stand with them to ensure your own future and the future of other beings. It's a good place to be with your friends and your family, as the growing shadows blanket our skies.

On September 17, 2018, I will go down to the river and wait. I will watch for sunlight gleaming on the salmon's caudal fins, standing proud of the surface of the water in the river's shallows. I will smell them on the evening air and watch the males converge on the females, shouldering each other out of the way. And I will concentrate on this thought: If I do not help them to keep doing this, my days too are numbered.

River

For Cort and Dave

THE BED OF A RIVER, A GEOLOGICAL FEATURE LIKE AN ARROYO, a canyon, or a wash, freights moving water from high ground to low. The river itself is in the class of flowing waters, which includes the run, the brook, and the kill, but it is distinguished from all these by its greater breadth and by its length. The Mississippi River is 2,340 miles long; and the distance from the mouth of the Mississippi to the headwaters of the Missouri River is 4,880 miles. The mouth of the Columbia is four miles across. Another measure of the river's primacy among bodies of moving water is how much more often its tributaries are called forks, branches, roots, and prongs, like the Coulter Branch of the Kentucky River in Kentucky, or the North and South Prongs of the Little Red River in Texas, or the Ross Fork of the Judith in Montana, or the Rat Root of Rainy Lake in Minnesota.

The flow of a river is insistent; it carries high water

during a flood and low water during a drought, but it does
not dry up or disappear like an ephemeral creek or the waters
of an arroyo (unless, like the Rio Grande or the Colorado, it
is periodically completely drained by irrigation pumps).

The rate of flow of a river might hardly be apparent, as
is the case with a back eddy; or wildly rushing, as whitewater
tumbling through a dalles; or plain sluggish, sprawling in a
leisurely way across the bottomlands of its floodplain. The
nature of a river, generally, is to be more obviously relentless
on its journey than a creek, to animate to a greater extent the
landscapes it moves through, and to grow more stately as it
broadens and deepens in its middle reaches. The bass voice
of the river can be found in the cataract, in the plunge of a
waterfall, and in the hollow cavitation of a rapids; but the
river speaks, too, with the susurrations, the gurgle, and the
delicate seethe of the narrower and shallower runs of water.

These characteristics are concerned only with the size,
the animation, the constancy, and the force of the river, as
well as its seeming parenthood in the family of rills, branches,
and their kin. It is to say nothing of the beings living comfortably within the river—trout, caddisfly larva, behemoth
sturgeon (a kind of once-upon-a-time fish), mussel, dace, and
salmon alevin—or of those who fish in them, like the mer-
ganser and the great blue heron, or those who sleep on their
quiet waters in the evening, the harlequin duck and the mal-
lard, or those who crawl their bottoms like the crayfish, or
who reside in their banks like the beaver and the ouzel, or
who prowl their quieter water in search of food like the sala-
mander, or who depend on them for life, like the otter.

It is to say nothing of how darkness does not stem their

flow, for they are sleepless, or how sunlight lambent on their surfaces strains the human eye, which can find no detail in the molten light and must therefore turn away. It is to say nothing of the sudden clack of cobbles shifting on the river's bed in the middle of the night, of the way rain hammers the surface flatter, or of how soundlessly it accepts the fall of snow.

It is to say nothing of the trickle of its headwaters or the sigh of its apparent extinction as it unbraids across its delta, or the turbulence and upwelling as it falls into the line of a larger river. It is to say nothing of its cutbanks and gravel bars, its salmon redds, pocket waters, islands, and holes.

This is to say that it is a kind of animal itself, containing other animals and abetting the lives of still others, like the osprey and the mountain lion sipping at its bank. It is to point out that rivers are older than humans, that they endure dams, pollution, and being channeled, and, one way or another, carry on. It is to say that despite our charts of cubic feet of flow per second, our topographic maps of the precise extent of their watersheds, our catalogs of their aquatic, avian, and terrestrial denizens, we hardly know them.

Residence

IN THE SPRING OF 1965 I DROVE A FRIEND FROM SOUTH BEND, Indiana, where we were both in school at the University of Notre Dame, to Santa Fe, New Mexico, before heading north to Jackson Hole, Wyoming, where I would work the summer wrangling horses on a dude ranch.

I liked Santa Fe, the look and feel of it. It felt like a place I should end up. I didn't, but the thought that I belonged there still occurs from time to time. I finished a master's degree at Notre Dame and then moved to Eugene, Oregon, to earn an MFA in creative writing, a degree I thought I needed to have if I was going to make any headway as a writer.

The program proved to be not what I was looking for. I decided to quit and try to make a living as a writer. I'd just gotten a check for a magazine article that would cover four months of rent on a house in Eugene, and I believed, as perhaps only the young can, that my wife and I would be all right. She'd just earned her master's degree in library science and had taken a job as the driver of the local library's book-mobile. It seemed workable, but we were neither of us enamored of Eugene. One night I asked her what she thought of moving to Santa Fe. She was game. I phoned my old friend to inquire about housing and work opportunities there.

We were nearly committed to the move when someone I'd known at the writing program, who knew I was eager to leave Eugene, told us about a house forty miles away on a whitewater river, the McKenzie, that was for rent. It was $80 a month, had septic and a well. It was right on the river and had a washer and dryer.

It seemed we had to take a look.

Our intention was to see if we could actually live forty miles out of town. Plant a garden, cut and split six cords of wood for winter, and so on. We moved in June 1970 and the place grew on us. I never again had a serious thought of moving.

Sandra and I separated in 1996 and then divorced. In 2007 I married again, and my wife, Debra, moved in after leaving her job at Portland State University. We had an apartment in Portland and discussed getting a larger place there and keeping our home on the river, which we had begun to call "the Finn Rock house." We soon let go of the idea of a Portland domicile. I was embedded at Finn Rock. What was missing for her at Finn Rock was a proximity of good friends and the rich cultural life of Portland. What was missing for me in Portland was deep darkness, deep silence, the presence of a big river, and the occasional black bear, bobcat, or herd of elk drifting past the house.

Two hundred seasons at Finn Rock have included plenty

of rain (about eighty inches per year), snowstorms in winter, ferocious winds, the unsettling presence of wildfires nearby, disruptive minor flooding during periods of high water, and, for a while, regular power outages. One might experience nearly all of these events living here for just a year or two.

Living here for fifty years, I realize that many of the individual wild animals I saw when I first moved in—deer, great blue heron, river otters, osprey, beaver, mink, coyotes—have passed away. When I see fox scat on the walkway to our guesthouse or the secreted nest of a winter wren in a pocket of moss under the wood ricks, or a ruby-throated hummingbird at the window of my studio, I know I've been here longer, for whatever that's worth. When I see salmon spawning in the river in front of the house in September, I can count back fifty seasons to the first time. And when I come upon the remains of an elk calf killed by a cougar I know this might be a once-in-a-lifetime event, of which there always seem to be more.

I have traveled to nearly eighty countries doing research as a writer, and when I am asked where I would most like to go in the world, I always say the same thing: here. Here is where I have had the longest conversation with the world outside myself. Here is where I have tested the depths of that world and found myself still an innocent. Here is where the woods are familiar and ever new.

In 1964, a flood at Christmastime washed out the old Finn Rock Bridge. A salvage crew hauled some of the ten-by-sixteen timbers up to a clearing on what is now my property. They are hidden by a farrago of brush—salal, Oregon grape, sword fern, young Indian plum trees, maturing cedar trees and western hemlock, huckleberry bushes, sorrel, thimbleberry thickets, dogwood trees, and California hazelnut. I know right where they are, if you'd like to look.

THE BIGGEST ANIMAL HERE, ITS aura larger than that of a deer mouse, a chickaree, a gray squirrel, a pileated woodpecker, but not better or more capable, is the river. In front of the house, it is 350 feet across. In late summer, it is not much more than four feet deep where the thalweg runs, the line that marks the course of the river's strongest current. In early spring, with snow melting in the high country to the east, the river might be ten feet deep and running so fast against the banks that to step near it is spine-tingling, like inching up on the edge of a cliff.

When the current is not so much a threat, I've taken a stout pole and walked the river bottom under a full moon. I've donned a wetsuit, and with my air tanks, have lain on the river floor in a back eddy behind a boulder and watched mergansers and wood ducks and mallards and harlequin ducks float past, their legs hanging down, turning to steer but not paddling. Riding the current. I've sat for hours in the riverside brush with my polarized glasses to watch trout hunt insects on the river's surface, and with my binoculars, I've watched ducks preen with meticulous care the feathers that keep them afloat.

I do not keep lists of those who live here, and must say I have over the years forgotten some of what I once knew: the different shapes of a hemlock cone and a red cedar cone, or of a deer's head orchid and a lady-slipper orchid before each blooms. I remember that the song of a winter wren, a bird smaller than the palm of your hand, lasts six seconds and that if you see a single chinquapin tree you'll spot half a dozen more if you halt and look deeply into the woods. I know that if I open a book on the deck in summer and begin reading, an insect I've never seen will soon cross the white page.

What's important to me here is not the natural history or even the richness and intricacy of local knowledge or accu-mulated experience of decade after decade of local weather. It's the scars on my hands and shins from years of cutting wood, the signs of belonging that say here and nowhere else is where you are incorporated. This is your history, what you've chosen and what has chosen you. Here is the record of your dedication and your allegiance to things you can't understand but still believe. Here is where you can lie down in the woods, at any spot you come upon, and not feel out of place, foreign. If you were eaten by an animal, this is what you would taste like.

Here is where you can stand on the deck at night and watch the stars and, with your hands in your pockets, not have to explain why it is here and not somewhere else that you stand defenseless. You are known here. You fit. You are welcome, even though, year by year, you know more of the ways that you are not in charge, not the decision-maker. You are an aspect of a moment in time in a particular place and you need be no more than that.

As I've grown older in this place I believe I have become more passive in my involvement. I no longer sleep with the windows always open so that I can smell the wild perfumes of the woods when I awaken in the night and hear the squawk of a bird struck by a night predator. Most days I walk down to the river to say my prayers, but stiffened joints no longer allow me to walk the woods every day, and so I miss a lot. But I am comfortable here, even as the particularity of my knowledge of this landscape shrinks. If I hear the crack of a limb breaking, and the limb crashing through the canopy, the whump as it hits the forest floor, I think: Me, too. If I see a fledgling osprey drop a writhing fish it has caught because it's too heavy and then try to regain its place in the air, I think: I've done that. If I see the afternoon sun light up the surface of the river like a sheet of gyrating metal, I close my eyes against the glare and think: One day I will enter right there and not return.

For now, I sit outside in the evening and in the middle of the day and am not afraid of the unknown. For many animals here, death awaits them a few feet from the house, and there are for some terrifying things waiting, but I have made my peace with that. Knowing this offers me a resolution I have found nowhere else.

Deterioration

I AM LOOKING BACKWARD AT ANOTHER DAY. IT'S RAINING IN western Oregon, temperatures in the low forties. I'm cutting wood with two other men, people I've cut wood with for years. When we're working we hardly talk. Everyone understands what needs to be done and the sequence in which the tasks need to be performed. One man is running the tractor, which is rigged with two chains, a skidder that will horse the twelve- and fifteen-foot logs out of the brush and into a clearing where we'll cut them into eighteen-inch rounds. The other man and I are setting the choker chains on logs, rigging them so the chains slide easily through the slip hooks, binding them against the bark, and rolling logs to the left or right to clear obstacles.

The rain is soft, a heavy mist. My rain gear keeps me dry except for the dampness of my own sweat, which the rubberized fabric keeps from evaporating. The same sweat across my forehead greases my skin so that, lying on the ground and trying to run chain under these two-ton logs, my hard hat occasionally slips on my head and blocks my view. I take it off for the moment. With chains under tension and broken limbs hung up in the crowns of trees above us—widow-makers, we call them—I put it on again while I'm still on my knees, before I stand up and give a hand signal to the man on the tractor. He knows I've forced a hook under the log and that in a moment the third fellow will have brought it up out of the tunnel he and I have fashioned by clawing one-handed toward each other, feeling for each other's fingers.

The choker's set. My partner makes a swirling motion with an upright index finger, telling the man on the tractor to cinch up the chain. He slows the swirling motion to tell him to tighten slowly. His closed fist raised high brings everything to a stop. The set of chain is good, the nose of the log is free. The last hand signal tells the man on the tractor to pull the log away. We've done this hundreds of times. My partner and I trail the butt end of the log, watching the play of it against the chain, ready to roll it left or right if it binds to the ground and bogs the tractor down.

We do this for hours. We start at first light and, except for breaks for coffee and maybe a sandwich, we don't quit until afternoon. That day we pull six or seven logs into the clearing and buck them into rounds, running all three saws at once until we have enough rounds to start splitting, allocating the work so anyone might take a break whenever he wishes but no one is forced to stand by idle. While two men run the splitter, a machine that uses pneumatic pressure to drive a steel wedge through each round, making the splits commonly referred to as firewood, the third man cuts the last of about sixty rounds. Toward the end of the operation, one man is pitching splits into the trailers behind three trucks, another is splitting rounds, and the third is alternating pitching splits into the trailers and helping the man at the splitter lift and heave the hundred-pound round into place on the splitter's carriage.

I might do this kind of work with my friends, who are also my neighbors, four or five times a year. On other occasions two of us might be working together to fall trees or split rounds at each other's homes. We all heat with wood, and this kind of physical labor has been part of my life for fifty years. I have made my living as a writer during those years. Indoor work. The physical exertion required to produce firewood and then rick it up in woodsheds—there are about nine cords, mostly Douglas fir, in my woodshed as I write here—is something I am always ready for and look forward to.

I look backward to that one day I am recalling because I no longer have the agility to set chokers or the endurance to operate a large chainsaw with a three-foot bar without drifting into that state of inattentive weariness that precedes an accident with this very dangerous tool.

I'm not what I used to be.

I don't recall any single moment when I began to notice that my body was starting to fail me, that I could no longer presume the strength would be there in my arms and shoulders, the stamina in my legs, the nimbleness to jump clear of a potentially lethal butt of a big tree twisting the wrong way off a stump as it began to fall. I have to plan more thoroughly, pace myself more thoughtfully. I'm older now.

My neighbor Larry and I got together to cut wood decades ago partly because we knew we had the same feelings about safety and that we'd both passed on the same men, other neighbors, as partners because they were careless. They stood too close to you when you were running a saw. They thought it unmanly to wear chaps (to stop a saw chain instantly, before it cut into your legs). They stood oblivious in the bight of a winch cable, though it could cut them in half if it broke.

Larry liked to move with deliberation, with forethought. He opted for mechanical advantage over approaches that depended on brute strength. When I started working around him, I knew I didn't have to watch out for him but could just watch over him, as you do when the machinery is dangerous and you're working with objects that could crush you and techniques that could ruin a hand.

Like me, Larry has had to adapt to growing older. Buying a splitter together, no longer splitting by hand, was adapting. Quitting at one in the afternoon instead of three was adapting. Having to wear glasses, which fogged up on cool damp days, forced adaptations. Getting a third guy to help us was adapting.

The pleasure of the work, the exhilaration of physical exhaustion, is no less sweet because we're slower now. We don't care, really, that we no longer do what we once did. We stand in awe of the men we once were, before the surgeries and the arthritis, the broken-down knees. We now have the understanding we didn't have forty years ago when we became impatient with the men much older than we were because they were slower or, to us, needlessly careful. We're old enough, finally, to understand what they were doing.

WHEN I WAS YOUNG I rode motorcycles, and then there came a time when I knew I didn't have the reflexes for it, considering where I'd chosen to live. My house was forty miles from town, and the road, which ran much of that way alongside a whitewater river, was unlit, serpentine, and narrow, the forest so close at some points there was no room to pull over. One night on a motorcycle I dropped into a swale to see a deer straddling the centerline, staring into my headlight. I was doing sixty. I was the span of one hand away from her as I shot past. I put the bike away.

When I turned seventy I wanted to make an inventory of the ways in which I was now compromised. A recently torn medial meniscus in my right knee. Arthritis in my lower spine. Rotator cuff surgery to grind down bone spurs. Loss of a sense of balance, which forces me to place each step I take in the uneven terrain of the woods more deliberately. Sprains take longer to heal. I'm not as quick or as strong.

Some of the diminishment—muscle strength, flexibility—can be remedied with exercise programs, but I don't find these programs appealing. I'd rather understand how to adapt. When I am no longer as physical an animal, I will settle comfortably into what remains.

ON THAT DAY I RECALL, dismantling that huge fir we'd felled the day before, the three of us took a coffee break in my truck. We brought so much moisture into the cab that the windows steamed up right away, but we were out of the rain, toweling the water and sweat off our heads and faces. Our soaked gloves sat limp and curled in our laps. We sipped coffee and speculated about how many more hours this might take. The other two, I knew, felt the day's work thus far in the big muscles—latissimus dorsi, gluteus maximus, quadriceps— and we shifted in the warm damp layers of our clothes, stretching, feeling how really strong we were, how taut and tuned these flexors and extensors were, how capable and dependable our bodies were. I'd gotten a broadside in the mail the morning before, a poem by Wendell Berry in which he spoke with affection and regard about the dignity of physical labor. My companions didn't know Berry's work, that he was a farmer with a physical life as well as a writer. But they understood deeply what he was talking about, and in the steamy air of that truck all three of us felt our own worth. We felt it physically, and in some way we were blessed to know this physical way of moving in the world, of using tools, of cooperating wordlessly, of turning something huge and, in its way, terrifying into heat for our homes on cool, wet winter nights.

The degree to which I have depended on my body to come through each day of my life, no matter what I chose to do, was not apparent until I could no longer assume it would. I was athletic and quick in high school and college. I was the starting point guard on my high-school basketball team, which won a city championship in my senior year. I started on the soccer team, a midfielder, and we won a city championship in my senior year in that sport, too. I played two years of soccer in college and after that a few years of pickup games wherever I was. I was agile and had excellent hand-eye coordination and balance. I can say this because I'm no longer agile, not very quick, and must use a staff to wade across creeks. I can no longer bound across, skipping from one exposed stone to the next, like a goat.

In the years when I felt, and was, fully capable, I knew many moments of near breakdown. Days of mind-addling heat working one summer in the stone deserts west of Lake Turkana in northern Kenya. Days camped on the polar plateau in the interior of Antarctica when it never got warmer than −29°F, and we had no heat in our tents but what our small cookstoves gave off. As a diver, I'd been swept away by unsuspected currents. Hunting with Inuit men in northern Baffin Island, I'd been accidentally stabbed in the wrist by someone who'd also been sleepless for about forty hours. We were a long way from medical help. I'd broken my left hand in an automobile accident. Fractured a humerus, a transverse process in a lumbar vertebra, and a right fibula. I'd become hypothermic at sea during a storm in Alaska and would not have survived without the help of companions. I'd contracted malaria and required stitches in my face and arms and legs.

Somehow the body carries on. The next morning or the next week or a little later, and you're good as you ever were. You look at the scars and marvel.

I was never reckless. I was prepared, a planner. And when I went off with the people whose work I wanted to write about, I chose seasoned, mature people to travel with, never young men with something to prove. I learned a lot, partly because whatever it was we were doing—diving under the ice in Antarctica, trapping wolves in Minnesota, tracking mountain lions in Arizona—I could depend on my body to come through, to not be a distraction or make me a burden to others. More than that, it was the body as much as the mind that was the source of what filled my notebooks. What the senses gathered from where I was: the sonic landscapes, the tactile sensations of the sandstone on which petroglyphs had been incised, the taste of wild ginger root, the violet light at dusk, the smell of creosote bush in the Mojave after a rain. At the end of a field day, when we were all exhausted, I might go alone to climb a ridge above our camp to get an overview. I would remember the difference later between gravel and sand and hardpan underfoot when we were traveling with heavy packs. My legs knew that. When I recalled an aggressive encounter with a black mamba in East Africa, my body—the muscles of the heart, of the throat, of the anus—remembered. The skin tightened again.

Once, on the Orinoco River in Venezuela, I fell into conversation with a man who was guiding a small group of us up a narrow tributary of the river to locate and watch rare tropical birds. He was a skilled ornithologist, and I could see from the way he moved and reacted to bird calls that he was at ease moving through the jungle, familiar with it, competent. He reacted like a pointer to the call of a bird, locating it before any of the rest of us could, when no one could actually see the bird.

The two of us were quickly comfortable with each other. I admired his skills and knew I would learn from him and so asked if I returned to Venezuela, could I travel with him, accompany him on one of the arduous trips he described to me. The birds of Venezuela are not well known and my new friend was at the forefront of the effort to learn who they were. His method was to lay out a compass bearing and follow it through the jungle for a hundred kilometers, identifying birds as he went. He would bring another ornithologist along. I would help carry equipment and prepare meals. I would assist with making recordings and keeping notes.

It was several years before I saw a time between other obligations to go with him, then there were a few years of trying to coordinate our schedules. In the end, I never went. It was becoming clear to me in my early sixties that I could not, as I had done for years without a second thought, rough it. It would be three weeks of heat and humidity, of hacking a trail through jungle vines and thickets, of dealing with leeches and insects, with fer-de-lance, rain, and thorns. I knew I might slow the others down, or be so distracted by discomfort that I could miss too much of what was going on.

I didn't think I had the stamina required. Or the flexibility.

Making my peace with this disappointment was not as difficult as I had anticipated. I would no longer be taking the physically demanding trips I had once thrived on. I'd be traveling in some other fashion, writing another kind of story. I would adapt. As I grew older I had come to admire this quality in my friends, the ability to adapt. To adapt in the face of trauma, certainly—financial devastation, divorce, sexual assault, war, robbery—but also to adapt to the history of the body, its disintegration, what some might call incremental betrayal.

I look back on the day eight years ago when I wrote to

my friend in Caracas to say I would not be able to join him, and coming forward I can see the accumulation of reservation, from that point, and the growing doubt about my capability. Do I need to worry about altitude sickness now at eleven thousand feet in Cuzco? Can I trust my knees to hold up over seventeen miles of steep terrain, a day hike? If I skip meals and sleep short hours in order to be present in a new place—Istanbul, Havana, Urumchi—the way I have always done, will I just collapse?

What will happen to me as a writer if I must remember what it was like because I am no longer able to stride out the door, cross the tangled field, vault the fence, and scramble to the heights that offer magnificent views and the wind in my face?

I'm not there yet. I don't expect the fierce desire I have felt since I was a child, to go and to see, will fade anytime soon. And the mind that drives the body is also the mind that strategizes about how to get more out of less, how to adapt to limitations instead of capitulating. I like being in this position. It's new, and it requires something of me that I am not familiar with.

I SEEM TO HAVE STAYED fit throughout my life with the physical work I've done around my home, like cutting firewood. I've been careful about what I eat, been conscientious about regular checkups, not shied away from strenuous physical tasks. What has interested me more than being able to run five-minute miles or marathons is the conversation between the body and that part of the mind, or spirit, that we call the will.

How is it that determination propels the body? How is it that the memory of what one has done before exerts pressure on the body to do it again? It seems to me, growing older, that all that changes is one's determination to get something done. It is a degree of caution, one's sense that over time the limits have changed, and one backs down from whatever the challenge is without embarrassment or regret.

I feel that's where I am now, managing a torn meniscus in my right knee, and the side effects of some treatment I am undergoing that makes me tired earlier in the day. I know what I can do, though it is not as much, not as quick as it once was. And, as used to happen regularly, I still surprise myself with the extra mile or the additional cord of wood thrown in the trailer.

LIKE MOST MEN MY AGE—I'VE just turned seventy—I've had a PSA test every six months to measure the prostate-specific antigens in my blood, the most common way to detect the onset of prostate cancer. During a period of time when I was dealing with a common but persistent infection in my urinary tract, I got a high PSA reading, five times higher than those I'd had consistently for years. My physician and urologist both thought this was a false reading triggered by antibiotics. The urologist decided to do a physical exam, even though I'd had one just six months prior with negative results. Moments after he started the finger palpation of my prostate, he said he didn't like what he was feeling. He scheduled me for a biopsy. Forty-eight hours later, he took the standard twelve core samples from my prostate. A few days later he called to say that all twelve were between fifty and ninety percent cancerous and the Gleason number—on a scale of ten, it measures the aggressiveness of the cancer—was nine.

Two days later a bone scan revealed that the cancer had metastasized into the pelvic bone. After that a CAT scan showed the cancer had moved into several lymph nodes. I began treatment in the Knight Cancer Institute in Portland. My wife located an oncologist there whom we both felt immediately comfortable with. I began with hormone therapy and at the same time worked on diet, nutrition, and exercise with a Chinese-medicine practitioner in San Anselmo, California. Between these three people—my wife, a young oncologist who specializes in advanced prostate cancer, and the naturopathic doctor who had helped a half dozen of my friends manage cancer—I felt I was in excellent hands. I was further supported by my four stepdaughters, all of whom had experience with herbs and homeopathy.

There is no cure for advanced prostate cancer, but with help and conscientious attention one can manage the disease. Considering the situation, the side effects of treatment, which now includes an antiandrogen in addition to hormone therapy, are little more than a distraction, an occasional annoyance. Hot flashes, loss of elasticity in my skin, loss of muscle mass, anemia. I'm not naïve or stupidly optimistic. I know what I am dealing with is a lethal disease, and after sixteen months of treatment I can feel that I am weaker. But whatever the cause of the cancer—genes or the chemicals on which commerce depends or random events—I do not feel like a victim, any more than I feel a victim of arthritis and bone spurs that come with aging. I don't seem to be anything more than another person tracking myself through a normal course of events.

I wish the cancer hadn't come. Or that the Gleason number had been two instead of nine. But that's not what happened.

CANCER, OF COURSE, IS A teacher. And I'm writing down the lessons. It teaches empathy and compassion. It teaches patience and forbearance with all that seems to be failing in the world. It teaches tolerance of the mess we and others make of our lives. It changes one's ambitions profoundly. It teaches the strengths to be found in community, which are different from the strengths to be found in individual striving. It teaches one to adapt.

Several years ago a tree fell in a storm and crushed our woodshed. The house and our close outbuildings are hemmed in by a forest of large trees, many over one hundred feet tall. For forty-five years I have lived in the shadows of these massive trees, watched them whip like fly rods in fierce winds and hoped they would not harm us. When the one fell across the woodshed, breaking its back, I had the shed rebuilt. There are now nine cords of wood decked in it, and in two days I will begin work with a friend on the next cord of wood we will put away there. I will put a heavy brace on one knee, a light brace on the other. I will don a pair of chaps to protect my legs and groin against an accident with the saw. I will cinch the brace that supports my back and we will go to work, reading the big trees that have come down in winter storms, determining how to cut them to keep saws from binding in the kerf and from nicking rocks in the forest duff and dulling instantly. We'll waste little energy and do things in the order that will make the best use of our time so we don't weary too fast. We'll enjoy each other's company and lean against our trucks, drinking from thermoses, and we'll watch fair-weather cumulus clouds scudding overhead, above the crowns of the Douglas firs and hemlocks and cedars, and feel the curious revitalization of physical exhaustion, the pleasure of mutual dependability, and the gift of life, still, in the waning body.

ACKNOWLEDGMENTS

Barry Lopez was deeply engaged in imagining and planning his final collection of nonfiction essays in the months before he died. Because of the serious nature of his illness, Barry relied more than ever on the encouragement and support of his longtime, cherished agent, Peter Matson, and the person he trusted most with his prose, Robin Desser. In the wake of Barry's death, many of Robin's colleagues at Random House and Peter's colleagues at Sterling Lord Literistic have helped make a beautiful and enduring collection that celebrates his literary legacy—thank you all.

Much appreciation to the editors Barry worked with over the years, including those who published many of these pieces: Chip Blake, Stephen Corey, Sigrid Rausing, Christopher Cox, John Freeman, Brian Doyle, and Frank Stewart among them.

If Barry were here, he would surely give thanks to the pals he leaned on, those who provided a sounding board, a dose of inspiration, a comforting word. It would be impossible to name each person in his far-reaching network of friends and colleagues—I trust you know who you are and that you know, too, how Barry relied on you. Special thanks to John and Cindy Adams, Alan and Monika Magee, Jane

Hirshfield, John and Claire Keeble, Dave Fross, Cort Conley, Tom Joyce, Susan O'Connor, Lillian Pitt, Richard and Patti Rowland, Julianne Warren, and Larry Wilcox. Also, Barry's brother and sister-in-law, John and Susan Brennan.

Toby Jurovics: Thank you for keeping Barry's devotion to art and the artistic process alive in the world. Thanks to Cody Upton and the American Academy of Arts and Letters and also the Sun Valley Writers' Conference for honoring Barry as you did. Thank you to Joe Moll and the entire staff of the McKenzie River Trust for protecting Barry's river home, our home, far into the future. Thanks to Robert Macfarlane for reading poems (from across the ocean) to Barry in his final hours.

James Warren, Barry's literary executor, was not only instrumental in bringing this collection to completion, he was also one to lift Barry's spirits over the last difficult year. Julie Polhemus and Chris Jones put in many long days and nights on this project, with an attention to fact-checking and to style detail that Barry would have appreciated (and then some).

In his final days, Barry was surrounded by love. We were with him, daughters and grandchildren, me, holding him as he died. Our family: Amanda Mae, Owen, Ezzy, Stephanie, Mary, Aaron, Mollie, Peter, Harry, and Edris. Barry was over the moon about all of you.

My husband often said that his profound desire was to live a life that helped. Barry, from those of us who loved you, your life helped.

Debra Gwartney
October 2021

PUBLICATION HISTORY

The essays in this book previously appeared in the following publications:

"Six Thousand Lessons," *Kyoto Journal* (2010)
"An Intimate Geography," *Portland* (2010)
"An Era of Emergencies Is Upon Us and We Cannot Look Away," *American Geography: Photographs of Land Use from 1840 to the Present* (Santa Fe, New Mexico: Radius Books, 2021)
"In Memoriam: Wallace Stegner," *The Geography of Hope: A Tribute to Wallace Stegner*, edited by Mary Stegner and Page Stegner (San Francisco, California: Sierra Club Books, 1996)
"Out West," *The Modern West: American Landscapes, 1890–1950* (New Haven, Connecticut: Yale University Press, 2006)
"A True Naturalist," foreword to *Raven's Witness: The Alaska Life of Richard K. Nelson*, by Hank Lentfer (Seattle, Washington: Mountaineers Books, 2020)
"Landscapes of the Shamans," *Orion* (2013)
"The Invitation," *Granta* (2015)
"An Afterword," *Literary Hub* (2020)

"On the Border," *The Georgia Review* (2009)

"Fourteen Aspects of Power," *Freeman's: The Best New Writing on Power*, edited by John Freeman (New York: Grove Press, 2018)

"Love in a Time of Terror," *Literary Hub* (2020)

"Southern Navigation," *The Georgia Review* (2003)

"Our Frail Planet in Cold, Clear View," *Harper's Magazine* (1989)

"¡Nunca Más!," *MĀNOA: A Pacific Journal of International Writing* (2008)

"State of Mind: Threshold," *Granta* (2017)

"Madre de Dios," *Portland* (2008)

"A Scary Abundance of Water," *L.A. Weekly* (2002)

"Sliver of Sky," *Harper's Magazine* (2013)

"The Near Woods," written in 2000; illustrations by Charles Hobson (Berkeley, California: Tangram Press, 2005, limited edition)

"Lessons from the River," Patagonia catalog (2018)

"River," *Orion* (2018)

The following essays were previously unpublished:

"On Location"

"Leaving California"

"Residence"

"Deterioration"

ABOUT THE AUTHOR

BARRY LOPEZ (1945–2020) was the author of four collections of essays; several story collections; *Arctic Dreams*, for which he received the National Book Award; *Of Wolves and Men*, a National Book Award finalist; and, most recently, *Horizon*, which was named a best book of the year by *The New York Times*, NPR, and *The Guardian*. He was a frequent contributor to both American and foreign journals, and traveled to nearly eighty countries to conduct research. He was the recipient of fellowships from the Guggenheim, Lannan, and National Science foundations and was honored by numerous institutions for his literary, humanitarian, and environmental work. He lived in Finn Rock, Oregon, with his wife, Debra Gwartney.

ABOUT THE TYPE

This book was set in Baskerville, a typeface designed by John Baskerville (1706–1775), an amateur printer and typefounder, and cut for him by John Handy in 1750. The type became popular again when the Lanston Monotype Corporation of London revived the classic roman face in 1923. The Mergenthaler Linotype Company in England and the United States cut a version of Baskerville in 1931, making it one of the most widely used typefaces today.